Custom Built by
McFarlan

ALSO BY RICHARD A. STANLEY

The Lexington Automobile: A Complete History
(McFarland, 2007; paperback 2012)

CUSTOM BUILT BY MCFARLAN

A History of the Carriage and
Automobile Manufacturer,
1856–1928

Richard A. Stanley

McFarland & Company, Inc., Publishers
Jefferson, North Carolina

The present work is a reprint of the illustrated case bound edition of Custom Built by McFarlan: A History of the Carriage and Automobile Manufacturer, 1856–1928, *first published in 2012 by McFarland.*

LIBRARY OF CONGRESS CATALOGUING-IN-PUBLICATION DATA

Stanley, Richard A., 1936–
Custom built by McFarlan : a history of the carriage and automobile manufacturer, 1856–1928 / Richard A. Stanley.
p. cm.
Includes bibliographical references and index.

ISBN 978-1-4766-8965-4
softcover : acid free paper ∞

1. McFarlan Motor Corporation — History. 2. Automobile industry and trade — Indiana — History. 3. Carriage and wagon making — Indiana — History. I. Title.
HD9710.U54M396 2022   338.7′6292220973 — dc23   2011036406

BRITISH LIBRARY CATALOGUING DATA ARE AVAILABLE

© 2012 Richard A. Stanley. All rights reserved

No part of this book may be reproduced or transmitted in any form or by any means, electronic or mechanical, including photocopying or recording, or by any information storage and retrieval system, without permission in writing from the publisher.

Front cover image: Painting by John Blommel (courtesy of the artist and Jeff Gabbard Photography); decorative frame © 2022 Shutterstock

Printed in the United States of America

*McFarland & Company, Inc., Publishers
Box 611, Jefferson, North Carolina 28640
www.mcfarlandpub.com*

Contents

ACKNOWLEDGMENTS	vii
PREFACE	1
1. Prize Winning Carriages by McFarlan	3
2. Six Cylinder Cars Exclusively	51
3. McFarlan at the Brickyard and on Tour	126
4. Professional Vehicles and Bodies Built to Order	148
5. Why the Stars Came to Connersville	171
6. McFarlans That Have Survived the Years	219
APPENDIX A: MCFARLAN AUTOMOBILE MODELS	239
APPENDIX B: BODY STYLES AVAILABLE, BY YEAR	242
CHAPTER NOTES	247
BIBLIOGRAPHY	255
INDEX	263

Acknowledgments

Soon after moving to Connersville, Indiana, in 1960, to take a teaching position, I became aware of this community's involvement in the manufacturing of automobiles and replacement parts. The most knowledgeable person about the history of Connersville's industries was Henry Blommel, who had grown up in the city and, as a young person, had paid visits to the Auburn and Cord factory as it was closing down. He used his knowledge as a contributing author with Keith Marvin and Alvin J. Arnheim for the book *What Was the McFarlan?* Henry's father had come to Connersville in 1909 at the invitation of Harry McFarlan to assist in getting automobile production underway. This author learned a great deal from numerous conversations with Henry, since deceased, and visited his basement archives at times to be exposed to some of the sources of his vast knowledge.

With this bit of background, it is a special delight that the cover for this book was created by Henry's son, John Blommel, a skilled artist and illustrator. Now retired, John had a career spanning many years at Stant Manufacturing Company, a Connersville institution since 1898 that has long served the automobile industry.

I owe a special debt to my wife of more than 50 years for her dedication in checking the manuscript for spelling and grammar infractions. This was purely a labor of love since she is not particularly fond of antique automobiles. My family has been very supportive in this endeavor including Diane Stanley in Richmond, Indiana, Lynn and Mike Engle in Xenia, Ohio, Alan and Charlene and Andrew and Anne Stanley in Connersville, and a cousin, Raymond Stanley, in Sebring, Ohio.

A number of people shared stories and information about the McFarlan Company and the family responsible for it. This book would have lacked much information without their contributions. Help came from people spread across the country. In Connersville, Indiana: the staff of the Fayette County recorder's office and auditor's office, the staff of the Fayette County Public Library, the Fayette County Historical Museum committee, the staff at Commercial Printing, the staff at Brunsman Graphic Design, photographer Jeff Gabbard, Paulette Hayes, Robert Nobbe, Robert Martin, Donald Squires, Bill Todd, Glen Smith, Henry Orschell, Richard Hankins, Erma Moore, Jim Wicker, Fire Chief Rick Free, John Blommel. In Auburn, Indiana: Mark Bill, archivist at the Auburn Cord Duesenberg Museum. In Cambridge City, Indiana: the staff of the Cambridge City Public Library. In Boston, Indiana: Bill Tyndall. In Liberty, Indiana: Robert Barnard. In Indianapolis, Indiana: Harry J. Cangany, Jr., Dennis Horvath, Shawn Miller, and from the Indianapolis Motor Speedway Museum, Dave Hilberry, Donald Davidson, Terry Gunter and Mary

Ellen Loscar. In LaFayette, Indiana: John R. Gambs. In Muncie, Indiana: Charles McNaughton. In Ft. Worth, Texas: Jim Raymond. In Detroit, Michigan: Ken Lane and the staff at the National Automotive History Collection of the Detroit Public Library. In Ann Arbor, Michigan: Peter Heydon. In Cincinnati, Ohio: Rick Donahoe. In Uniontown, Ohio: Phillip Marquette. In Menlo Park, California: Albert Mroz and Mike Moskowitz. In Canton, Ohio: Char Lautzenheiser, Director of Canton Classic Car Museum. In Dayton, Ohio: the staff at the Dayton Public Library. In Lynchburg, Virginia: Mark Smith. In Richmond, California: Keith Marvin. In Oakland, California: J.W. and Barbara Selveira. In Orange, California: Randy Ema. In Eureka, California: Harvey Harper and Floyd Myers. In Wilmington, Massachusetts: Brian Anderson, Jr. In Sylmar, California: Skip Marketti, director of the Nethercutt Collection. In El Segundo, California: Craig Karr. Elkton, Florida: David Ansted. St. Johns, Florida: Wellington Morton III. In Hershey, Pennsylvania: Kim Miller and the staff of the AACA Library & Research Center. I extend my heartfelt appreciation to the contributions of any person whom I may have omitted.

I have collected automobile literature for more than 65 years and have been a resident of the Connersville community for over 50 of those years. My collection contains a significant selection of McFarlan materials including brochures, trade magazine articles and advertisements that aided in this undertaking.

I have been diligent in my research. In addition to using my own extensive collection, I have gone through Connersville newspapers on microfilm from the 1850s into 1929 at the Fayette County Public Library. I also

Artist John Blommel holding the painting he did for the front cover as a courtesy to the author. John's involvement with this publication is especially appropriate because his grandfather, William, came to Connersville in 1909 to assist with getting McFarlan automobiles into production. His father, Henry, was a contributing author for the book *What Was the McFarlan?* published in 1967. John's talent and his willingness to share it are much appreciated (photograph by author).

visited the Antique Automobile Club of America Library and Research Center at Hershey, Pennsylvania; the National Automotive History Collection at the Detroit Public Library in Detroit, Michigan; the Cambridge City and Richmond, Indiana, public libraries; the Dayton, Ohio, Public Library; the Indiana Historical Society; the Marion County Public Library; the Indianapolis Motor Speedway Museum in Indianapolis; and the Auburn Cord Duesenberg Museum at Auburn, Indiana.

Assembling all the data I gathered in a meaningful form has been a challenge, but certainly an exciting and satisfying experience. My hope is that the reader will receive some of the knowledge and satisfaction that I have had during this process.

Preface

Connersville, Indiana, is much like hundreds of other small to medium sized cities in the United States, struggling to maintain a vibrant business climate and to keep its population employed. As this Eastern Indiana community nears its 200th birthday, it is appropriate to look back at one of the town's prominent families and a significant business that they created and nourished, witnessing its growth and decline.

The McFarlan Company was founded by John B. McFarlan, an immigrant to the United States as a child, who became the community's most influential industrialist and developer. J.B., as he was known, was already a successful carriage maker when he came to Connersville in 1856. He focused on building high quality light duty horse-drawn vehicles, expanding his business with a minimum of advertising, except by word of mouth from satisfied customers. Investing some of his profits in land that he developed, he aided in the city's expansion. The nation's first industrial park was formed on land owned by McFarlan to encourage businesses related to his own carriage manufacturing to locate nearby. McFarlan may indeed have done more to ensure the growth and development of this town than any other single individual. The McFarlan company became virtually an institution in Connersville, where it was in operation for more than 70 years. It had ranked first in the nation for a few years in the production of light-duty horse-drawn vehicles. Generations of workers, mostly men, earned a living, raised families, learned and practiced their skilled trades and took pride in their workmanship.

Like many companies that built wagons and carriages, McFarlan entered the automobile business soon after the turn of the twentieth century, but instead of trying to outproduce and outsell their competition, they gravitated toward the more exclusive market by catering to individual desires and whims of clientele with money enough to indulge their wishes. For nearly 20 years, McFarlan automobiles were recognized for their quality, custom features, powerful engines and enormous size. They were sought after by the rich and famous and sometimes infamous, including such personalities as Wallace Reid, Fatty Arbuckle, Jack Dempsey and even Al Capone.

McFarlan also built a number of ambulances, hearses and even a few fire trucks. Several other prominent manufacturers of automobiles such as Locomobile, Auburn, Premier and Duesenberg called upon the McFarlan company to supply high quality bodies for their own products.

Although not a widely known marque even throughout the antique automobile fraternity, McFarlan has been the subject of several articles in periodicals and at least one book. The excellent publication *What Was the McFarlan?* by Keith Marvin, Alvin J. Arnheim and Henry H. Blommel helped pique this author's desire to expand its coverage to include the carriage trade that initially built the institution. In more than 40 years since that book came on the market, materials became available to this author that were not included in the earlier publication. This effort expands a great deal on anything previously written about McFarlan to show the impact an obscure company in a small city left on the carriage and automotive industry.

1

Prize Winning Carriages by McFarlan

The story of the McFarlan carriage and the McFarlan automobile is that of a family owned and family run business that stressed quality more than quantity. The business was first based on the carriage trade and later evolved into production of motorized vehicles as many other carriage builders did, with quality workmanship always emphasized over the number of vehicles produced. An important part of the local economy, McFarlan provided employment for Fayette County citizens over a period of more than 70 years. Therefore the company's story is entwined with the development of Connersville, Indiana, as it grew from a village into a small industrial city.

Connersville was founded in 1813 by Indian trader frontiersman John Conner, while it was very much a part of the Indiana wilderness. It remained a typical small Hoosier settlement much like hundreds of others until the Whitewater Canal arrived in 1845, providing much easier transportation for passengers and freight to and from Cincinnati and points beyond via the Ohio River. The canal's use as a transportation artery was short lived because of the 490-foot variation in elevation between Connersville and the Ohio River, in a distance of just over 70 miles. Fifty-six locks were necessary to raise and lower boats and seven feeder dams diverted water from the Whitewater River. Heavy rains frequently caused freshets or wash-outs that shut down the canal until repairs could be made. The final death blow for the canal as a means for hauling passengers and freight was the arrival of railroads that were built within a few years, providing quicker, more reliable service. In spite of becoming obsolete as a transportation artery, the canal still helped transform this community into an industrial center by providing a practical source of water power with its flowing current.

The availability of water for power attracted two brothers, P.H. and F.M. Roots, who, in 1854, established the Roots Woolen Mill alongside the Whitewater Canal. Their plan was to use the flow of water in the canal to power their mill, and as they attempted to design a better water wheel for the slow current, they discovered an unusual principle for moving air that became known as the Roots Positive Rotary Principle. This discovery led to the production of the Roots Blower that has been applied to a myriad of uses throughout the world. Roots type blowers, or superchargers, have even been adapted to boost the power on various automobiles from 1900 to the present day. The Roots brothers established the first major industry in Connersville, and they were energetic participants in promoting the growth of the town.

Whether or not the Roots brothers influenced businessman John B. McFarlan to locate in this emerging industrial community is not known for certain, but it seems entirely possible. Both the Roots and McFarlan families had been raised in southwestern Ohio before coming to Indiana. Lydia McFarlan was a staunch member of the Presbyterian church, as were the Rootses, and they may have become acquainted through church activities. These two families were very close friends and both were extremely important influences in the growth and development of Connersville. As an indication of their friendship, when Francis Roots died in 1889, J.B. McFarlan served as a pallbearer.[1]

Another potential influence on J.B. McFarlan was the Rev. William Pelan, the Presbyterian minister in Connersville at the time the McFarlans moved from Cambridge City. The Rev. Pelan told the story that they had been friends since childhood, that both of them had come over from England together and that he, Pelan, had persuaded McFarlan to relocate and assisted him in doing so. Whether his influence or that of the Roots family was decisive, it appears to have been a Presbyterian connection that brought the McFarlan family to Connersville.[2]

John Becraft McFarlan was born in London, England, of Scottish ancestry on November 7, 1822, and was about eight years of age when his parents, James and Ann (Becraft) McFarlan, immigrated to the United States, settling in Hamilton County, Ohio, near the rapidly growing city of Cincinnati. James settled onto a farm to raise his large family, which, besides John, included James, Thomas, Robert, Edward, Ann, Martha, Elizabeth and Mary.[3]

Lydia Jackson McFarlan, born 1822 in southwestern Ohio, died 1906 in Indiana (courtesy Jim Wicker).

Though just a young boy upon arrival in Ohio, John helped his father develop their farm into a productive property. He also completed his schooling in the Cincinnati neighborhood, and, when about seventeen years of age, he apprenticed into carriage blacksmithing at the factory of George C. Miller and Sons in Cincinnati. In 1841, McFarlan began business for himself, opening a carriage and wagon repair shop in the village of Cheviot, now a part of Cincinnati.[4] On October 16, 1845, he married Lydia C. Jackson, who was born and raised in Ohio. John and Lydia were the parents of seven children; Clara, who died when about twelve years of age, Maria J., who never married, Charles E.J., James Edward, William W., Lucy, who died when 2 years of age and John B., Jr.

In 1849, John and Lydia moved to the small village of Cambridge City, Indiana, about 75 miles northwest of Cincinnati, transporting their belongings in a covered wagon.[5] The attractions of Cambridge City included its location on the newly constructed Whitewater Canal and on the National

Road, a major East-West thoroughfare and the first federally funded interstate road. Cambridge City would seem to have been the ideal location for this enterprising young businessman to set up operations supplying and repairing vehicles for adventurous travelers. He established a factory in a desirable location on Main Street, which was also the National Road. In addition to the major East-West transportation artery, the Whitewater Canal offered easy, though not always reliable, passage to points South as far as Cincinnati, Ohio. John's passion, however, wasn't in the heavy-duty wagons needed for the Western movement, but, instead, the high grade light-duty carriage, spring wagon and buggy used regularly by the average family.

His preference in vehicle manufacture may also have been one of the reasons for another move. In 1856, J.B. chose to pick up and relocate again, this time downstream on the Whitewater Canal about fifteen miles to Connersville. By that time he had substantial experience in building and repairing

John Becraft McFarlan, born 1822 near London, England, died 1909 in Indiana (courtesy Jim Wicker).

horse-drawn vehicles and had developed some ideas on how he could see his business expand. The buggy manufacturing business was already operating in Connersville when McFarlan arrived. However, he used that as a springboard to expand his customer base by purchasing the going concern owned by Ware and Veatch.[6] McFarlan's new shop was located in a small building at the northeast corner of 6th Street and Grand Avenue and close to the canal boat loading docks. Here he continued his practice of manufacturing small wagons, buggies and carriages. On the ground floor was his forge which was used to pound out the iron parts. Trimming and finishing were done on the second floor.[7]

Once he settled in Connersville, McFarlan would not move his business outside of Fayette County, even though some offers were made with handsome incentives to relocate to another community. Instead, he helped Connersville by expanding his own business, developing land that he was able to purchase and investing in other local industries.

Conservative by nature, McFarlan rarely chose to spend hard earned funds on advertising, instead relying mainly on satisfied customers to spread the word. In later years, company ads claimed that J.B. McFarlan, Sr., established his business for the purpose of building quality carriages. His idea was that there were enough people who appreciated quality transportation to ensure a substantial market for his product and provide an excellent return on his investment. He was careful to instill his ideals in the minds of his sons, all of whom worked with him at one time or another. C.E.J. and J.B. McFarlan, Jr., remained active in the carriage building business for its duration, carrying on the same high standards that had been established by their father.[8]

As time went on, McFarlan continued to focus his efforts on improving the quality

ADVERTISEMENTS. 11

CONNERSVILLE
CARRIAGE SHOP.

JOHN D. McFARLAN

Keeps on hand and manufactures to order,

Family Carriages,

BUGGIES, SPRING WAGONS, and SULKIES,

VERY LOW FOR CASH OR APPROVED PAPER.

Shop on Head st., near the Canal—Sales room on corner of Monroe and Head sts., at sign of the

BLUE BUGGY.

The earliest known advertising by McFarlan appeared in 1858 in a county fair publication and made reference to the "Connersville Carriage Shop." The sales room was located on the corner of Monroe and Head Street, now 6th and Grand Avenue. The shop was in a small building next door.

of his product, and business was good. Soon outgrowing the limited space of his factory in the small shop on 6th Street, he added shops next door and close by until the company occupied quite a cluster of buildings on both sides of the street, all the way east to Central Avenue.[9] After about 15 years of working and expanding, McFarlan purchased additional property from William Merrell and had a large factory building erected on the southwest corner of 6th and Central Avenue. This building became known as McFarlan's ware room where finishing work was done and completed vehicles were displayed.[10] The McFarlan Hotel, for many years the most prominent building in the city, would later be built on this site after additional property was added. In true Horatio Alger form, John B. McFarlan had come into this country an immigrant with humble beginnings, but through hard work and fair dealings, had become a wealthy industrialist.

Being recognized as "successful" financially also meant the privilege of paying taxes. An article in an 1870 local newspaper listed the names of prominent citizens who paid $100 or more in taxes with the following comment: "We doubt whether there is another county in the Union that can give so many. Fayette is one of the wealthiest counties in the Union, if not the wealthiest, according to population." Although that claim was probably a significant overstatement, J.B. McFarlan was listed as having paid taxes amounting to $207.15, a tidy sum for that day.[11]

Twenty years after J.B.'s arrival in Connersville, there were two McFarlans in business when one of his sons posted the following announcement; "Having purchased D. H. Sellers interest in the stock of boots, shoes, hats, caps, etc., of Sellers & McFarland, I will continue the business at the old stand, where I will be pleased to see all of their old customers and many new ones. I have a large and well selected stock, which will be sold very low. Thanking you for your past liberal patronage, and soliciting continuance of the same, I remain, Respectfully yours, C. E. J. McFarland." Confusion about the family name spelling, McFarlan or McFarland, not only existed in those days but continues to the present.[12] A few years later, a second son, J. Edward, opened a livery stable in partnership with Tom Shields. In addition to boarding and supplying horses as needed, the livery also had a line of buggies and carriages for rent or purchase. Ed kept this business interest for several years, even after joining with his father in carriage manufacturing.

J.B.'s philosophy about advertising seemed to agree with Horace Greeley, who was credited with having said, "The man who moves his business as the Arab moves his tent, must use the flashy, sensation style; but he who pursues his business in a legitimate way, year after year, needs a straightforward, continuous advertisement."[13] McFarlan's straightforward, continuous advertising relied mainly on word of mouth from satisfied customers and it seemed to work to attract more business. He was developing a reputation for quality products, both locally and in other market areas where he chose to participate, but his approach remained very conservative, choosing happy customers instead of flashy, sensational ads.

One ad that appeared in the *Connersville Times,* a weekly newspaper, offered "a splendid new buggy, one of McFarlan manufacture, for sale at a sacrifice." Interested persons were to contact the newspaper office for details.[14] This ad was apparently placed by a private individual and not by McFarlan. However, the following week, a statement from the editor of the *Times* read as follows: "Mr. J A [sic] McFarlan has a more extensive carriage factory than we supposed. We were shown through his establishment the other day. We saw about forty carriages and buggies of a fine quality, all ready for

An early carriage photograph from the McFarlan family (courtesy Jim Wicker).

1870s carriage built by J.B. McFarlan (photograph by author).

horse and driver, besides many others in process of completion. Mac is a driving business man and a clever gentleman."[15]

J.B. McFarlan was more than an industrialist; he was also a developer. He invested his profits in land, being fortunate and farsighted enough to obtain the old Jonathan Johns farm containing 160 acres adjacent to the growing village of Connersville, north of what is now West 8th Street and west of the canal. He first developed a residential district that became known as McFarlantown, but was eventually annexed into the city of Connersville as McFarlan's Plat. *The Connersville Examiner* of Dec. 24, 1867, was quite complimentary in referring to McFarlan's accomplishments, noting, "The best evidence that a town will be successful is to see that its moneyed men are possessed with enterprise and energy. That some of ours have the requisite qualifications is shown by the improvements made during the past season. One of them Mr. J B McFarland, commenced the erection of nine commodious, two story, brick residences during the summer and has completed six already."[16] In the spring of 1868 McFarlan announced that he would be building several houses on his plat to accommodate the influx of workers needed in the local industries. Another news item noted, "By October next, Mr. J B McFarland, the most enterprising citizen of this place, will have twenty-six houses for rent. A large number of them are now finished and occupied."[17] Eight new houses were entered onto the tax rolls by year's end at a total assessed value of $12,500.[18]

This area became almost a community within itself, as noted in the local newspaper in 1871: "McFarland town is becoming noted for its general thrift and healthy condition.

The cultural growth of the village being more than ordinary, in attracting the attention of persons in search of an earthly home."[19] Within a short time, the name of this new suburb to Connersville was written as one word, "McFarlantown." J.B. could probably have turned his town into a company run establishment where he controlled prices and allowed only his employees to live. Instead, he chose to rent or sell properties to whoever could afford them and even helped finance young men who were good prospects to build a home and make small payments toward ownership. One of the newly built houses was sold late in 1868 to Moses Long for the sum of $3,000.[20] J.B.'s own large house was located well up the hill off of what would later become 10th Street.

In those days, the most exciting happening in the community was the yearly county fair. One local newspaper was maybe a bit boastful in its description of this local gathering place: "The Fair Grounds, for convenience of location, picturesque beauty, native and artificial adornments, are not excelled by any other grounds in the state. They are on the north of the city, about a stone's throw from the suburbs, and extend east of the Ft. Wayne, Muncie & Cincinnati Railroad to the White Water River, and contain an area of 27 acres."[21] At the 1869 Fayette County Fair, held Sept. 3–10 at the fairgrounds north of what is now 10th Street, "Mr. Enoch Carson exhibited ... one of McFarlan's splendid late style topped buggies, which took the first premium. For beauty of finish, harmony of taste, and fine workmanship, nothing else there near equaled it." Another note in the same newspaper stated, "That fine carriage in which Mr. Levi Pike and family attended the Fair, is one of McFarlan's manufacture, and took the first premium."[22] When the awards for the fair were posted, the local carriage maker received further recognition, winning both first and second place for two-horse carriages, first place for top buggies, and first place for open buggies.[23] In Wayne County, which adjoins Fayette to the northeast, the county fair was held in October near Centerville. Again, Connersville workmanship was recognized as McFarlan received the first premium on one of his top buggies, and John Manlove received the first premium on his fine saddle horse.[24] The following year brought more recognition for McFarlan at the Fayette County Fair with the best two-horse carriages and second place for his spring wagon.[25] At the 1871 county fair McFarlan was again recognized with first and second prizes for the best two-horse carriage and first place for the best top buggy.[26]

Excitement at the fairgrounds wasn't limited to viewing the exhibits and socializing. Bantering back and forth among exhibitors over whose product was the best was a common pastime that was usually given and taken in good humor, but could lead to flaring tempers and fisticuffs or more serious eruptions. Such was the case at the 1881 county fair. The account in one of the local newspapers read as follows: "Some of the employees of the carriage factories of J.B. McFarlan, of this city, and George Loper, of Fairfield [Indiana], indulged in a row Thursday afternoon on the fair grounds over the merits of the work on exhibition from their respective shops. Fortunately the fracas was quelled before much blood was let."[27] The arm of the law apparently felt the situation should not be passed over as the "McFarlan boys" who participated in the fight were charged with inciting a riot. The case was settled a few months later in January 1882, when the local court acquitted them of the charge.[28] Both J.B. McFarlan and George Loper had records of high quality workmanship and had previously won premiums at the county fair. The workers that were involved were showing a certain amount of pride by their actions, but not everybody found it to be acceptable behavior at an event geared for family entertainment.

The 1882 County Fair was apparently less exciting as there was no record of anyone running afoul of the law. However, McFarlan found it to be quite profitable as he sold 16 vehicles to fairgoers. Those purchasing side-bar buggies were Lee Roberts, Horry Clifford, Charles Jackson, Elijah Jemison, Berry Meek, Wellington Beeson, Lycurgus Beeson, John Murphy, Alf Corbin, W.V. Spivey, Clark Porter, William Bertch, and Lewis Simler. Alex Edwards and Doc Sparks each purchased a Jagger wagon and J.H. Manlove a platform Kellog.[29]

Even without investing locally in advertising, McFarlan gained substantial notoriety through the various awards and his business continued to grow to the extent that he enlarged his trimming shop in September of 1871 by purchasing an additional building across the street.[30] After being in business for 20 years in Connersville, McFarlan invested in a small ad that ran for several issues in one of the local newspapers. The local paper also announced that J.B. McFarlan was going to have a big sale of buggies, phaetons and spring wagons on May 20, 1876, at Fayetteville, a small village, west of Connersville, located on the Fayette Rush county line (now known as the town of Orange).[31] Why McFarlan chose to have his sale at Fayetteville instead of Connersville is not clear. There was a competitor, Phillip Heeb and Sons, in the carriage building business in Fayetteville, and McFarlan may have wanted to put his products close enough to the competition that they could be easily compared for quality. The sale may also indicate McFarlan was feeling the business recession that was affecting businesses throughout the area at that time. At any rate, a few months after the sale at Fayetteville the competition had closed up shop and was no longer in business.

J.B. McFarlan's earliest local newspaper advertising appeared in *The Connersville Examiner*, May 2, 1876.

If sales were slow at the time, the lull apparently didn't last because within a couple of months, the same newspaper reported that J.B. McFarlan had shipped a carload of fine buggies to Hagerstown, a prospering town about 20 miles north of Connersville.

Even though McFarlan carriages and buggies were known for quality construction, they were not immune to problems. One summer evening in 1876, Charles McFarlan broke his buggy wheel while out Sunday driving. C.E.J. gave the reason as "too many drives of late."[32] Another Sunday evening outing proved to be less enjoyable than expected when Will McFarlan and Miss Maud Davis were out driving. The horse became frightened and made a sudden lunge, throwing both passengers to the ground and badly damaging the buggy.[33] Courting had its dangers even in those days. A few years later another incident was recorded. John McFarlan, Jr., had left his horse and spring wagon unattended at the Courthouse when the horse broke loose from the hitching rack, and running up Central Avenue, collided with John Mulheeren's sign post. The wagon was badly damaged and the horse had slight injuries, but no one on the crowded street was hurt.[34]

As McFarlan's business prospered, the family was recognized as being at the top of the social ladder. They already lived in a large house near the top of 10th Street hill that looked down on McFarlantown, but success tended to create a need for an even finer residence. An announcement came in April 1872 that J.B. was planning a new $20,000 residence.[35] By June, the foundation had been completed and the estimated value of the residence had been raised to $30,000 upon completion. This amount would be considered exorbitant by many folks as 10 comfortable houses could have been built for that amount.[36] Construction progressed rapidly throughout the summer months so that by September McFarlan's new residence was about ready for the roof.[37] Work continued throughout the winter months and by April 1873, a full year after construction began, plasterers were at work at what the newspaper labeled "McFarland's palatial residence."[38] By early October the residence was about ready for occupancy as it was reported that the observatory was nearing completion on McFarlan's new house west of town.[39] Construction of this magnificent house took 1½ years, but it was done well and is still a part of the local landscape.

McFarlan was a robust, hard-working man who knew few illnesses, but during the time that his new residence was being completed, he became seriously ill with erysipelas, an acute infectious disease of the skin.[40] He recovered from this illness and went on with his active lifestyle for many more years.

In a small community where everyone thinks they know everyone else's business, excitement and gossip ran rampant whenever a visiting dignitary or person of notoriety arrived in town. Such was the case in early February 1882, when a visit by Mr. Studebaker (which of the brothers was not mentioned) and Fred Parsehel of the South Bend wagon manufactory caused concern and speculation among locals. Could they be interested in working a deal that would give a boost to the local carriage industry, or were they making offers trying to lure McFarlan away?[41] Whatever the mission the two men had with McFarlan, their conversation was never revealed.

Within a week after the visitors from South Bend had been in town, McFarlan's workers had walked out on strike for higher wages. At least, that is the way *The Connersville*

Times described it.[42] The other weekly paper, *The Connersville Examiner*, told something of a different version: "The reported strike at J.B. McFarlan's carriage factory on Saturday was not a strike at all. Three or four helpers in the blacksmithing department demanded more wages, and were given permission to quit. The factory is still running on full time and with a full set of hands." One wonders just how forcefully the "permission to quit" was offered. There was also a near catastrophe when a pot of varnish caught fire in McFarlan's large frame building at the corner of 6th and Central Avenue. The excitement soon subsided when the flames were extinguished without damage.[43] Fire was probably the most dreaded thing that could happen to this type of business because virtually all of the materials on hand were quite flammable, the buildings were of wood construction, and what fire fighting equipment the city had was mostly ineffective. This time it was fortunately a near miss as the fire was taken care of quickly.

The very week of the fire scare and labor unrest, there was work to be done as McFarlan had received orders for 30 vehicles, 20 of which were to go to Springfield, Illinois.[44] The reputation of McFarlan's quality carriages was spreading well beyond the borders of its home state.

Labor troubles were making the news throughout the nation during this time and there had been issues in some departments at the carriage factory. One effort in fostering improved relations between workers and management was noted early in 1882. "All the buggy trimmers at McFarlan's shop took tea with foreman Carson Monday evening, at the solicitation of his estimable wife."[45] Even as the business was growing, there was still a family atmosphere that helped maintain favorable labor-

Top: Residence of J.B. and Lydia McFarlan, built in 1872–73. *Bottom:* Residence of C.E.J. McFarlan, located on 8th Street hill across the street from his parents' home (both photographs: the Rev. Julius F. Schwarz, *Pen and Camera of Connersville Indiana*, 1906).

management relations most of the time. At least one employee who had left for "greener pastures" returned as noted in another news item: "John Kensinger, a real good boy of Troy, Ohio, employed in the gear department of McFarlan's carriage works last year, is back at his old bench."[46] Another who thought the grass looked greener on the other side of the fence was John Henry, who, after being a foreman in the blacksmith department for 14 years, resigned so he could erect a shop on his property and start his own business. He was a master of his trade, and a worker that was surely missed.[47]

Skilled employees were often recruited from other towns whenever they were receptive to the invitation to change jobs. This may have been the case when John Kirkpatrick, of Rushville, accepted a position in the McFarlan Carriage factory and later moved his family to Connersville.[48] Many employees started as young men. Such was the case with Will Jameson, a worker at McFarlan, who married Miss Fannie Schrank. After

Has Stood the Test for 25 Years!

We mean the

McFARLAN BUGGY.

A trial for twenty-five years by the people of this vicinity fully warrants us in pronouncing the McFarlan Buggy the

Best Buggy Made in the West.

I have now on hand a large stock of this work which

I Must and Will Sell.

My stock consists of

Carriages, Kellogg's Buggies and Phaetons.

"Brewster Side-Bars" a Specialty.

All this work is made of the Best Material and by First-Class Mechanics.

ALL WORK WARRANTED.

Call and examine work and learn prices before purchasing elsewhere.

Repairing promptly done in the best style and at lowest rates. Remember the place, 6th street, opposite Dale, Rhodes & Co.'s lumber yard.

N. B.—I sell none but my own manufacture.

J. B. McFARLAN.

April 24-3m

J.B.'s establishment was on the northeast corner of 6th Street and Grand Avenue, across from Dale, Rhode & Co.'s lumber yard, as indicated in this ad in *The Connersville Examiner*, May 22, 1879.

the wedding, the couple was blessed with a furnished house, waiting in McFarlantown.[49] McFarlan often helped young men purchase their homes, accepting small payments until the home was paid for. With numerous factories in the area, workers had the opportunity to change jobs and many did when they tired of one company. They might leave for what seemed like a more appealing work situation, then a few months or years later, return as job openings became available. Although some employees came and went at the McFarlan Company, many of the faithful stayed and worked year in and year out, and were even loyal to the company generation after generation as McFarlan became almost an institution in its more than 70 year tenure in Connersville.

The spring of 1882 brought about a flurry of activity as demand for McFarlan vehicles dramatically increased. Saturdays proved to be quite busy as country folks came into town to shop. On Saturday, April 14, a dozen McFarlan buggies were sold,[50] but two weeks later on the 28th, McFarlan sold 25 buggies, probably keeping the entire staff of salesmen jumping.[51] These numbers likely included carriages and spring wagons. By the end of

May, it was reported that the McFarlan carriage factory had sold 455 buggies and carriages so far that season and had orders for 80 additional units. They also noted that the carriage factory provided employment for 65 men and boys.[52] One of the newspapers offered its support for Connersville's largest industry with the following claim: "The McFarlan works is the largest carriage manufactory in Indiana, turning out annually over fifteen hundred buggies and carriages. Why shouldn't Connersville people rejoice at its rapid growth and prosperity?"[53] There were other major producers of horse drawn vehicles such as Parry Manufacturing in Indianapolis and Studebaker in South Bend, but the Connersville community had arrived as a major player in the industry and would become even more prominent in coming years. Another news item noted, "The McFarlan carriage works continue to make things fly. They will sell 1,500 buggies and carriages during the present season."[54] It was evident that the facilities were being strained to their limit and plans would have to be made to enlarge. One way to increase production was to make the present facility more useable year round. During the summer of 1883, McFarlan installed natural gas throughout his factory building with the plan of running full time all winter.[55] Prior to that time, most vehicles were built "in season," during the warmer months when most sales were made. The installation of gas would benefit J.B. McFarlan twice, as he gained year round use of his carriage factory and was part owner of the gas company. The factory was able to work through the following winter as they turned out several elegant sleighs that were said to have been perfect little beauties.[56]

Traveling salesmen had become an important part of the McFarlan operation. Working mainly through the warmer months, they were to make contacts and open new territories with the end result being increased sales. One such salesman was Joshua Greer who worked the Wabash valley in western and northern Indiana, calling upon prospective distributors. Two years later, Greer had moved to Shelbyville, Indiana, working for a McFarlan dealer.[57] The sales job could be lucrative, as demonstrated by Tom McDaniel, who had had exceptional sales providing a salary plus commission netting $3,052 for the first seven

"Don't forget the place" in this ad from *The Connersville Examiner*, Aug. 11, 1881, referred to McFarlan's new salesroom, located where the majestic McFarlan Hotel would be built several years later.

months of 1882,[58] certainly an extraordinary income for a salesman of that time. Another who accepted a position of traveling for the McFarlan Company was Fred Smith, a young man considered to be a clever gentleman and expected to have good success.[59] Smith kept his sales position with the company for a number of years and covered a great deal of territory. Reaching out to new markets was showing its rewards as McFarlan shipped an order to Denver, Colorado, consisting of one carriage, one basket phaeton and two buggies.[60] There seemed to be few boundaries within the United States that McFarlan could not conquer.

The success of the McFarlan Carriage Company was certain to attract competition from others. The George Loper Company of Fairfield, Indiana, established a salesroom in Connersville and announced plans to build a factory. This was the company whose employees had gotten into an altercation with some McFarlan workers at the local fair a few years earlier. Loper's plans for construction in Connersville did not materialize, but another new buggy manufacturing company, the Connersville Buggy Company, did go into production in 1883 building quality low-priced buggies. This company lasted for about 30 years producing large numbers of inexpensive vehicles. A few years later in 1898, another major player entered the buggy business locally when Rex Manufacturing began producing low priced, high quality horse-drawn vehicles that sold by the thousands for a few years. McFarlan seemed to thrive with competition as their business also continued to grow and prosper.

J.B. McFarlan was one of the major influences in turning the Connersville community into a bustling industrial city. He established several significant businesses that would contribute to the city for many years. His carriage company also underwent change when J.B. brought his sons into the business and changed the name to McFarlan Carriage Company. The first announcement of the reorganization was made on November 1, 1883, when sons Charles E.J. and William W. assumed equal interests with their father.[61] The next change was made public in late April of 1884, when J. Edward McFarlan took a fourth interest and was given personal supervision of one of the departments of the

Having 34 buggies in stock showed preparation for the upcoming county fair where brisk sales were expected (*The Connersville Examiner*, Sept. 1, 1881).

For a Fine
BUGGY,

GO TO THE

McFarlan Carriage Works,

The Leading Manufacturer of Fat FULL

Carriages and Buggies

In the West.

TESTIMONIALS:

GENTS: Your buggies have not failed in a single instance to give entire satisfaction. We have never had one of your jobs returned to us for repairs, neither have we heard a single complaint. Yours truly,
H. B. BUCKLEY & CO.

Springfield, Illinois, December 31, 1881.
N. B.—Since writing the above, Messrs. B. & Co. have ordered twenty-two buggies from us.

GENTS: I have used your buggies for the past five years in my livery, and they have given entire satisfaction. Yours truly,
CHARLES BUNDY.

New Castle, Indiana, January 19, 1882.

DEAR SIR: Having during the past season handled your carriages and buggies, I am pleased to state that my customers have been fully satisfied with their purchases. Please send me catalogue and price-list for coming season. Yours truly,
JOHN SWANSON.

Joliet, Illinois, January 7, 1882.

GENTS: In handling your work in the past, I have become satisfied that it is first-class all through, and my customers are pleased with it and speak well of it. I can recommend your goods without any hesitancy. By the way it has been selling, I think I shall be able to order often.
Yours truly, S. C. BARLEY.

Marion, Indiana, December 26.

Please call and examine the work before purchasing elsewhere.

April 5-tf   J. B. McFarlan.

STILL IN THE FIELD!

The Old Reliable

McFARLAN CARRIAGE FACTORY

— Where you can get the —

BEST WORK IN THE WORLD FOR THE LEAST MONEY!

Do Not be misled by the idle talk about Shyster Work, Etc., by Small Dealers in Foreign Work, but

COME DIRECT to HEADQUARTERS

AND

EXAMINE OUR WORK

for yourselves, and you will be convinced that

All We Claim is True.

SALESROOM,

South-west Corner Sixth Street & Central Avenue

J. B. McFARLAN.

8-16-tf

Left: Including testimonials gave credence to the claim of the quality of McFarlan built vehicles (*The Connersville Examiner*, April 15, 1883). *Above:* "The Old Reliable McFarlan Carriage Factory" had served the community for many years before other buggy manufacturers opened their doors for business (*The Connersville Examiner*, May 16, 1883).

factory. Very strong in family ties, the new company had as officers the elder McFarlan and his four sons: John B. McFarlan, president; C.E.J. McFarlan, vice-president; J.E. McFarlan, superintendent; W.W. McFarlan, secretary; and J.B. McFarlan, Jr., assistant secretary.[62] It was a completely family owned and family run business. There was also evidence that, after building his business for thirty years, J.B., Sr., was ready to turn part of the operation over to the younger generation; however, he still kept his finger on the pulse and continued to have the final say on decisions of significance.

In mid–1884, another company was formed for the purpose of breaking into the lowest priced vehicle market. This was described by the local newspaper as follows; "A new Buck Board Company has been organized in this city with J.B. McFarlan (Sr.) as president, C.E.J. McFarlan vice-president, W.W. McFarlan secretary and treasurer, and J.E. McFarlan, superintendent. Until a more suitable place can be had, the new enterprise will be carried in connection with the McFarlan Carriage Works." The new company had been negotiating with the Connersville Buck Board Factory with a view of buying that establishment, but had failed to agree upon terms.[63] The lower priced buckboards had found a niche in the market because near the end of the year, McFarlan and Sons had sent out what was described as "a long train of carts and buggies," headed for Richmond, Indiana.[64] There was definitely a market for the lower priced vehicle and the Buck Board Company was probably formed at the urging of one of the younger McFarlans. It didn't last because it did not meet the quality standards on which J.B. had built his business.

Charles E.J. McFarlan was born Dec. 1, 1853, while his parents lived in Cambridge City. As a boy, he learned the trade of carriage painter while also attending local schools. Additional education was gained at the Chickering Institute at Cincinnati. After selling boots, shoes and the like for three years, Charles joined his father in the carriage business. He was united in marriage to Ella S. Hughes in 1880, and they had one son, Alfred Harry McFarlan, who would later become very much involved in the family business. In addition to his involvement building carriages, C.E.J. became secretary and treasurer of the Connersville Natural Gas Company, vice-president of the McFarlan Realty Company and a member of the local school board for 12 years. Charles E.J. was quite active in the First Methodist Episcopal Church and other local organizations. He died in 1920 at his home in Connersville.

Charles E.J. McFarlan, who with two of his brothers entered the business with their father in 1883. C.E.J. stayed with the carriage business until it ended (courtesy Jim Wicker).

James Edward McFarlan was born in 1856 in Connersville and attended the local schools. He became a partner in the McFarlan Carriage Company before migrating south to spend a large part of his adult life in St. Petersburg, Florida.[65] James died August 13, 1929, at his home in Connersville. He and his wife had one son, James Edward, Jr.

William W. McFarlan was raised in Connersville and joined with his father and older brother, Charles, as an equal partner in the newly formed McFarlan Carriage Company on November 4, 1883. Within three weeks after entering into business with his father, Will was united in marriage with Miss Roe Mount, also of Connersville.[66] William remained active in the carriage business for several years until becoming president of the Central State Bank at the time it was founded. He retired from the bank in 1908, moving to Los Angeles, California. William and Roe had one son, Herbert M. who married Helen Louise Mount and left the area to settle on a cattle ranch in Texas. He returned for a couple of years to help with the marketing of the McFarlan automobile in its early years, but could not ignore the call of the West.[67] Herbert eventually moved to California where he died in 1937.

John B. McFarlan, Jr. the youngest of the clan, was born November 7, 1866, and was reared in Connersville. After completing public school education he attended Miami University in Oxford, Ohio, for two years before returning to his hometown to become a partner in the newly formed McFarlan Carriage Company. He later became president of the People's Service Company and owned a fine farm in Rush County that he had inherited from his father. John was long considered one of the most eligible bachelors in the area until he finally married Nellie Brown, also of Connersville, on October 12, 1910.[68] John B. Jr. died in 1953. John and Nellie had one son, John B. McFarlan III, born in 1918.

The buggy and carriage business had grown dramatically in the early 1880s to the point that J.B. decided to put up a new four-story brick building. It was to be in downtown Connersville at the corner of Central Avenue and 6th Street where his large frame factory and ware room stood. Community leaders received the news with enthusiasm.[69] In view of J.B. McFarlan's status as head of the most prestigious family in town and a respected businessman, it might be expected that his desire to purchase additional property to accommodate a new building downtown would be applauded by all citizens. In fact, however, some opposition apparently arose to the proposed location of the carriage factory, prompting one local newspaper to comment, "The McFarlan Carriage Company, having failed to agree on terms for the purchase of J. L. Bailey's property, now talk of building their new factory up town. It is to be hoped that the matter will be so adjusted as to enable them to go ahead with the building down town. Connersville is sadly in need of good business rooms, and this building would furnish a half dozen first-class ones. Give 'em a chance."[70] McFarlan had already spent a good deal of money at the 6th and Central location by installing gas throughout the building and he now wanted to make a much larger facility that would provide increased employment.

The downtown location did not materialize, but as sometimes happens when a plan falls through, a better solution was soon to come. In the short run, McFarlan built two small additions onto their 6th and Central location. The first of those adjoined Gipe's Fruit Store and was completed by July of 1884 to be used as the office area.[71] For the long run, an announcement came early in 1884 of plans to build the new carriage factory on ground that McFarlan already owned at the north edge of town across the Cincinnati Hamilton & Dayton Railroad tracks. This decision elicited less enthusiasm from city leaders because it would not add the impressive new building to the downtown landscape that they had hoped for. It was not initially McFarlan's preference either, because the land on which he was to build was crop land that he preferred not to take out of production. The various utilities also had to be run to the proposed plant location and would take additional time and expenditure. After McFarlan announced its plan to relocate along the edge of the city, it would be nearly three years before construction actually began on the new factory building. However, had it not been for J.B.'s inability to purchase more land at that time in downtown Connersville, the nation's first industrial park might not have been developed in Fayette County, Indiana.

As soon as the news got out that a new factory building was planned, other cities sat up and took an interest to see if McFarlan could be enticed to move to their community. Already cities were offering incentives to factories that would provide jobs. A committee from Kokomo, Indiana, offered five acres of ground and an operating natural gas well without charge if McFarlan would relocate there.[72] That was an attractive offer for sure, but the elder McFarlan was too well entrenched in Connersville with property he owned, interests in other local businesses and close family ties to seriously consider such a move.

A few years passed before serious action occurred with the new building. In February 1887, the following announcement was made: "The McFarlan Carriage Company is making preparations to build a commodious new factory on their vacant grounds, near the Connersville Furniture Company's buildings during the coming season. They will burn their own brick and commence building about the 1st of August."[73] Work started early in the spring putting in gas and water lines and laying the foundation. By July, the contract had been awarded to Wertlake Brothers of Muncie, Indiana, for laying the bricks.[74] Work progressed rapidly on the large factory building so that by mid–August, the brick walls were reported to be three stories high.[75] By mid–October, factory equipment was being moved to the new building and the Central Avenue side of McFarlan's old factory building was being remodeled into business rooms.[76]

This impressive new carriage manufacturing facility was located on five acres of land at what later became Mount and Columbia Streets next to the Cincinnati Hamilton and Dayton Railroad. The main building was a substantial four-story brick structure measuring 270 feet by 60 feet. There were also two large wings, the first measuring 150 by 60 feet, and the second wing, 110 by 60 feet. The latest powered machinery available at that time enabled increased production of high quality vehicles with less effort on the part of the workers. With the exception of wheels, springs and axles, the entire process of building carriages, from raw materials to finished product, was accomplished "in house." This building was certainly a tremendous change from the small quarters near the corner of 6th and Grand in which J.B. McFarlan started his business some thirty years earlier.

Production started at the new four-story brick factory as soon as the building was under roof and equipment could be moved in. Additional improvements to the manufacturing facility were added soon after. By mid–December, a natural gas well had been drilled nearby that provided gas for factory stoves.[77] Several pockets of natural gas had been located in the area and were useful for short periods of time as a source of energy, but the wells didn't maintain adequate pressure for very long. It was several years before a reliable source of natural gas would become available to the community.

The new McFarlan Carriage Company main building was built in 1887 (courtesy Robert Martin).

To aid in receiving materials and shipping finished products, two switches were installed on the C. H. & D. Railroad and side tracks were brought along next to the factory building. One track was for bringing in raw materials such as steel, wood and fabric, and the other for exporting the finished products.[78] A major improvement was added about one year later with the installation of an electric light plant, so the building was brilliantly lighted and work was no longer restricted to daylight hours.[79] McFarlan management was better able to keep the night-watchman on task when an electric register with 25 stations was installed. The man on duty was compelled to check in at each station every hour and the visit was recorded by electrical impulse in the office.[80]

With the new building completed and equipment installed, production would be increased significantly. Within two years of their relocation, McFarlan announced plans to put on additional workers. At times, from 300 to 400 men were employed, many of whom were considered to be artisans at their trade, from woodworkers to blacksmiths, to upholsterers, painters and polishers.[81] A significant change in policy came about when they decided to hire 25 women to run the sewing machines in the trimming department.[82] For the first time in company history, the fairer sex was permitted to work in the factory. The women were expected to contribute that special touch of meticulous detail that McFarlan had become known for, and they would be expected to do the work quicker than men for less pay. The McFarlan Carriage Company was, by far, the community's largest employer. The local economy was a sure beneficiary of the wages workers received.

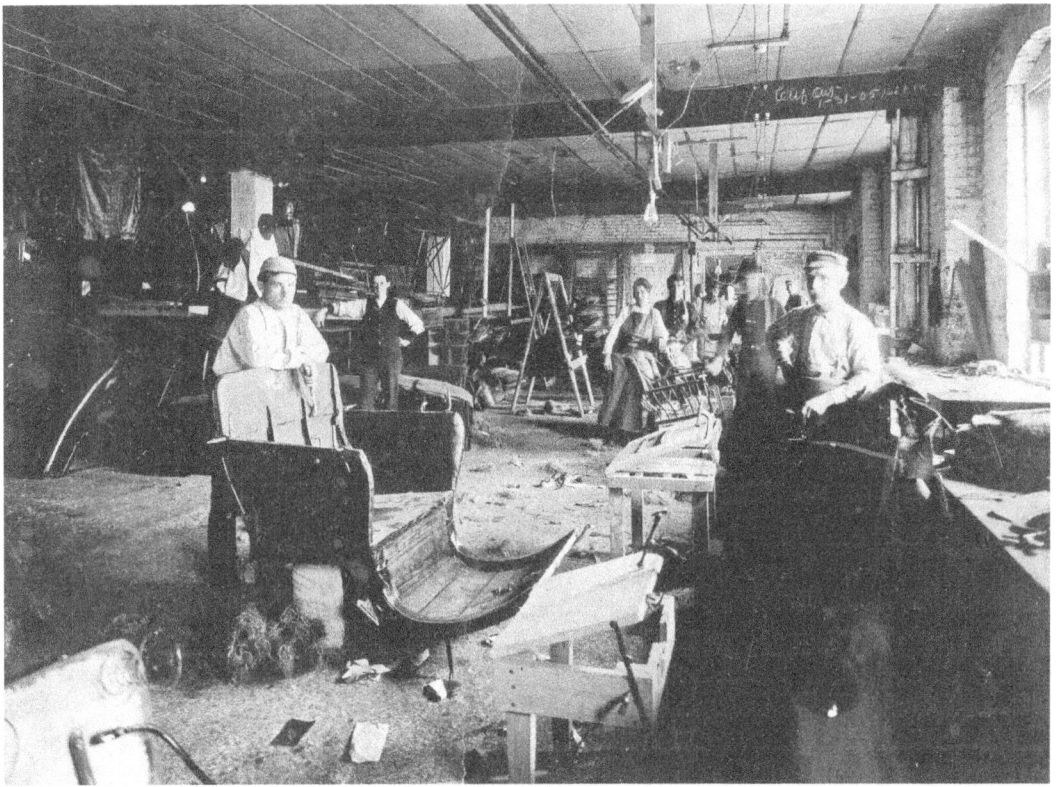

Inside the big McFarlan carriage factory on Mount Street (courtesy Fayette County Historical Museum).

Every Monday, approximately $1,800 in pay was taken home, and that figure increased as business prospered and additional people were put to work.[83]

Increased plant production was showing results with new records being set. For 1890, the prediction was that 10,000 vehicles would leave the factory. The very week that the optimistic prediction was printed, though, a breakdown left the factory in darkness. It seems that a belt on the electric light generator broke, causing a loss of valuable time toward meeting the production goal for that day. In spite of occasional delays, production did set records for the company.[84] One year later in January 1891, 10 train car loads of McFarlan vehicles were shipped at one time to Kansas City, Missouri. This was an exceptional shipment, recognized even by the C. H. & D. Railroad, which decorated the cars with advertisements that made the train look somewhat like a circus train.[85] Company management didn't miss the opportunity to brag just a bit because they had shipped an order of vehicles to Australia.[86] In another shipment two years later, a number of vehicles were sent on consignment to a firm Down Under.[87] The local company had reached another milestone. Not even the borders of the United States would limit their sales for customers who recognized the quality of McFarlan's products.

Once J.B. could see his new carriage factory running at full speed, he decided to turn more of the management duties over to his sons, but he didn't drop out of the picture.

Employees of the McFarlan Carriage Company about 1890 (courtesy Fayette County Historical museum).

He still had the final say on any issue of significance. J.B. was at a period in his life when many men would think of retirement or traveling. He didn't think that way as he was purely a business man, conservative, but a liberal contributor toward worthy enterprises.[88] He did travel a bit more, though, and even took his wife on enjoyable trips to Cedar Rapids, Iowa, and Kansas City, Missouri. These cities probably did provide cultural attractions they could enjoy, but they also had McFarlan distributors he could check on. His employees recognized J.B.'s advancing age and, in recognition of his 71st birthday, presented him with an elegant plush rocker as a token of their respect and esteem. The gift was a delightful surprise for the aging gentleman, who sincerely thanked them with words of appreciation.[89] The rocking chair provided welcome relaxation when used, but did not keep the senior McFarlan from remaining active in his businesses.

As J.B. spent less time at the factory, he had energy to pursue other interests. He decided there would be an advantage for his business if other manufacturers chose to locate nearby. Of special interest to McFarlan were firms involved in the production of carriage parts. Having such businesses close by would provide easy access to parts he might need without relying on the sometimes unpredictable railroads. Therefore, the decision was made to develop additional land that he owned near the carriage plant.

Early in 1891, the Connersville Land and Improvement Company was founded by the elder McFarlan and other prominent local men. This company was incorporated and began holding regular meetings with the express purpose of planning the development of land near the carriage factory, an area that became known as Edgewood.[90] Through the

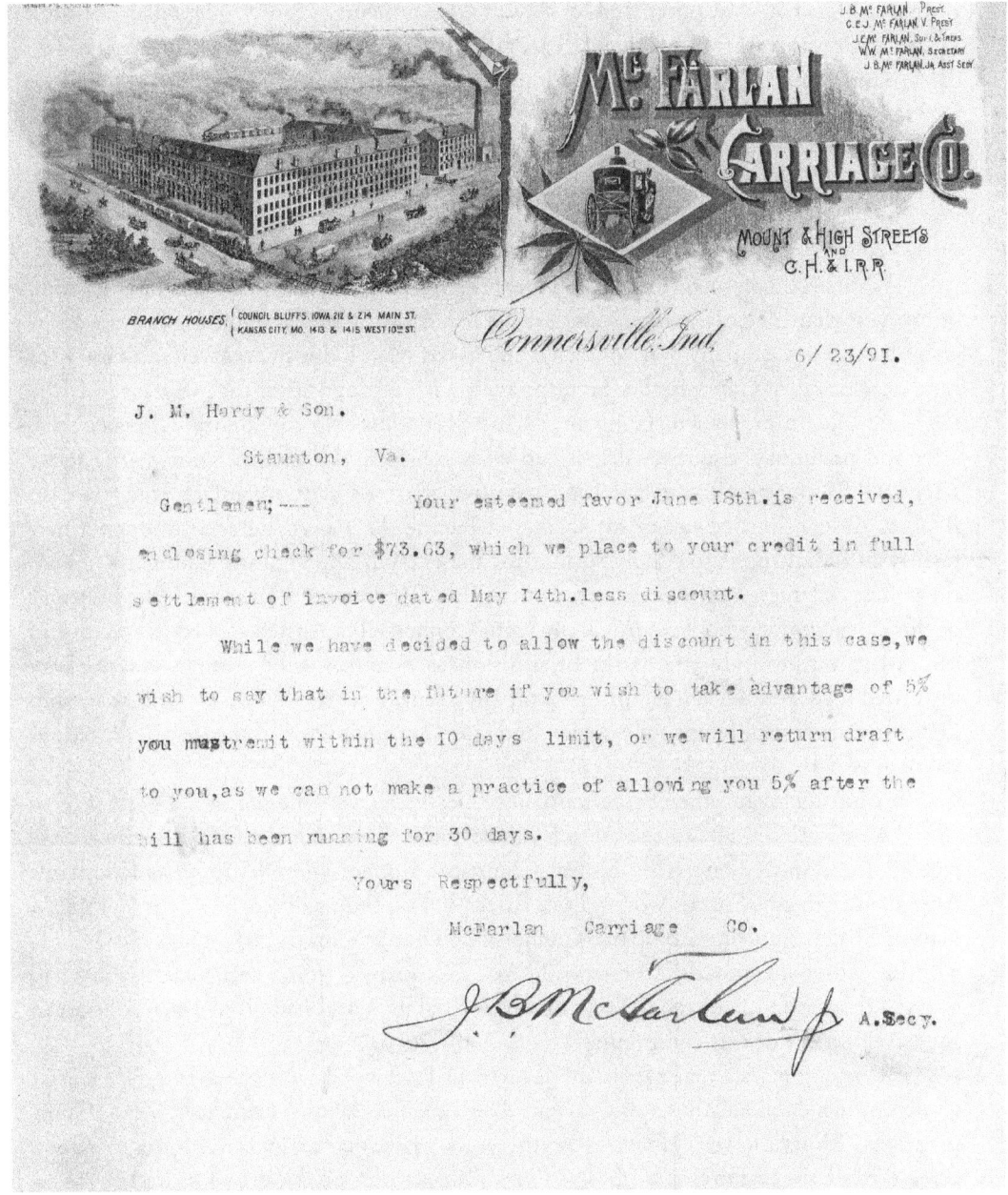

The McFarlan Carriage Co. letterhead conveyed the message of a large operation. J.B. McFarlan, Jr., had joined the company as secretary.

Land and Improvement Company, additional property was purchased from the County Commissioners and from private individuals. Then, contacts were made with various manufacturing firms asking what kind of incentives would be required for them to relocate in this new development. Land was also platted for residential use. It was expected that homes would be built for factory workers who chose to live near their place of employment.

Individual lots could be purchased for $200 with payments as low as one dollar per week until the lot was paid for. A residential area did develop, much of which still exists today.

Many people in that day did not understand the significance of McFarlan's venture in Edgewood. It had originally been cultivated farmland that they considered to be useful, but as they watched the laying of gas and water pipes, the development was often ridiculed as "John's corn patch." Little did they understand that this project was to become what was probably the nation's first industrial park and a source of employment for hundreds of east central Indiana residents for generations to come.

The first out-of-town industry to locate in the new development was just the kind of business that McFarlan was looking for. When Edward W. Ansted, owner of the Indianapolis Spring Company, was contacted and asked what inducements were necessary for him to relocate to Connersville, he responded with a proposition that was accepted by the Land and Improvement Company.[91] Ansted made a trip to Connersville very soon after and finalized the agreement. A man with youthful vigor when he made the move later in 1892, he previously had been part owner of a spring manufacturing plant in Racine, Wisconsin. Because of his success at Racine, he was encouraged to open a new factory in Indianapolis to supply springs for the Parry Manufacturing Company, one of the country's largest buggy producers at that time.[92] Three years later, with the blessings of the Parry family, who were originally from Connersville, Ansted moved his factory to the just sprouting industrial park. In addition to manufacturing springs, Ansted later organized the Central Manufacturing Company to make vehicle bodies, the Indiana Lamp Company, makers of lamps for buggies, and later, automobiles and the Hoosier Castings Company.

Within ten years, there were ten companies located in the industrial park, five of which were entirely new to the city of Connersville. In addition to McFarlan's carriage factory, there was Connersville Blower Company, Connersville Natural Gas Company, Ansted and Higgins Spring Works, Fries Brick Works, Indiana French Mirror Company, National Manufacturing Company, Connersville Lounge Company, Connersville Woodworking Company and the Connersville Axle Company. "John's corn patch" truly had sparked the beginning of the nation's first industrial park and had given a major boost to the development of this community.

Other companies that eventually located in Edgewood were the George R. Carter Company, which did leather upholstering; the Rex Wheel Works; Lexington Motor Company; and Roots Blower Company. As the years passed by, many other industries took advantage of the location and chose to locate near other businesses to share the transportation arteries and draw from a plentiful supply of labor.

McFarlan was not interested in developing all of his property. He appreciated good farm land as he owned two fine farms in Rush County and two in Fayette County. Occasionally he would opt out of working at his factory so he could spend time looking after his farm interests. As he got older, these occasions became more frequent. As his sons were entrusted with the responsibility of managing the factory, J.B. felt more freedom to be away from the plant. There is no indication that J.B. ever actually took a vacation or cared to travel extensively. He was a company man and he manned the company that he

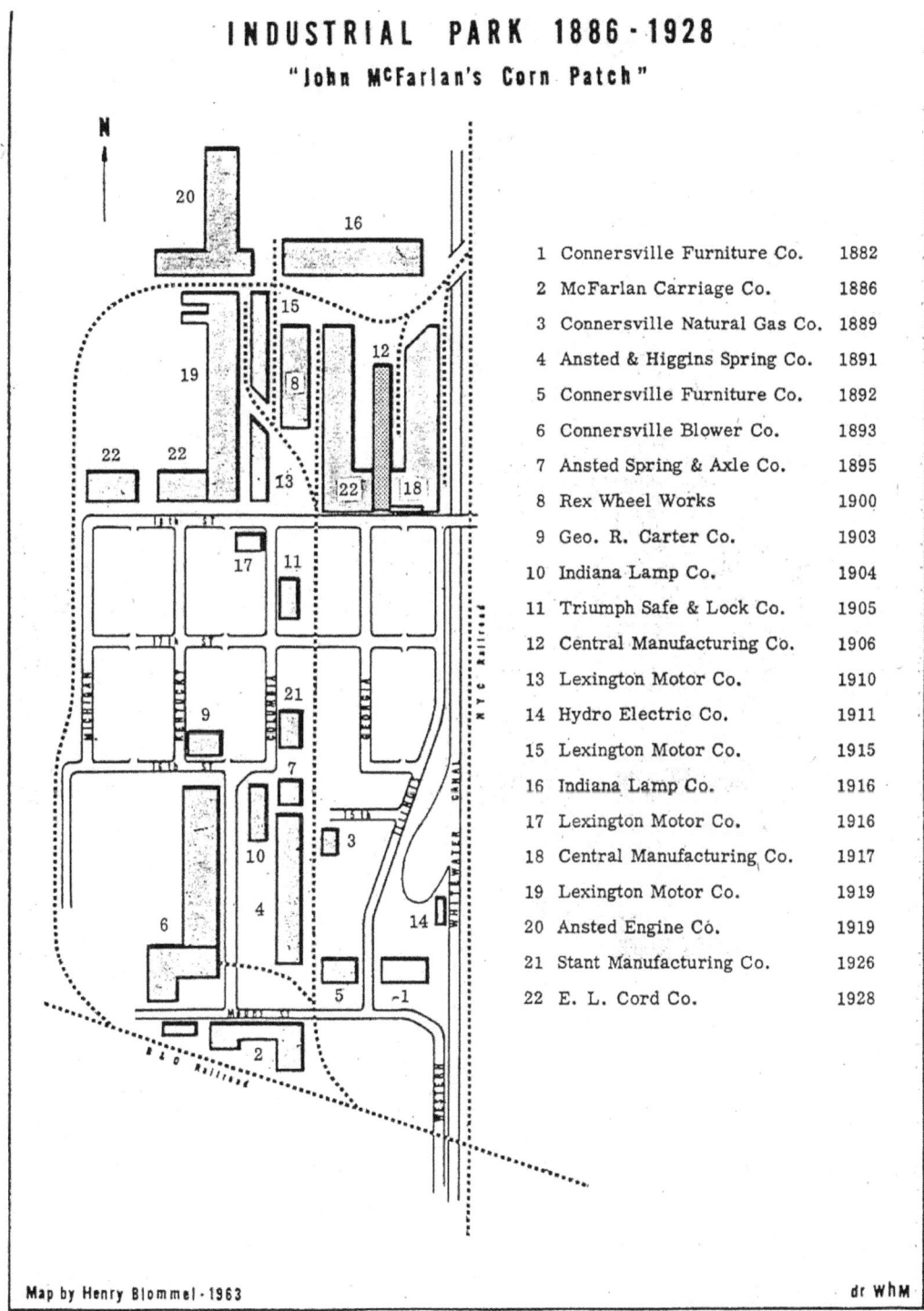

"John McFarlan's corn patch" became the nation's first industrial park (*Connersville News-Examiner*, October 19, 1987).

A temporary shelter was used to display this new McFarlan carriage (courtesy Fayette County Historical Museum).

had built and nurtured through the years. The few extended trips that J.B. and Lydia took still permitted him to keep a finger on business while not having to deal with the day to day problems of the factory.

J.B. McFarlan gave little concern for social involvement. While living at Cambridge City, he had joined the Masonic lodge and was at one time Worshipful Master. After moving to Connersville, he was a member of a lodge for a short time, but generally shunned community organizations. Not a member of any church, he did contribute liberally to many causes, usually without notoriety. Although he was Connersville's most conspicuous citizen, J.B. preferred to stay out of the public eye, opting instead for the quietness of home.[93] The single exception was his leadership with the local Board of Trade, an organization similar to today's Chamber of Commerce.

At the Board of Trade meeting that was held on New Year's Day, 1891, the topic of discussion was the need for a fine hotel in Connersville. The men of wealth had been invited and all seemed to agree regarding the need, but no one offered to take on such a project.[94] J.B. McFarlan, however, began mulling over the idea of building just such a structure. If the McFarlan name was to be connected with it, the building would have to be grand indeed. Within three years, definite plans had been formulated and the necessary land had been acquired.

Sometimes collecting money owed was more difficult than making the sale.

To facilitate this venture, the McFarlan Building Company was organized. Its main purpose was to oversee the erection the largest, most ostentatious building in downtown Connersville, the McFarlan Block. More than just a grand hotel, this structure was to contain an opera house, a location for the Central State bank, recently founded principally by the McFarlan family, plus a number of spaces for stores.[95] Construction was expected

The McFarlan Hotel and Office Building opened January 1, 1895 (the Rev. Julius F. Schwarz, *Pen and Camera of Connersville Indiana*, 1906).

to begin in 1893, and workers did move a substantial amount of dirt that year while digging the basement for the building, but difficulties with some details held construction up until the following year. The first stone was laid in the foundation early in 1894 on the half-block lot at 6th and Central Ave. that formerly had been the location of J.B.'s two-story wood frame carriage factory and ware room. Construction progressed rapidly, allowing for the building to formally be declared open on January 1, 1895.[96] This magnificent building became the center of local social events for many years, but it lost favor with a younger generation and was razed in 1963 to be replaced with a more modern but much less picturesque bank building.

At the carriage factory, business remained good. In April 1895, McFarlan shipped 11 carloads of buggies and carriages. Much of this business was generated by the traveling salesmen who represented the carriage factory throughout the country. One example of the company's outreach was a display of vehicles in Atlanta, Georgia, at the Cotton States Exhibition in the fall of 1895. Fred Smith, a longtime traveling representative for McFarlan, was put in charge of the company's exhibit. Hailed in some ads as the Atlanta World's Fair, the event was a major attraction that had many features of the previously held

Chicago World's Fair plus many new ones. It ran from September 18 through the remainder of the year and attracted large numbers of onlookers.[97]

Accidents at the factory seemed to be few, but an unusual one happened in the new building when Charlie Jacobs was on the third story bridge that connected two parts of the facility. He somehow lost his balance and fell off of the building. While falling, he was able to turn two complete somersaults, landing on his feet in such a manner that he was not hurt. Charlie was considered to be one lucky fellow that day.[98] A more painful accident occurred when William Brown got two fingers on his right hand crushed by a tire setting machine.[99] One of the McFarlan family, J. Edward, suffered a rather spectacular accident in 1907. He was on the roof of one of the factory buildings inspecting the repair of storm damage from the previous week, when he slipped and fell through a broken skylight, landing on the floor about 15 feet below. Nearby workers went to his aid and a physician was summoned to attend to his serious injuries.[100]

With the beginning of a new century Connersville was reaching its full potential in manufacturing and was rated as third in the nation in production of light-duty horse-drawn vehicles, behind only Cincinnati, Ohio, and Flint, Michigan. For the year 1900, Connersville was expected to turn out an average of 185 vehicles each day or over 50,000 for the year. The major producers were listed as follows:

Company	Employees
McFarlan Carriage Company	350
Rex Buggy Company (one year old)	225
Connersville Buggy Company	150
Central Manufacturing Company — bodies	150
Connersville Axle Company	75
Ansted Spring Company	75
Connersville Wagon Company — wheels	200[101]

By 1900, the J.B. McFarlan Carriage Company had established several distribution houses to strengthen their marketing position. Distributors were located in Minneapolis, Minnesota; Des Moines, Iowa; Kansas City and Moberly, Missouri; Dallas, Texas; Lincoln, Nebraska; and Atlanta, Georgia.[102]

An illustration of the large scale of business the McFarlan Company was engaged in was shown on January 8, 1900. An unusual celebration of sorts was held at the factory as a trainload of McFarlan vehicles left Connersville for dealers in Texas. Hundreds of people gathered along the C.H. & D. tracks to watch the train leave. There were 30 carloads of vehicles, each 50 feet long with a full length banner hung on each side proclaiming "McFarlan Vehicles, Connersville, Indiana," plus the name of the Texas dealer who was to receive them, and the statement "Largest Single Shipment of Vehicles Ever Sent Out of The State."[103] With nearly 1,000 vehicles on board worth an estimated $55,000, this was believed to be the largest single shipment of already sold vehicles ever made in the United States.[104]

A great deal of credit was given to the Texas sales representative, Dan M. Hankins, formerly of Connersville, for his fine sales performance. Hankins was employed by McFarlan from 1894 until 1905 at a salary that started at $50 per month, increasing to $175 per month, by yearly contract, as he had sold upwards of $100,000 worth of the company's output in a single year.[105]

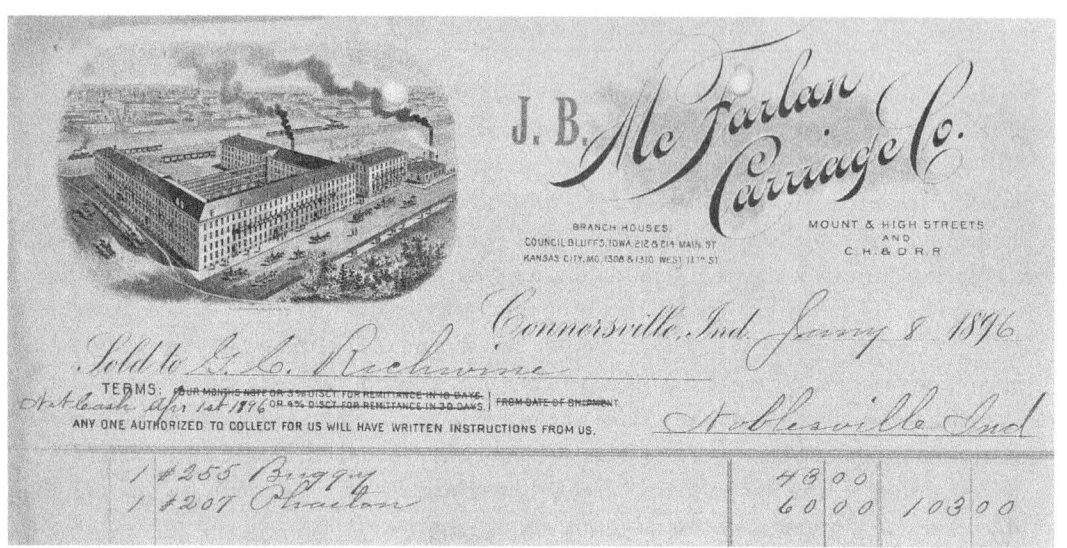

Top: G.C. Richwine, a dealer in Noblesville, Indiana, purchased a buggy and a phaeton in 1896 and was billed $103. *Bottom:* Payment was received promptly and was acknowledged by J.B. McFarlan, Jr.

Opposite: A major distributor was located at Kansas City, Missouri (*Millard's Implement Directory*, vol. IX, 1895).

McFARLAN CARRIAGE CO.

WHOLESALE MANUFACTURERS **CONNERSVILLE, IND.**

BRANCH HOUSES:

KANSAS CITY, MO., 1308 and 1310 West 11th Street.
COUNCIL BLUFFS, IOWA, 212-214 Main St., and 213-215 Pearl St. Tel. 63.

MANUFACTURERS OF

Carriages, Surreys, Phaetons, Buggies, Road and Spring Wagons.

SEE OUR LARGE LINE OF NEW SURREYS AND PHAETONS!

HOLD YOUR ORDERS FOR OUR TRAVELING SALESMEN OR WRITE TO US DIRECT AND WE WILL GIVE IT PROMPT ATTENTION.
☞ SEND FOR CATALOGUE AND PRICES.

McFARLAN CARRIAGE CO., KANSAS CITY, MO.

W. J. HANKINS, Manager.

No. 203, Physician Phaeton, as advertised in a January 1896 catalog.

Another sale of unusual proportions was noted in Connersville in April. The local McFarlan distributor, Mart Meyer, had 52 McFarlan vehicles on display along Central Avenue. This was quite an impressive display for a small city distributor, but it was all the more impressive because all 52 vehicles had already been sold. Another unusual thing about the display was that 42 of the vehicles rode on rubber tires, at a time when McFarlan was only equipping about one in six vehicles with rubber tires for normal distribution. Local purchasers obviously recognized the improved riding qualities of rubber over steel tires. Mart Meyer provided entertainment and a sumptuous meal at the McFarlan Hotel for this exceptionally large number of purchasers.[106]

McFarlan vehicles offered three grades of quality: Imperial, Standard, and Royal. The nomenclature of grades seems odd as the Imperial listed the fewest amenities. Even at that, Imperial carriages had refinements such as leather, cloth or fancy corduroy upholstery, tops of leather except for the side curtains, and Sarven patent wheels. Colors for the running gear were black, green or wine. The middle level Standard Grade offered wool, leather or fancy plush upholstery in any of eight different patterns and a high spring seat back with fancy welts if the customer preferred. The top was of leather or had leather

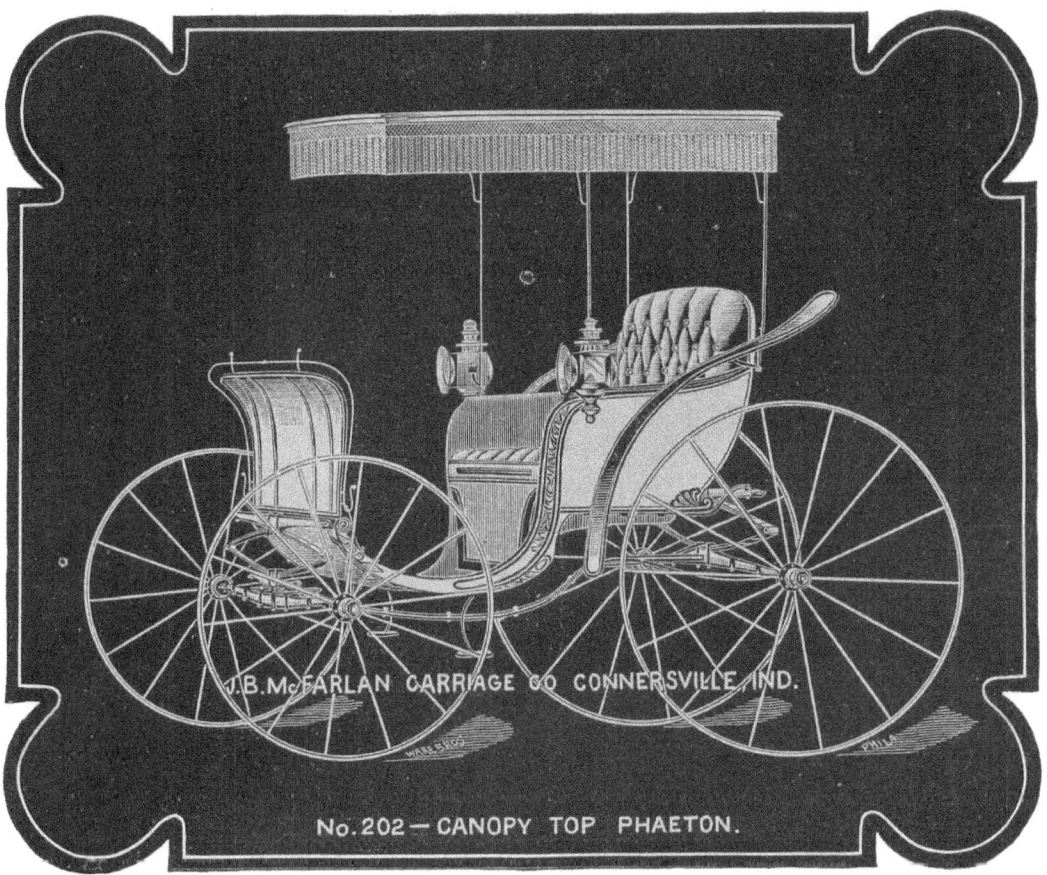

No. 202, Canopy Top Phaeton, from January 1896 catalog.

quarters with rubber roof and curtains. The Brewster style fifth wheel was furnished with double collar steel axles. Colors for the running gear were black, bronze green, carmine or dark green with neat striping. The top-of-the-line Royal Grade offered upholstery of heavy wool cloth, M.B. leather, whipcord or fancy corduroys, a top of the best machine buffed leather with four roll-up straps and four knobs across the bottom of the back curtain. The Royal Grade boasted thousand mile axles and quick shifting shaft shackles and a wrought iron Brewster slot fifth wheel. The final touch, in addition to rubber covered steps, was a black or rosewood painted body with striping as preferred and black, green or carmine for the chassis. If the specified colors didn't satisfy the discriminating buyer, other colors were available if the company was given extra time. One popular option that was available on all vehicles was rubber tires, which added comfort and extended the life of the vehicle. The McFarlan warranty covered all vehicles for one year from date of sale, with fair and reasonable usage, as a private vehicle only. Shipping instructions stated that all goods were packed and crated carefully and delivered in good order at the depot in Connersville. They went on to say, "with this delivery our responsibility ceases." Presumably, any damage upon arrival would have to be settled between the railroad and the

No. 183, Extension Top Surrey, from 1900 catalog.

purchaser. The catalog for 1900 listed 71 different vehicles that were available for order ranging from the Smith Undertaker's Buggy to the Stanhope Phaeton.[107]

The year 1901 marked a significant change in company policy. Up until that time, the business had been wholly family owned, but as a means of rewarding several employees who had demonstrated their commitment to the company through years of faithful service, a step toward profit sharing was introduced. One fifth of the company stock, valued at

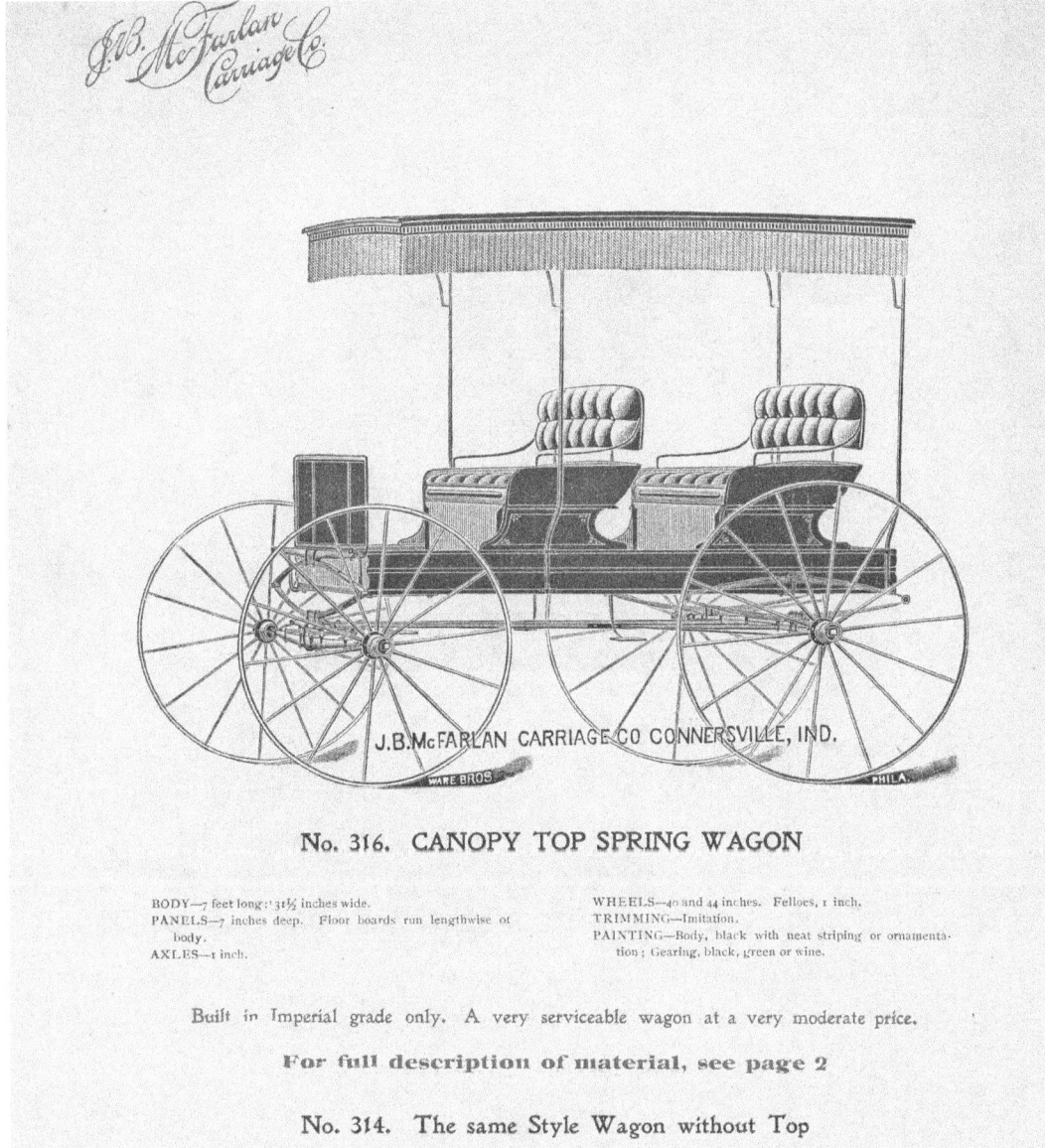

No. 316, Canopy Top Spring Wagon, from 1900 catalog.

$25,000, was made available to nine trusted employees, Charles Reeder, Charles Manor, Will Silvers, Scott Webb, Edward Moore, Andrew Jackson, Wright Holter, Fred Smith and Bert Barrows. These men had been with McFarlan from seven to twenty years and had gained the trust of the family. It was expected that additional employees would be given the same opportunity in the future. One local newspaper was quite complimentary in saying, "They [McFarlans] are always in the right place when the welfare of the town or their employees is at stake."[108]

No. 243. COMBINATION ELLIPTIC SPRING AND SIDE BAR TOP BUGGY

BODY—18, 20 or 23 inches wide; 54 inches long.
TOP—Made with shifting rail so the top can be removed, leaving the back with the buggy when used as an open vehicle.
WHEELS—Sarven or compressed band, 36 and 40, 38 and 42, 40 and 44 or 42 and 46 inches. Felloes, ¾, ⅞ or 1 inch.

TRIMMING—Cloth, whipcord or leather. See page 57 for styles.
PAINTING—Body, black, plain or striped, or will finish in fancy colors as preferred; Gearing, black, green, wine, carmine or vermilion, with striping to correspond.

Built in Imperial, Standard and Royal grades. Furnished with straight dash and dash rail or curved dash without dash rail.

For full description of grades, see page 2

No. 243, Combination Elliptic Spring and Side Bar Top Buggy, from 1900 catalog.

The McFarlan organization was very well thought of throughout the community, but not all employees had the same regard for it. One of them, William Potter, even went to court to challenge the company's unwillingness to pay damages for an injury allegedly caused by company negligence. The case dragged on from one court to another until the Indiana Supreme Court found that the employer had known of a defect in the rip saw being used by Potter and had asked him to continue using the faulty equipment until the

1. *Prize Winning Carriages by McFarlan* 37

No. 300. GENTLEMAN'S DRIVING WAGON

BODY—24 x 58 inches.
WHEELS—Sarven or compressed band, 38 and 42, 40 and 44 or 42 and 46 inches. Felloes, ¾, ⅞ or 1 inch.
Oval edge steel tire, ¼ inch thick, bolted between each spoke.

TRIMMING—M. B. leather, wool cloth or whipcord.
PAINTING—Body, black; Gearing, black, green, wine, carmine or New York red.
AXLES—Either arched or dropped, as preferred.

Built in Royal and Standard grades.

For full description of grades, see page 2

No. 300, Gentleman's Driving Wagon, from 1900 catalog.

job was completed, at which time repairs would be made. Potter received a serious injury before the job was finished. The court awarded $2,000 as compensation.[109]

McFarlan produced all of the materials that were used in manufacturing its vehicles with the exception of the wheels, springs and axles.[110] Since McFarlan didn't manufacture its own wheels, it relied on outside suppliers to provide the quantity needed to keep up with production schedules. In a rare move, a lawsuit was filed in 1902 through company attorneys Conner and Conner against the Connersville Wagon Company for damages of

An ad for "One of Our '1905 Winners'" that appeared in *The Vehicle Dealer*.

$8,000. The complaint alleged that a contract, agreed upon a year earlier, for 10,000 sets of wheels had not been filled and that the McFarlan Carriage Company had had to cancel a number of orders causing a loss of profit of $4,000.[111]

The case was finally heard in court at New Castle, Indiana, by change of venue. What amounted to a countersuit for $6,000 damages was filed against McFarlan by the Parry Manufacturing Company of Indianapolis. In a complicated series of events, the account for payment of the wheels, which McFarlan would have owed the Connersville Wagon Company, had been transferred to the Sarven Wheel Company and later to the Parry Manufacturing Company.[112] The case dragged on for several years before finally being settled in 1908.

Advertising for the past several years had been concentrated mainly in trade journals. The company also published an excellent catalog each year. A description of the publication for 1903 indicated it was a handsome book, illustrated throughout with fine halftone engravings of the different styles of business and pleasure vehicles McFarlan would manufacture. Styles listed included stanhopes, phaetons, carriages, buggies, surreys, driving carts, and special makes such as physician's and undertaker's phaetons and mail delivery wagons.[113] Catalogs were mailed to prospective customers upon request or could be obtained from a distributor.

In spite of the elaborate catalog and other limited advertising, vehicle sales were slower than in the past few years. Although the outlook for 1904 was optimistic as the factory was busy preparing for spring orders,[114] the carriage industry was experiencing

1. Prize Winning Carriages by McFarlan

This ad for McFarlan's carriages appeared in *The Vehicle Dealer*, March 1906.

No. 718. Southern Spindle Wagon.

Body—18 x 52 or 22 x 52 inches.   Wheels—⅝ or ¾-inch.

Can also be furnished with buggy seat with drop back.

A very easy running wagon.

No. 719—Same job with No. 603 buggy seat and top.

Built in Royal, Standard and Imperial Grades.

No. 718, Southern Spindle Wagon, from 1908 catalog.

No. 813. Platform Spring Wagon.

Detail of gear construction on page 81.

Body—7 feet long, 2 feet 10 inches wide.

Panels—8½ inches deep. All measurements outside. Drop end gate. Edge of panels protected by iron.

Springs—Elliptic or Hayes in front, full platform in rear. Kingsley fifth wheel.

Axles—1⅛ or 1¼-inch, Collinge collar.

Wheels—Sarven patent, 1⅛ or 1¼-inch.

This wagon is built to meet the growing demand for a strictly high class job of this kind; the sort that always brings you home.

No. 814—Same job open.

Built in Imperial Grade only.

No. 813, Platform Spring Wagon, from 1908 catalog.

more variation in demand than would be indicated by economic conditions. It was becoming apparent that another factor was influencing their trade. Self-propelled vehicles were beginning to make an impact. Within 10 years, McFarlan's horse-drawn vehicle production would cease.

In 1907, a financial panic hurt business even as carriage and buggy sales were already faltering in the face of the automobile's growing popularity. Factory owners looked for ways to maintain profits. In an unprecedented move, McFarlan joined with 75 other carriage manufacturers from the Midwestern states of Indiana, Ohio, Illinois and Michigan, agreeing to raise prices on their products by 10 percent. Although this action gave the appearance of forming a gigantic "buggy trust," the group claimed it was just a combine for the purpose of raising prices.[115] The very fact that McFarlan chose to become a part of such an effort indicates that it was feeling financial pains that it had not known for some years.

By 1908, McFarlan advertised only three distribution centers, Kansas City, Missouri, Omaha, Nebraska and Enid, Oklahoma. Their product grades remained the same as they had for several years, Imperial, Standard and Royal. The Imperial Grade was touted as "our popular priced line; equal to much of the so-called high-grade work." Trimmings included the choice of deep buffed leather, 14-ounce wool cloth or whipcord with 15 springs in each cushion and a full Brussels rug for the feet. Wheels offered were banded wood hub or Sarven patent with screwed rims. The Standard Grade was described bluntly as "just what the name implies." It was upgraded by offering, in addition to base equipment, 16-ounce wool cloth upholstering and a full length rug, 13 inch padded dash, either plain or with solid nickel mold, and heavy rubber aprons and rubber boot. For the running gear, a full wrought Brewster slot fifth wheel and oil tempered springs came without extra cost and one could choose the Sarven patent wheels or Pinneo & Daniels wood hub wheels. Advertising for the top-of-the line Royal confidently stated that the "work in this grade is the equal of any custom built vehicle on the market." It offered the heaviest 18-ounce wool cloth in addition to leather or whipcord trim, full length Wilton carpet, heavy melodian apron and a leather boot. Steps featured a three-prong wrought iron shank with rubber-covered pad. The number of models offered in the 1908 McFarlan catalog increased to 134, ranging all the way from No. 746 Bike Wagon to No. 486 Surrey.[116]

With the onslaught of the automobile, the market for horse-drawn vehicles was on a sharp decline. This was felt especially hard in Connersville because several industries were connected directly with carriage and buggy production. The local community had not recovered from the nationwide financial panic of 1907, even two years later. One newspaper referred to this as "the recent period of depression."[117] Just as the carriage and buggy industry was winding down toward its end, the man who developed that industry in Connersville was "called to rest" after suffering a number of sinking spells.

The passing of John Becraft McFarlan was a major blow to the community. From the very beginning of his residence in Connersville, J.B. had taken an active part in the business and industrial life of this city. In addition to establishing and maintaining his carriage building business, he developed what became known as McFarlantown, an attractive residential area that eventually became part of the city of Connersville. When natural

1. Prize Winning Carriages by McFarlan 43

No. 509. Export Phaeton.

Body—29½ x 47½ inches on bottom.   Back—26½ inches high.
Cushions—20 x 35 inches.   Width between bows, 44 inches.
Can also be built with two springs in rear on special orders.
Built in Royal, Standard and Imperial Grades.

No. 509, Export Phaeton, from 1908 catalog.

No. 241, Cabriolet, from 1908 catalog.

gas was discovered in an adjoining county, he became one of the chief organizers of the Connersville Natural Gas Company and was elected its president. He also helped organize the Indiana Furniture Company and the Connersville Land and Improvement Company, was president of the McFarlan Building Company, which financed the McFarlan block in Connersville, was president of the Fayette Banking Company and held the position of president of the Connersville Blower Company until his death. Indeed he had been styled the "father of Connersville." Even as his health deteriorated, J.B. would make nearly daily visits to the carriage factory and to the Blower Company plant, the industries in which

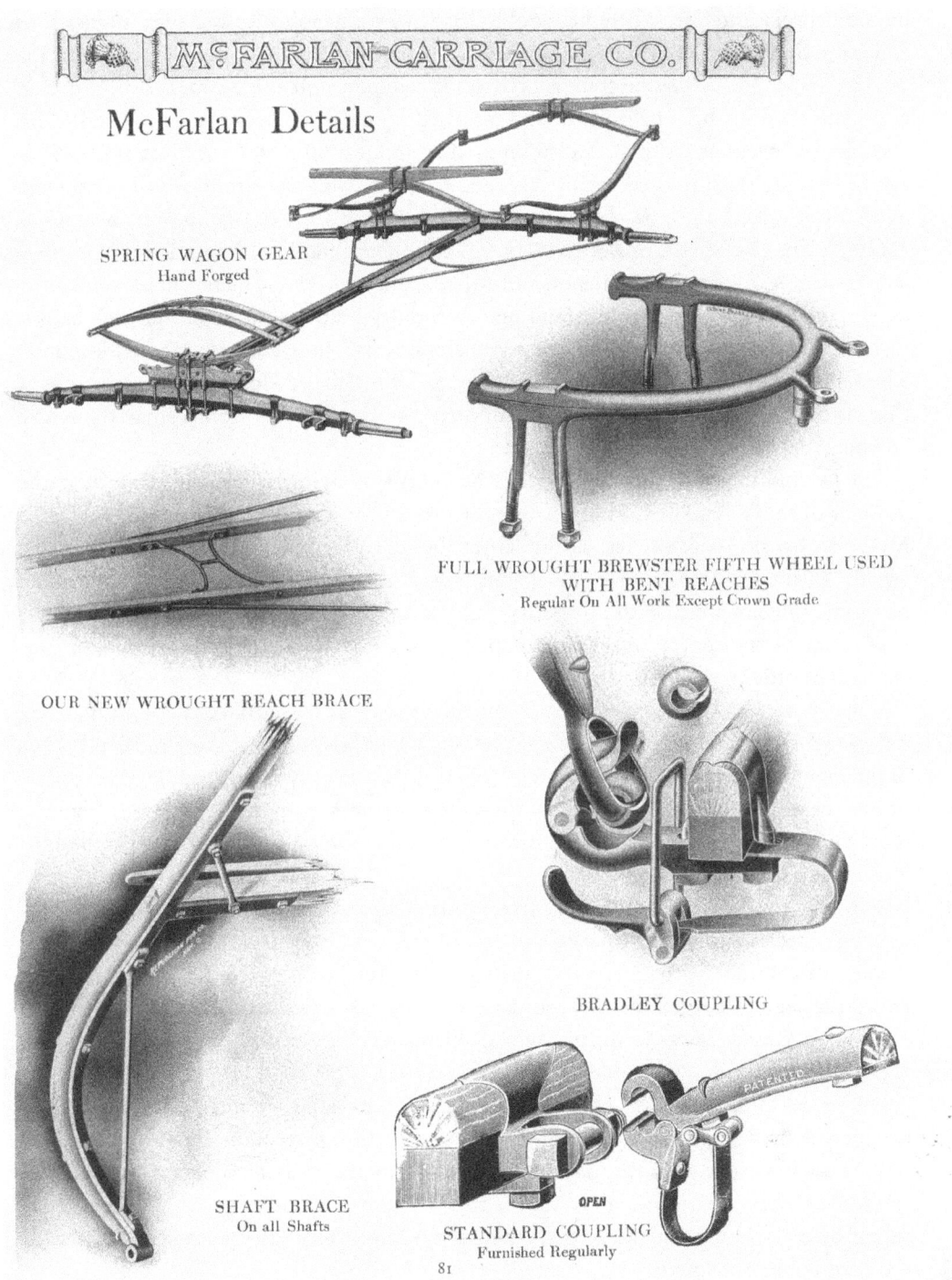

Some of the features that made McFarlan a top seller, as touted in 1908 catalog.

he took special interest. There he would chat with the employees and offer suggestions or instructions as to their work. On Friday, before his death on Sunday, he visited the carriage factory in which he took special pride, having built the business over a period of 53 years, but he became quite ill and returned home. His sons were summoned to his bedside that evening. John B. McFarlan died at about 4:00 A.M. on August 15, 1909, at age 86, having far surpassed the life expectancy of the time. The funeral was conducted by the Rev. G.C. Lamb, pastor of the First Presbyterian Church. Pall bearers were O.V. Handley, Thomas Norris, Edward Moore, Charles Rieder and John Edwards of the McFarlan Carriage Company, R.T. Huston and Mike Ganley, of the Connersville Blower Company. Out of respect for this outstanding community leader, all of Connersville's banks, most manufacturing concerns and many businesses had shut down for the afternoon.[118] Though a very modest and unassuming person, John Becraft McFarlan was truly one of the outstanding influences that saw his adopted community grow from a small town into an energetic industrial city.

It is almost ironic that the carriage business was dying at the very time that the founder of the McFarlan Carriage Company was laid to rest. From 1886 until 1900, the McFarlan concern was ranked as the largest builder of medium grade carriages in the world.[119] True, the horse-drawn vehicle business continued for a few more years and even had some hints of a return to prosperity, but the handwriting was clearly on the wall. As new forms of transportation became popular the company would have to make major changes in order to survive.

Early in 1910, there was reason for encouragement at the carriage factory. One local newspaper noted that all of the carriage and buggy factories were working full-time. One of the manufacturers gave the following reasoning for the upswing. A couple of years ago, horses seemed to be frightened every time they saw an automobile. "But somehow the horses have become educated or accustomed to the benzene wagons, and, everybody is buying buggies again."[120]

By the time the large four-story factory building was 25 years old, the company was seeking other uses to occupy space no longer needed for horse-drawn vehicle production. Even with automobile manufacturing using part of the facilities, considerable space was going unused. In September 1912, an agreement was reached to produce parts for the Krell Auto Grand Piano Company, also of Connersville, using one empty wing of the carriage factory.[121]

New ideas continued to offer improvements to McFarlan products. One interesting gadget was the Catley Top Lift that would close the top in seconds. Moving the Catley lever caused the spring loaded top frame to jump into place, giving shelter from a sudden thunderstorm or the steaming rays of the sun.[122] In an attempt to retain customers who might be considering defecting to the motorized ranks, one carriage model was named the automobile runabout.

No gimmicks, however, could counter the fast-growing automobile industry. Horse-drawn vehicle sales were plummeting to the point that it was no longer profitable to keep McFarlan's carriage business going. Late in 1913 it slipped into receivership.

In October of that year, R.N. Elliott, trustee of the bankrupt McFarlan Carriage

1. Prize Winning Carriages by McFarlan

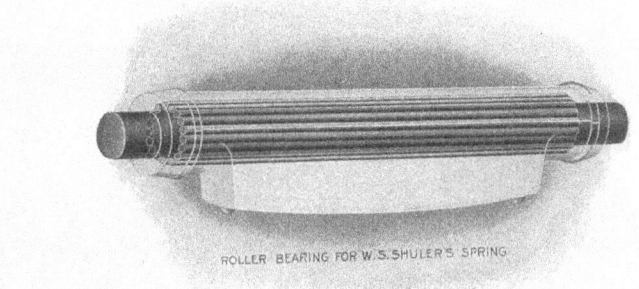

No. 228 Featherweight Wagon

Body—18 or 20 x 52 inches. Springs—Shuler or any style shown in catalog.
Weight—about 240 pounds.

No. 228, Featherweight Wagon, from 1911 catalog.

No. 300 Stanhope

Body—25½ x 56 inches.
Cushion—17 x 32 inches.
Springs—4 and 4 leaf.
Axles—arch only.

Single reach gear.

No. 309—Same style body with Physician's Top like **No. 307** on page 45.
No. 311—Same style body with top like **No. 301** on page 42.

No. 300, Stanhope, from 1911 catalog.

No. 23½ Automobile Runabout with Top

Body—23 x 56 inches.
Cushion—17 x 31½ inches.
Twin seat steel construction. Mohair or auto cloth top.

Springs—two four leaf.
Wood bars only.

McFarlan's 1911 catalog featured the No. 23½ Automobile Runabout, for those who were tempted by the newfangled vehicles but couldn't let go of the faithful horse.

Co., filed a petition asking for authority to sell the real estate belonging to the company. The petition came up for hearing at the office of H.C. Sheridan, the referee in bankruptcy, on November 3, 1913.[123]

On December 31, 1913, it was announced that the large plant of the McFarlan Carriage Company had been sold to Edward W. Ansted, one of the successful industrialists who, 20 years earlier, had been encouraged to set up shop in J.B. McFarlan's new industrial park. Ansted manufactured springs and axles that were used in the construction of carriages, buggies and also in McFarlan automobiles.[124] Ansted demonstrated the same type of entrepreneurial energy that had made J.B. McFarlan so successful many years earlier.

2

Six Cylinder Cars Exclusively

Rumors of major changes in modes of transportation had begun as early as the 1870s. Horses would be replaced, some said, by machines propelled by steam or some other means, although few normal folks paid much attention to such chatter. In most localities, the city fathers were not interested in anything that would speed up traffic on the streets. Six miles per hour was the fastest gait allowed for riding or driving through Connersville. Complaints were still voiced regularly that the law was violated almost daily.[1] Efforts of the local constable to judge speed accurately and issue citations to violators became a matter of lawful judgment, subject to interpretation and perhaps to influence.

The first real threat to horse power came from human power with the popularization of the bicycle. The velocipede craze was just getting under way in the 1860s but already had reached small communities. In 1868, a local newspaper proclaimed, "The velocipede excitement has at last reached Connersville, and the efforts of sundry persons to ride the two wheeled of H.O. Dorsey or the three wheeled one of John Henry, have furnished our citizens with a vast amount of amusement during the past week. The man most determined in his efforts to learn, that we noticed, was Deacon Applegate — he says, 'that in time, he'll learn to ride it, or vice versa, he isn't sure which.'"[2] The cycling clubs that formed in the coming years began an organized effort for improved roads and streets.

The first mention of a motorized vehicle's possible appearance on the streets of this small Hoosier community came in an 1870 article stating, "Captain Johnson of our city will, in a few weeks, be riding through the streets of Connersville on a velocipede to be propelled by steam. So says rumor. The thing is to have three wheels. The city dads will please make a note of this, so as to be in time for a new ordinance."[3] Whether or not that effort actually came to fruition is not recorded, but it shows evidence that, in some people's minds, vehicles would, in time, be propelled by some means other than horses or humans.

Even in rural eastern Indiana, where a good horse was considered a treasure, there were people interested in displacing them. Harvin Tryon apparently was one such person and is given credit for having built the first successful self-propelled 4 wheel vehicle in Connersville. Tryon, who was a mechanic or blacksmith, and his wife, Fannie, lived at the corner of 6th Street and Eastern Avenue. In the late 1870s, he conceived the idea of hitching a small steam engine to his large sturdy wagon for the purpose of taking a trip to his old home in Georgia.[4] Many who knew of his project thought him to be of unsound mind, or even downright insane, but he continued undaunted. Tryon finished the mechanicals to his satisfaction and loaded his wagon. On a certain balmy day in late summer, he climbed aboard and rode triumphantly out of Connersville, headed south, down through Brookville and on to Cincinnati. All went well until he attempted to ford a stream in southern Kentucky and got into quicksand whereupon the wagon sank. When water reached the boiler an explosion occurred, sending Fayette County's first motorized vehicle into oblivion.[5]

By the 1890s, several groups openly lobbied for improvements in the highways. Their efforts were two-pronged: to do away with the turnpike system where toll gates were used to extract funds from anyone wanting to travel that particular road, and to have roads graded and graveled to make travel safer. The popularization of bicycles spawned an industry directed toward personal transportation. In 1890, two separate bicycle groups visited Connersville, the Indianapolis Bicycle Club and the Indiana Wheelmen. The former group rode in from the capital city in time for dinner at the Buckley House, then left for Brookville, Indiana, and Harrison and Cincinnati, Ohio.[6] Travelers often related stories about the toll charges made every few miles for the privilege of traversing poorly maintained roads. These experiences did little to encourage others who might have considered venturing forth on their own.

The turn of a new century, 1900, saw the McFarlan Carriage Company reaching new pinnacles of production as 1,000 already sold carriages and buggies were shipped to Texas in January. The glow of a bright-looking future soon started to fade, however, as the newfangled horseless carriage began to make inroads into buggy and carriage sales. On November 15, 1901, Miss Kathryn Derbyshire caused quite a sensation when she drove her father's new "one lunger" curved-dash Oldsmobile through town at an estimated speed of 12 miles per hour, twice the legal limit.[7] Horses reared on their hind feet, dogs barked and mouths dropped open as the curious crowd watched, but kept their distance. The car, emitting considerable smoke, stopped at 5th and Central where Derbyshire and J.F.L. Moore, a factory mechanic and driver instructor, stepped out onto the street. Earl Walker, just a young lad, approached Moore and said, "Mister, your teakettle is steaming." The old gray mare and spring wagon was good enough for Joe Moffett. "By gosh, they'll never get me into a thing like that," said Chief of Police Scott Thomas. "It'll never be a success" was the opinion of "several onlookers."[8]

As those "play things" gained popularity, it was only a matter of time until such a happening occurred. Miss Derbyshire apparently also had the first auto accident locally. Just six days after her first trip through town, it was reported that the young lady, while driving on North Central Avenue, had lost control of the "horseless carriage." For an unknown reason, she had turned into the gutter near Mrs. Cornelia Conwell's residence and collided with a tree. Derbyshire sustained painful bruises to her face and the Olds was badly damaged with the front wheels being broken off.[9]

Then there was mutiny in the ranks when one of the "carriage family," William McFarlan, showed up in his new electric automobile in 1902. William also experienced an automobile accident in late May of that year. He and his son, Herbert, were on 8th Street, returning home in the auto, running at a lively gait, when a dog ran in front of the vehicle. The dog was run over, causing the car to swerve. The condition of the canine was not given, but the car ended up in the gutter and on the sidewalk in front of the John

Schweikle home at 8th and Walnut streets. The occupants were unhurt, but the vehicle sustained heavy damage.[10]

The city of Connersville had nothing but dirt, graveled or macadamized street surfaces from the beginning of its history until 1903. Macadamized surfaces were crushed gravel mixed with tar oil, packed to make a somewhat firmer road. As if preparing for the onslaught of the motor car, the City Council approved an ordinance on August 25, 1903, to pave Central Avenue and adjoining streets with brick from 1st to 7th streets.[11] The first street paving with concrete was not done locally until 1912, but by 1917, Connersville claimed to have more miles of hard surfaced streets than any other city of its size in the state.[12] These efforts at street improvement were none too soon, because by 1910, there were 85 automobiles registered in Fayette County.[13] Although slow getting started, this small city provided well for the new automobilist. This effort may have been influenced by a very active local automobile industry, since Empire, Lexington, Howard, McFarlan and Van Auken Electric vehicles were all produced here during that time period.

The Central Manufacturing Company, a local concern that supplied bodies for buggies and the fledgling automobile industry, including Cadillac in their initial year, was putting together an automobile of its own design. A prototype was nearly ready to be test driven when the building in which it was housed burned in 1905, destroying another locally built self-propelled vehicle and ending that company's horseless carriage venture.[14] However, interest in this new form of transportation was growing throughout the community.

The forerunner of the Chamber of Commerce, the Manufacturers Club, was made up of the city's "movers and shakers." This organization had been actively recruiting industries with considerable success, but had become especially interested in attracting builders of automobiles. Connersville had been one of the nation's leading cities in carriage and buggy production, but industry observers were aware of a softening of the market in horse-drawn vehicles. These men realized that more and more customers were turning to the automobile. Through the efforts of local leaders, at least three separate concerns expressed an interest in the manufacture of self-propelled vehicles in Connersville.

Frank Burns of the Chicago Manufacturing Company, maker of the Chicago steam car, visited Connersville in June of 1906, investigating the possibility of relocating his plant in this southeastern Indiana city. He claimed his company was losing its factory lease and was also having problems keeping an adequate labor force.[15] The deal raised local hopes but did not materialize.

In November 1906, the Ray Motor Company filed articles of association with the Fayette County Recorder. One newspaper optimistically predicted that Connersville was destined to become a great automobile manufacturing city.[16] This company was interested enough to contract with W.W. Wainwright, a local iron works and machine shop owner, to build a prototype.[17] Although the Ray Motor Company never went into business in Connersville, its car may have been the first locally built factory produced automobile.

In February 1908 a third company, the Hatfield Motor Company, came to town with its "Buggyabout," expressing interest in relocating its factory from Miamisburg, Ohio. One of the local newspapers was rather flowery in stating that everyone who saw the buggylike vehicle was much impressed with it. Many people were impatiently waiting for self-propelled vehicles to come down in price to within the limit of their pocketbooks. The Buggyabout was supposed to sell for $650. It was later decided that officials from the Hatfield Motor Company may have been more interested in extracting money from local capitalists than in relocating to Connersville.[18]

Meanwhile, management at the McFarlan Carriage Company saw that the market was changing, as sales of top-of-the-line carriages sagged and the horseless carriage continued to make inroads. Hoping for a share of the profits this new mode of transportation would generate, they founded the Connersville Motor Vehicle Company in November of 1906, with $50,000 capital stock.[19] The incorporators were John B. McFarlan Sr., by that time 84 years of age; John B. McFarlan Jr., Charles E.J. McFarlan, Dr. Joshua H. Morrison and Scott Michener.[20] J.B's grandson A.H. McFarlan was also involved, which meant that three generations had joined in forming the new company. One out-of-towner was included, L.M. Ellis of Chicago. Despite having zero experience with internal combustion power, the company had ambitious plans. It was understood that they possessed valuable patents and original designs on engines.[21] Besides engines, they hoped to turn out automobiles, street sweepers and farm implements.[22]

The organizers of the Connersville Motor Vehicle Company spent about two and a half years studying their options with seemingly little progress before announcing in June 1909 that they planned to enter into the manufacture of automobiles as the McFarlan Carriage Company. The company claimed to have their plans fully worked out so production could start in short order.[23] News of this announcement traveled quickly through the community and was received with enthusiasm. There had been rumors before from out-of-town companies planning to set up shop, but McFarlan had been in business locally for more than 50 years and had established a fine reputation. The person who would take charge of the new endeavor was the youngest generation of McFarlans, 28 year old Harry.

Alfred Harry McFarlan was born November 18, 1881, to Charles E.J. and his wife, Ella. The announcement in the *Connersville Times*, a bit male chauvinistic, noted, "Charles McFarlan is now a happy father. His boy was not a girl, which affords him a very joyful reflection."[24] Harry grew up a member of the most prominent family in Connersville. For his 14th birthday, his parents entertained about 50 of his young friends in McFarlan Hall, the ballroom of the magnificent new McFarlan

Alfred Harry McFarlan as a young child (courtesy Jim Wicker).

Hotel, which of course, had family connections. Entertainment included crokinole, checkers, charades and music, with assurances of proper supervision and a prohibition of dancing. Refreshments of Neapolitan cream and cake were served with the party ending at 10:00 P.M.[25] Harry attended local schools and, after graduating from high school, went on to higher education at Greencastle, Indiana. Like many young people then and now, he brought back a spouse as well as a degree. While attending DePauw University, he met an attractive young lady, Jessica Manlove, who grew up in Sheridan, Indiana. Harry and Jessica were married on February 4, 1904. They had no children.

Since his family owned a carriage factory, Harry was well grounded in the horse-drawn vehicle business, but he was also aware of what was happening in the transportation industry. He believed that the automobile was here to stay and that this new fad would only grow much stronger. Harry had also formed some opinions about steam versus electricity versus gasoline as a source of power. Although just a young man, Harry gained approval from the 86 year old family patriarch and was granted permission to build automobiles that he intended to market using the family name.

The news that there was to be a McFarlan automobile was not a great surprise, at least to some. In June of 1909, an article in *The Horseless Age* magazine stated, "The McFarlan Carriage Company of Connersville, Ind., will soon begin the manufacture of a motor buggy, following the example of the majority of buggy manufacturing concerns in Indiana."[26] Harry McFarlan would not have been pleased with the suggestion that he was to build a "motor buggy." Such a crude vehicle was just not his style. Several months later, the same publication more formally announced that the McFarlan Car Company was planning to turn out a six cylinder automobile that would sell for about $2,100. It was to use a Brownell power unit and Weston-Mott axles.[27] Plans were to build a touring car and a roadster to begin with. The company proclaimed its ambition to make as good a car as could possibly be made for its chosen class.

Following the tradition set by his grandfather, Harry built his cars to favor the "carriage" trade rather than the "buggy" trade. Many newcomers in the automobile industry had started by tinkering with engines of one or two cylinders before progressing to larger

Harry loved the wilderness (courtesy Jim Wicker).

Above: Harry as a young man (courtesy Jim Wicker). *Right:* Jessica Manlove McFarlan (courtesy Jim Wicker).

power plants. By 1909, automobiles were almost exclusively running on four cylinders. Harry moved up to the next level — a bold decision, especially for a first-timer. His cars were powered exclusively by six cylinder, four-cycle, water-cooled gasoline engines. This pointed toward the quality of vehicle he intended to produce. Harry, having had no previous experience in automobile manufacturing or marketing, was convinced that providing a quality product a step ahead of the competition would bring success.

By early August, two sample cars had been assembled except for bodies and wheels.[28] Wheels and tires were mounted within a week, but testing was delayed a few days because of the impending death of the family patriarch and founder of the company. He had approved the project and watched the cars take shape, but never had the satisfaction of riding in one.

The passing of J.B. McFarlan on August 15, 1909, slowed the development progress for just a few days until proper respects could be paid. One test car had been taken from the shop and given a brief trial the day before J.B.'s passing, but owing to his grave condition at that time, there was no demonstration for the public. However, the day after the funeral, Harry and his nephew, Herbert, had the McFarlan "40" test car out on the streets, the "40" designating its horsepower rating. The body had not been mounted yet, but the chassis was given a thorough test with complete satisfaction.[29]

Possibly as a means of recognizing the Scottish ancestry of J.B., McFarlan adopted as its nameplate a round badge with a Scottish thistle and the "McFarlan Six" logo. This identification stayed with the company, largely unchanged, throughout its history.

In early September, one local newspaper claimed the McFarlan Carriage Company was already in the automobile business as they had a "large number of machines in course of construction" at their factory. In order to get into production as soon as possible, most of the parts were purchased from suppliers for assembly at the same building where carriages were still being built.[30] The company already had vast experience at building bodies, so that essential component was made in-house.

Harry and his associates assumed the management responsibilities for the automobile venture and saw it grow to become a prestigious marque. Not being known for his mechanical ability, Harry sought advice from a friend and was directed to two men who lived in Indianapolis, William Blommel and Stanley Kepler, who were employed by the Atlas Engine Company. They both came to Connersville at Harry's request to help with technical details, arriving in town via the interurban on October 25, 1909, several weeks after the first McFarlan cars had hit the streets.[31] Both men became problem solvers for Harry and the team of workmen he had put together. Blommel became a permanent resident, working for Wainwright Engineering and later operating his own auto repair shop.[32]

From late October into early November, a finished McFarlan was exhibited at the tri-state convention of dealers held at the armory in Cincinnati, Ohio. As a test of dependability, Harry drove the show car over primitive roads to and from the Queen City without difficulty. The car made a statement for itself by bringing a number of orders from dealers who were attending the show. After it was returned to Connersville, the McFarlan was exhibited and driven on the streets to show its quality.[33]

Test cars were seen frequently on the streets of Connersville as they were used regularly to run errands and to gain technical information. Even as winter set in and the streets became slippery, a McFarlan test car saw continued use. In February 1910, it was involved in a minor accident. While rounding the corner at 7th Street and Western Avenue, the car slid a little and came too close to an I & C interurban train car. A few spokes were knocked out of the "right fore wheel," but no other damage was done and no one was injured.[34]

The price range in which McFarlan chose to compete was right in the middle of the field. Lots of small cars were available for considerably less money, and several makers offered vehicles for thousands of dollars more. Harry's "carriage trade" provided a quality product at a reasonable price. McFarlan didn't enter the exclusive market for several years, but gradually moved up in price and prominence while stressing limited production and customer choice as long as the customer wanted a six cylinder engine. Company advertising would later claim, "We believe we were the first American manufacturers to build six cylinder cars exclusively. Winton and Pierce may have beaten us to it by a nose. However, it is enough to say we were among the first."[35]

By late November, one local newspaper reported, "There are at this time twenty-five machines on different factory floors at the McFarlan plant in various stages of construction and parts for a hundred like them ready to be assembled as they pass on through

The earliest advertisements for the McFarlan Six made it clear that the company had no interest in participating in racing (*Cycle and Automobile Trade Journal*, Jan. 1, 1910).

the final finishing stages and thence to the market."[36] Inquiries for information were being received and answered as the following correspondence indicates.

> The McFarlan Motor Car Company
> BUILDERS OF SIX CYLINDER AUTOMOBILES EXCLUSIVELY
> Connersville, Indiana
> December 1-09

Mr. William S. Crowe,
Manistique, Mich.

Dear Sir;

We have been somewhat delayed in getting out our printed matter, but in accordance with our recent letter to you we are sending you under separate cover today copy of our preliminary catalogue showing what we have to offer.

The car in question is different from many of these on the market in many particulars. One of the most important among these is the great pains which have been taken in designing to give the utmost comfort to the passengers.

The front seats instead of being placed up close to the dash necessitating a very straight post and uncomfortable position, have been set back 29" allowing for very low seat and a great deal of leg room with a good deal rake to the post.

The rear seat passengers are also carried very low. This being taken care of by dropping the floor between the frame. The entire car is built low, the top of the frame measuring only 24" from the ground even with 36" wheels. There is good clearance however and fresh gravel and rough roads offer no inconvenience to the McFarlan Six.

Owing to our limited capacity and our present contract we are in position to take on only a limited amount of additional business and if interested we would be very glad indeed to correspond with you further with a view of reserving positive delivery date of demonstrator which would best suit your convenience.

Awaiting your further pleasure, we remain,
    Yours respectfully,
    McFarlan Motor Car Co.
    A H McFarlan
AHM/BB   Manager.[37]

The first McFarlans available for sale appeared in late 1909 and were considered to be 1910 models. They were impressive in appearance, being offered in a variety of paint colors and featuring glistening brass plating on the radiator, headlights, side and tail lamps, horn, acetylene tank and windshield frame to add sparkle and luster. The headlights were fueled by acetylene, cowl and tail lamps by kerosene. The Brownell gasoline engine was a six cylinder valve-in-head, rated at 30–40 horsepower. It was suspended at three points, had a bore of 3⅝ inches and stroke of 4 inches with cylinders cast in pairs for a displacement of 248 cubic inches. Carburetion came from a Stromberg water jacketed unit intended to overcome the inertia of gasses. A dual ignition was provided using a Splitdorf magneto for one system and a battery and coil for the other, with imported Mercedes plugs providing the spark. Cooling was accomplished with water through a tubular radiator using centrifugal circulation. Engine lubrication was by automatic force-feed with a single sight feed on the dash so the driver could observe the movement of the circulating oil. The clutch, a multiplate unit with 30 discs that ran in oil, permitted shifting the transmission's non-synchronized three forward gears plus reverse. The transmission, clutch and engine were combined into a unit power plant.[38]

As was common on most automobiles in those years, the steering wheel was on the right-hand side, with gear shift and emergency brake to the right of the driver on the outside of the car body. The speed in third gear direct drive could be controlled from 3 to 60 miles per hour. The car weighed in at 2,700 pounds and rode on a 120 inch wheelbase with plenty of ground clearance provided by the 36 × 3½ inch front tires and 36 × 4 rear tires. The five-passenger touring or four-passenger Toy Tonneau came equipped with English mohair top, five lamps, tools, jack, and tire pump. The car was advertised as being "ready for the road," meaning it was fully equipped. Included were the lights and top, but no windshield. At $2,000, or $2,100 with doors, the car was priced competitively against the Kissel Kar D-10 while offering six cylinders to Kissel Kar's four. Comparatively few other six cylinder cars were on the market in 1910, and the others required considerably more financial commitment. The Alco 60 listed at $5,000, the Apperson 6-40 at $4,200, Chadwick Great Six from $5,500 to $6,500, Franklin H at $6,750, Kissel Kar G 10 and the Winton Six at $3,000 and the Lozier at $6,000. The Kline Kar 6-40, one of the nearest six cylinder competitors pricewise, was still priced $500 higher than this newest of six-cylinder cars. McFarlan clearly had a bargain priced, quality product to offer as it sought to find its niche in the automobile market.[39]

The steering wheel was located on the right-hand side with the gear shift lever and hand brake to the right of the driver on the outside of the body. Doors were an option that added $100 to the price (*Motor*, Feb. 1910).

A change in company policy saw McFarlan participate in racing and proudly proclaim the results. Two hundred miles without a stop was an unusual feat in that day (*The Saturday Evening Post*, Nov. 12, 1910).

There is no known record of who became the lucky owner of the first McFarlan automobile, but the second car produced is believed to have been purchased by Rylie Clark, a gentleman who owned a local coal yard and lived in Edgewood on Georgia Avenue. He regularly took his family and neighborhood children for rides. Sometimes on Saturdays, he would get on the Milton Pike at the 24th Street toll gate and drive the 30 mile round trip to Cambridge City and back. Rylie drove his McFarlan for several years, but what eventually happened to his car is not known.[40]

Among the very early McFarlan owners was Mr. A.J. Brown, who was president of a Noblesville, Indiana, bank. Enthusiastic over the excellent service he was getting, he suggested that his son, James, who was visiting from California, give the car a test drive. James was so impressed with the car's performance with the Brownell six cylinder engine, he visited the factory and acquired the agency for the Golden State.[41]

Through the efforts of James A. Brown, a substantial market developed for McFarlan automobiles early on in California. Dealers who had sold carriages knew about McFarlan quality and they found a lucrative market for this new type of transportation. Brown had become known as "the vehicle man from Healdsburg," having begun in a small way selling horse-drawn vehicles and soon expanded his business to other communities. With the advent of the automobile, Brown saw opportunities for more profit. After acquiring control of McFarlan sales for the state of California, he then orchestrated a merger between his own establishment and the Miller and Miller Company of San Francisco, forming the Consolidated Vehicle Company. Officers of the new organization were James Brown, president; Glen Miller of Miller and Miller, vice-president; and Clyde C. Kennedy, secretary.[42] By mid–1910, Consolidated Vehicle was considered to be one of the largest automobile dealers in the Sonoma Valley with branches in Healdsburg, Santa Rosa, and San Francisco and more being planned. A train carload of McFarlans was delivered on or about April 1, 1910. Included were one pony tonneau and 2 tourings; all were painted royal blue with cream running gear.[43] In June, a contract was made with Allen and Arthur Bryant to represent the Consolidated Vehicle Company in San Jose. The new agency was known as the McFarlan Sales Company.[44]

After making another trip back east, Brown had expanded his territory to include the entire Pacific coast comprising the states of Washington and Oregon, in addition to California.[45] When the trip was made from San Francisco to Los Angeles to open an agency and give demonstrations, the McFarlan was shipped by water. After finishing at L.A., Brown drove the six cylinder car to Bakersfield, a distance of 190 miles, making the journey in less than 8 hours. The slightly used demonstrator was immediately sold to C.L. Taylor, owner of a large department store.[46] Before the end of the year, Brown had made an arrangement with Charles T. Peterson, of Spokane, Washington, to assume the McFarlan agency for eastern Washington state and the southern part of British Columbia. Peterson was confident enough in the product to wire deposit monies for 15 McFarlans, hoping for immediate delivery.[47] James A. Brown had quickly taken control of McFarlan sales in the far west and was calling for more cars than the company was prepared to produce.

This new six-cylinder Hoosier product was well received on the West Coast. At the

A new and larger McFarlan entered the scene mid-year, equipped with a 50–60 hp engine made by Wainwright (*Horseless Age*, Feb. 15, 1911).

Santa Rosa Carnival held in June 1910, the winner of the first prize was a McFarlan Six entered by the Consolidated Vehicle Company.[48] At the California State Fair in Sacramento, a gold medal was awarded to the McFarlan dealer for its display.[49] Another West Coast newspaper pictured Verne Dumas with his family in their McFarlan Six, noting they were motoring with carefree enjoyment.[50]

James Brown was known as a hustler and a go-getter. That was adequately demonstrated in the sale to Frank Robinson of Albion in Mendocino County. Robinson lived on a mountain ranch located at the bottom of a deep canyon about 10 miles from Albion. Plenty of automobile salesmen had tried to convince Robinson of the advantages of their motor car, but they were satisfied to stop at Albion and conduct negations there. Brown and Edward Jackson, manager of the Healdsburg agency, decided to "beard the lion in his den." Consequently, they drove right into the canyon, ending up at Robinson's front door. Their demonstration that the car was able to travel the rugged canyon roads satisfied the rancher and he purchased a McFarlan.[51]

Brown had Indiana roots, having been raised in Noblesville, just north of Indianapolis. When he took the McFarlan agency for California, he also specified that his father should be the dealer for Hamilton County, of which Noblesville was the county seat.[52] A.J. Brown was already a McFarlan owner, and his car had been the motivating force for his son taking the marque to the West Coast, so it was only natural that the agency should be awarded to him.

Another market that developed early on was close to home in the Midwest. C.A. Chambers took an agency and incorporated it under the name McFarlan Six Sales Company. His office was in the State Life Insurance building in Indianapolis. Mr. Chambers was quite famous in the state for being a racehorse devotee. Sportsmen seemed to take a

The Little Six Model 30 Roadster listed for just $2000. Doors were an extra $100 (McFarlan Six catalog, 1911).

special liking to the new 6 cylinder machine. C.A. Coey, an aeronaut who had participated in the national balloon race, took the agency for the Chicago area.[53]

The McFarlan company was not modest in early advertising, as they boastfully stated, "It is not 5000 cars built to sell only, but instead a limited number, each properly road tested, each a perfect individual in which you and ourselves can have a lasting pride and satisfaction." Early advertising also made it clear that the company had no intention of becoming involved in racing competition; however, before the year was over, McFarlan, along with many other manufacturers, would realize that a victory on Saturday could lead to sales on Monday. They would enter two cars in the new Indianapolis Speedway's Labor Day events where they made a respectable showing, which brought bragging rights that were soon touted in their advertising.

Ads that appeared after the Labor Day races proclaimed success on the racetrack. They proudly stated how the McFarlan Motor Car Company had entered two of their regular stock model six-cylinder cars in the Labor Day weekend races at the "Indianapolis Motordrome." One significant success was in a 200-mile event on Monday, Sept. 5. Although this was their first experience at racing, one of the cars made the 200 miles in 183 minutes and 15 seconds while averaging 17 miles per gallon of gasoline. Additional bragging rights came because the McFarlans won first and second in the free-for-all handicap that same weekend. Later ads proclaimed success from making a respectable showing at Atlanta, Georgia, on November 7. There was no hesitation to make it known that the McFarlan six-cylinder car was very competitive in racing against established makes of automobiles while still being quite economical.[54] If nothing else, McFarlan's successes on the track had proved the car to be a reliable vehicle since it had gone the distance at racing speed without having to stop for gasoline, oil or repairs.

McFarlan seemed satisfied with their limited production and apparently intended to keep it that way. They claimed that the slowdown in mid–1910 for many manufacturers had not affected them, because they still had orders booked far ahead, and other factories shutting down elsewhere might make it easier to get more skilled labor. The local work force might be substantially increased if the demand for McFarlan cars continued.[55] By indicated orders, production of over 100 units seems likely.

Even though customers were having to wait for the privilege of owning their chosen marque, new areas were opening up giving the opportunities for increased sales. An agreement was made with an agent in Australia who had contracted for 25 cars. That was believed to have been one of the largest shipments of automobiles to be sent by an Indiana company to a foreign country up to that time.[56]

The introduction of the 1911 models came with an announcement that they were continuing, without change, the same car that had created more demand than the company was able to supply. The Toy Tonneau did, however, gain a more aggressive sounding name, "Torpedo." McFarlan started the model year using one standard chassis with the Brownell model A-6 overhead valve, 246 cubic inch displacement engine just as they had done the previous model year.[57]

Soon, however, company management developed a desire to market a larger vehicle, which called for a more powerful engine. The larger engine that was introduced later in

Top: The Big Six. In the 4-Passenger Torpedo, the driver entered through the passenger door. The top and windshield were both extras. *Bottom:* The chassis for the Big Six used an engine manufactured by the Wainwright Engineering Company, also of Connersville (both images, McFarlan Six catalog, 1911).

the 1911 season was one of local manufacture, being built in the Wainwright shop in Connersville. Labeled the Big Six, it was developed for the McFarlan Motor Company with a bore and stroke of 4 by 5 inches, displacing 377 cubic inches with cylinders cast in pairs. It was said to run up to 2,500 rpm without undue vibration. The engine was designed with integral water jackets and valves in the head that were set at an angle. Pistons were fitted with four rings. Valves were two inches in diameter and were ground so as to be interchangeable.[58]

One unusual feature of the engine, advanced for its time, was the complete enclosure of the pushrods and most other moving parts, thereby giving protection from dirt and cutting down on wear. Another design feature that made this power plant unique was that the engine and transmission used one continuous aluminum crankcase with the entire system being lubricated by the same oil. This engine was completed and tested in August of 1910. It was then installed in a McFarlan chassis for a thorough road evaluation before being put on the market.

A great deal of credit was given the Wainwright establishment for quickly getting the new engine on line. Wainwright Engineering was founded by William Warren Wainwright in 1903 as a machine shop. Being dissatisfied with the castings he purchased from other sources, he built his own foundry and began producing engine parts.[59] His oldest son, Harry A. Wainwright, a graduate of Purdue University, had returned to Connersville to work with his father in the shop after doing a stint with the Sullivan Machine Company in Chicago. Using suggestions given by Harry and plans drawn up by the McFarlan Company, the shop took just 12 weeks from the time they actually began work on the engine and transmission until it was being tested.[60] When McFarlan company management was convinced of the engine's merits, it was added mid-year to the 1911 lineup.

Another significant change mid-year was an improved Brownell engine that developed 35–40 horsepower. An announcement in *The Evening News* stated that a new shipment of engines had arrived and were not essentially different from motors used in McFarlan cars in the past, "aside from the fact that they are more refined and more perfect." A news reporter had been given a test ride with A.H. McFarlan at the wheel and an employee of the company walking alongside; the car was kept at a snail's pace without changing the "clutch from high speed."[61] The power plant still used overhead valves and carried the same cubic inch displacement but gave a slight increase in horsepower.

The chassis for the early 1911 Little Six was shown with the 30–40 hp Brownell engine, the same as had been used in 1910.

In spite of the company's earlier intentions, there developed a proliferation of McFarlan models that were built on two separate chassis. The 120 inch wheelbase offered body styles including model 26, a two-passenger runabout, and model 30, a five-passenger touring; these could be had without doors for $2,000 or with doors for $2,100. Their weight was listed at 2,650 pounds. Some purchasers thought they would prefer a car without doors because they were accustomed to riding in slower moving horse-drawn vehicles and enjoyed unobstructed entrance and exits. Doors were often purchased later after those riding in their new higher speed conveyance realized that being partially enclosed made them more comfortable and secure. The Small Six power plant continued the same engine, clutch, and transmission as were used on earlier cars. Cooling was by tubular radiator with centrifugal pump, and all models rode on 36 × 3½ inch front and 36 × 4 inch rear tires.[62]

The new Big Six rode on a 128 inch wheelbase. It was offered in model 34 two-passenger runabout with trunk for $2,500, model 36 four-passenger torpedo with top for $2,600, a five-passenger touring for $2,500 or a seven-passenger touring with two jump seats for $2,575. Each weighed approximately 3,000 pounds. The torpedo body was unusual in that the sides were higher and it had only three doors. The driver entered from the passenger side. Steering from the right-hand side was continued; however, on the Big Six, the gear shift and emergency brake controls were moved inside the body requiring left hand manipulation. This arrangement was referred to as "center control." Pricewise, McFarlan continued competing in the mid-range of cars, most of which offered only 4 cylinder engines. One example was the other Connersville make, Lexington, that had a price range from $1,650 to $2,500, but would not offer a 6 cylinder engine for another year.[63]

McFarlan literature for 1911 showed what a bargain their 6-cylinder cars were by comparing them against other makes that were available.

	Price	Horsepower	Bore and Stroke	Ignition	Wheelbase	Drive
McF Little Six	$2,000	35–40	3⅝ × 4	Dual System	120	I-Beam
McF Big Six	$2,500	50–60	4 × 5	Dual System	128	I-Beam
Alco	$6,000	60	4¾ × 5½	Jump Spark	126	2 Chains
Apperson	$4,200	50	4½ × 5	Jump Spark	128	Shaft or 2 Chains
Chadwick	$5,500	60	5 × 6	Double 2 Sets of Plugs	133	2 Chains
Franklin	$3,750	42	4¼ × 4	Jump Spark	127	Shaft
Locomobile	$4,800	48	4½ × 4½	Dual		Shaft
Matheson 18	$3,500	50	4½ × 5	Double 2 Sets of Plugs	125½	Shaft
National	$4,200	50	4½ × 4¾	Jump Spark	125	Shaft
Oldsmobile	$5,000	60	5 × 6	Jump Spark	138	Shaft
Palmer-Singer	$4,000	60	4⅞ × 5½	Jump Spark	138	Shaft
Peerless	$6,000	50	5 × 5½	Double 2 Sets of Plugs	136	Shaft
Pierce-Arrow	$4,000	36	4 × 4¾	Double 2 Sets of Plugs	125	Shaft
Premier	$3,500	60	4½ × 5¼	Jump Start Make and Break	140	Shaft

	Price	Horsepower	Bore and Stroke	Ignition	Wheelbase	Drive
Stevens-Duryea	$3,300	35	4¼ × 4¾	Jump Spark	128	Shaft
Thomas	$3,750	40	4¼ × 5½	Double 2 Sets of Plugs	125	Shaft
Winton	$3,000	48.6	4½ × 5	Jump Spark	124	Shaft[64]

The Brownell engine was manufactured by the F.A. Brownell Motor Co. of Rochester, New York (*Motor Age*, March 16, 1911).

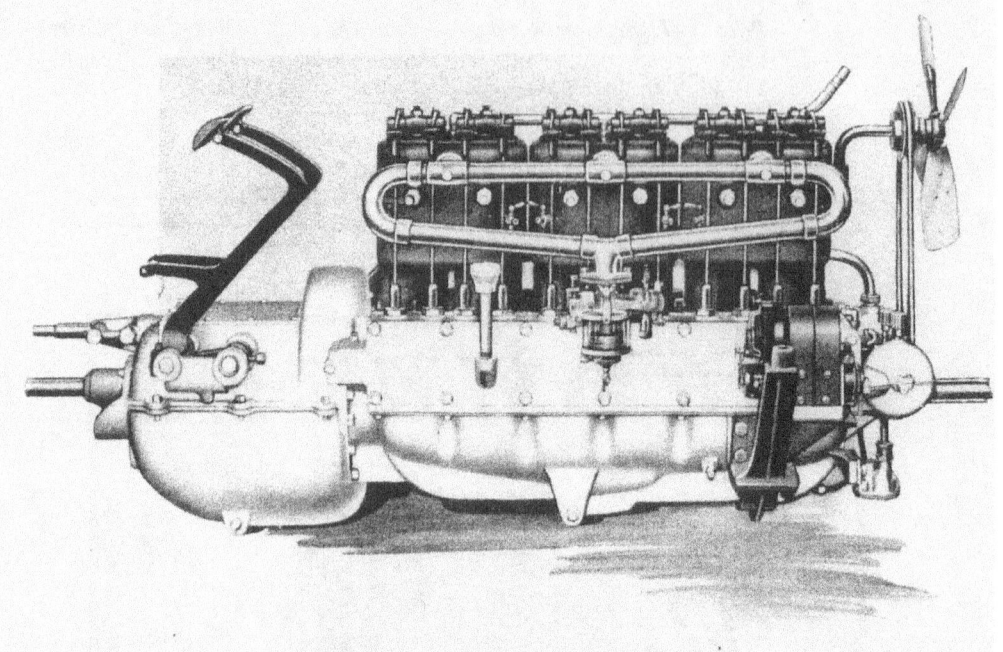

Little Six Power Plant

A mid-year upgrade, this engine by Brownell provided 35–40 hp for the Little Six (McFarlan Six catalog, 1911).

As the season for auto shows approached, McFarlan decided, almost at the last minute, to take five cars to New York City. There were two automobile shows held in the Big Apple. One was in Madison Square Garden for members of the Association of Licensed Automobile Manufacturers (A.L.A.M.) who were paying royalties brought about by the Selden patent that had been issued in 1895 to George B. Selden. The other show, for manufacturers who refused to join the A.L.A.M., was held at the Grand Central Palace.

McFarlan had not acquiesced to pay tribute to the A.L.A.M. and, therefore, displayed their cars at the Palace. Of the five cars taken to New York City, three were displayed inside; because of the lateness of their decision, though, their space was number 17 in the basement.[65] The other two cars were used on the streets as demonstrators. Herbert McFarlan, nephew of Harry, had assumed the position of sales manager and was in charge of the exhibit. The three cars shown inside were a black roadster, a 4-passenger tonneau finished in rich seal brown and a gray 5-passenger touring with nickel trim. Bert Adams, a test driver for McFarlan who had driven in the Atlanta races the previous fall, was in charge of giving rides and demonstrations. This was the first time McFarlan cars had been exhibited in the East, creating an opportunity for new sales contacts to be made.[66]

The company was quite ambitious in their advertising, using not only the usual trade journals, but also nationally circulated magazines of general interest such as *The*

Auto shows provided an outstanding opportunity to display the product for prospective customers (National Automotive History Collection, Detroit Public Library).

Saturday Evening Post, Life, Everybody's Magazine and *McClure's*. The advertising blitz, along with their participation in shows and racing events, would logically signal a desire to expand their market, presumably with the intention of significantly increasing production. It was definitely a sellers' market as financially able prospective customers were willing to spend dollars for their chosen machine. Instead, McFarlan remained a very small producer that found its niche by providing special appointments to satisfy customers' desires.

The city of Connersville was basking in the limelight of the rapidly expanding automobile industry, and was supporting it by improving their system of streets. One of the major north-south thoroughfares, Grand Avenue, dead-ended at the railroad embankment north of 10th Street. The city had been after the Cincinnati Hamilton and Dayton Railroad to construct an underpass in order that Grand Avenue could be extended, but the railroad refused to comply, preferring not to spend the money. The case ended up in the courts, dragging on for years before reaching the state Supreme Court. Finally, the railroad was convinced to spend the $40,000 or so required and in 1911, workmen dug through the embankment. Little six-year-old Charles McNaughton, who lived nearby, couldn't pass up this exciting event. As he was watching the goings on, closer to the action than he probably should have been, a workman grabbed him, put him through the hole that had been dug, and said, "You are the first one to go through this opening." Several years later, after graduating from high school, McNaughton was employed by McFarlan. Some of his memorable experiences while working there are noted in another chapter.[67] The first motor vehicle to pass through the not yet completed opening was a McFarlan Six driven by noted mechanic, test car and race driver Bert Adams. The opening was still so restricted that Adams had to duck his head in order to pass through, but a locally built car got the honors of being "first."[68]

An unusual use was found for the McFarlan Big Six that demonstrated their superb pulling power. When the race track at Connersville's Roberts Park needed grading, a Big Six was commandeered to pull two heavy harrows over the track surface. It worked so well that management for six other county fairs plus the Indiana State Fair put the powerful Big Six to work for them. Ezra Brown and Bert Adams were kept busy as they delivered 10 cars in the Indianapolis area within a few months.[69]

The new models for 1912 were introduced quite early, only to receive major changes during the model year. The McFarlan Six was advertised in Indianapolis newspapers prior to the first 500 mile race in late May of 1911, no doubt an effort to capitalize on their anticipated racing success. The Little Six wheelbase was bumped to 121 inches with the price of the touring or roadster remaining at $2,100. The 35–40 horsepower engine provided by Brownell continued the same power plant that had been introduced midway through the previous year. The engine had overhead valves that were mounted in a special cage so they could be easily inspected or taken out for grinding. The engine, clutch and transmission formed the power unit. The 16 inch flywheel, the multiple disc clutch and the transmission were enclosed in oiltight cases to protect the parts. The Little Six could be had in the five-passenger touring, four-passenger torpedo or Runabout. All body styles could be purchased with or without front doors. Colors offered included Golden Brown body and running gear, Royal Blue body with the choice of blue or cream running gear, Torpedo Gray or McFarlan dull finish green.[70]

Within six months of its introduction, the Little Six had undergone major changes, including a completely different power train and a longer wheelbase. The revised model acquired a larger power plant made by Herschell-Spillman with a 4 inch bore and 5 inch stroke for 377 cubic inches displacement, rated at 40–45 horsepower. The new engine was of T-head design with cylinders cast in two blocks of three cylinders each. Both the cylinder castings and pistons were machined accurately enough so as to be interchangeable. The clutch was a multiple disc type having 40 steel plates, each 8 inches in diameter with tension maintained with a single spring. The clutch ran in oil and was part of the power unit, but the transmission was attached to the rear axle. This was the same engine-transmission combination that was being used by Palmer-Singer. McFarlan claimed that only Palmer-Singer and themselves had the exclusive contract to use that particular power train combination. Several other manufacturers chose to use similar transmission-differential units including the makers of the renowned Stutz Bearcat. The wheelbase was increased to 124 inches with the 17 gallon gas tank mounted at the rear attached to the

McFarlan introduced its 1912 models in the summer of 1911. The self-starter was not yet available on McFarlans when this ad appeared in *Everybody's Magazine* in July.

Though added later in the year, the self-starter was the big news for 1912. McFarlan used a system powered by compressed air (*Motor Age*, Jan. 25, 1912).

1912 Model 38, 4 Passenger Special. The gas tank was mounted high at the rear so gravity could be used to supply fuel to the engine (*Self Starting McFarlan Six*, Catalog 31, 1912).

outside of the back seat. Fuel was fed by gravity to the carburetor, and was said to work flawlessly no matter the nature of the road surface. However, for emergencies, there was a 2½ gallon reserve tank. The car sold for $2,300 including self-starter and a full set of shock absorbers.[71] Models 25, 26, 28 and 30 were built on this chassis.

The Big Six engine developed 55–60 horsepower and was still manufactured by Wainwright. Its size had been increased to 4½ by 5 inch bore and stroke raising the displacement to 477 cubic inches.[72] This engine continued using the valve-in-head design with circulating splash lubricating system. A multiple disc clutch unit with 28 plates, each 12 inches in diameter and running in oil, connected the engine and transmission.[73] The clutch and transmission were combined with the power plant into a single unit. The rear axle was of the full floating type using New Departure bearings. Models 32, 33, 34, 36 and 38 rode on the 128 inch wheelbase chassis. Model 38, a special long distance touring, offered increased fuel and oil capacity for a week's ordinary touring.

On all models, a sight feed on the dash allowed the operator to monitor oil movement to the bearings. The Stromberg carburetor included a water jacket to aid in maintaining uniform temperatures and assist in perfect fuel vaporization. Aluminum, a very high priced metal at the time, was used for the crankcase with supports at three points, one at the front and two at the rear, all of which were connected to the main frame. All models

The Model 25, Colonial Coupe 3 Passenger, McFarlan's first closed car, accounted for only a small percentage of sales in 1912 (*Self Starting McFarlan Six*, Catalog 31, 1912).

were upholstered using buffed leather over oil tempered springs stuffed with the best grade white curled hair.[74]

Purchasers were given the choice of wheel sizes, with 32, 34 or 36 inch being available depending on the amount of ground clearance required for road conditions they expected to encounter. One unique feature offered was the "curtain cupboard," a cylindrical container mounted at the rear of the body, for storing the side curtains when not in use. The steering wheel, still on the right-hand side, was 18 inches in diameter and made of walnut with spark and throttle levers located in the center for easy access. All models now had "Center Control," placing the gearshift and emergency brake levers in the middle of the front compartment.[75]

Although not yet available when the 1912 models were first introduced, the major innovation that became available during the year was a self-starter. Virtually every auto manufacturer was jumping on the self-starter bandwagon, trying to keep up with the stunning announcement made by Cadillac when they introduced their electric powered unit. Henry M. Leland, manager of Cadillac during the winter of 1910, had an established reputation of encouraging new ideas. During one month, five employees of Cadillac had suffered broken arms from what Mr. Leland called the "unruly, turbulent, vicious starting crank." A very close friend of Leland's suffered a broken jaw while helping a woman start her car. Charles F. Kettering, of Dayton, Ohio, was summoned to Detroit where he

CURTAIN CARRIER

CENTER CONTROL

The unusual Curtain Carrier permitted storage of side curtains, but required rolling them to fit the container. Center Control referred to placement of the gearshift and hand brake levers to the left of the driver, in the center of the floor (*Self Starting McFarlan Six*, Catalog 31, 1912).

40-45 H. P. MOTOR, INTAKE SIDE

40-45 H. P. MOTOR, EXHAUST SIDE

40–45 hp engine by Herschell Spillman with rear mounted transmission came on line in mid–1912 (*Self Starting McFarlan Six*, Catalog 31, 1912).

worked with Cadillac engineers, and the first Cadillac car equipped with an electric self-starter was built on February 17, 1911.[76]

By 1912, the industry was inundated with all kinds of different configurations to take away the danger and the burden of turning the crank. In addition to electric starters there were wind-up impulse units, acetylene gas systems and some powered by compressed air. McFarlan opted for the latter type, probably because it was easily adaptable to the present engine without major modifications and there were benefits having a power air pump available to assist with inflating tires that all too frequently went flat. A small four-cylinder Kellogg compressor, driven by offset gears, powered by the automobile engine, pressurized air in a cylindrical steel tank.[77] When starting the engine, air pressure from the storage tank spun the engine which was expected to fire up promptly. Included as standard equipment, this device made it much safer for anyone to start the engine, and women found new freedom behind the wheel.

One method of assessing the true quality of any product was to ask the locals what they thought about an item made in their community. A demonstration was offered to Connersville folk using a McFarlan as a livery or taxi service transporting passengers to and from the Fayette County Free Fair, for a small fee. The Free Fair was probably the most anticipated yearly community event in those days, and one of the only such attractions in the country that remains without charge to this day. Several operators used various makes of automobiles for taxis as a way of earning a few dollars while showcasing a particular brand of vehicle. The fairgrounds was located a little over two miles north of downtown Connersville, and the company claimed that their McFarlan car, driven by "Hurry Up Geezer Merrell," made two trips for every one of the other fellows, traveled 1,457 miles during fair week, and took in more money than any other livery. The expectation was that some of the persons who rode to the fair would eventually become buyers. Purchasers of 1912 McFarlans in Fayette County included F.A. Bosler, J.E. Huston, Howard Mount and Charles McGraw. Customers from nearby included William Overlesse from Milroy and John Noble from Morristown.[78]

The year 1913 brought several challenges beginning with the terrible flood that struck the community on March 22 and 23. Virtually all of the roads, railroads and interurban lines running into and out of the city were washed out, and electric poles and telephone poles were down. People had a great deal of difficulty getting from one place to another, even within the city. A few weeks later, McFarlan reported optimistically that the flood did not damage their plant at all and their plans were to turn out as many cars as possible and that production would not be held up one moment. The factory was close to the electric generating plant, so power was available, though in limited supply. The truth was that production was hampered because any materials that were not available through local suppliers could not be delivered, and real problems came when it was time for the finished product to go to the customer. Most roads were soon made passable again; however, the road leading to the covered bridge at East Connersville had been completely washed out and thus took several weeks to replace. Shipments were resumed April 1 on a limited basis as rail transportation slowly returned to normal.[79]

Among the new car shows in which McFarlan participated was the one held at Buffalo,

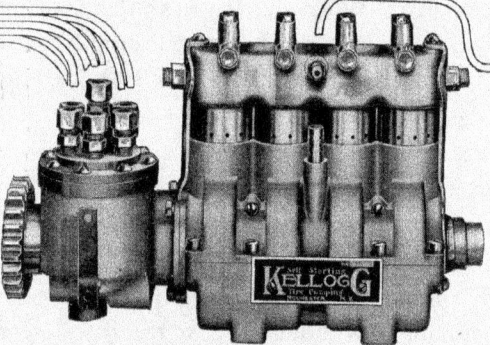

A Positive Self-Starter and Tire Pump Combined

Both Pump and Starter controlled by gauge and button on the front dashboard.

Entirely eliminates the most disagreeable features of motoring.

Sets motors humming that no other starter can move.

Patent Applied For

A NEW STARTER WITH 100% EFFICIENCY PLUS THE ADVANTAGE OF THE KELLOGG POWER TIRE PUMP

CONSTRUCTION

This is a compressed air Motor Starter, consisting of the well-known Kellogg Four Cylinder Air Pump coupled with a distributor of the rotary disk type and designed to be operated by the simple pressure of a button on the dashboard of a car.

The Kellogg Pump attached to and operated by the engine is used for pumping air in a storage tank which can be mounted most conveniently under the body of the car. By means of a foot pedal the pump is started and one hundred and fifty or two hundred pounds of air can be compressed into the storage tank. The Distributor Disk is timed with the motor in such manner that the opening in the Distributor Disk corresponds to the piston in the firing position so that by pressing the operating valve, air passes from the storage tank through proper piping, to the cylinder, and then into the other cylinders in rotation, instantly setting the engine in operation.

POWER

150 lbs. of air pressure, properly applied, is sufficient to readily turn over the heaviest engines, even in the coldest weather, and in the actual tests, this starter has easily run at more than 300 revolutions per minute, engines that no other starter has been able to move.

POSITIVE

On a six-cylinder engine, the Kellogg Starter will do its work 100 times out of 100 trials—it is absolutely positive in operation. On a four cylinder engine, it is positive except when the engine has stopped on dead center, a situation that may never occur, or that does not occur, according to statistics more than once in eighty times. A partial turn of the crank, however, is all that is necessary to move the engine from dead center and the Kellogg Unit will work.

SIMPLICITY

There are few moving parts, no batteries, no intricate, complicated wiring, nothing to get out of order. Both Air Pump and Starter are controlled from the dashboard, and connections are made with strong piping that can easily be replaced in case of an accident to the car.

WEIGHT

As the Kellogg Unit is made largely of aluminum, it is extremely light in weight, and the complete outfit will add less than 40 pounds to the weight of any car. This is an important feature for the owners of heavy cars.

COST

The Kellogg Unit complete, while it is the simplest, most powerful and most practical starter yet produced, costs from $75.00 to $150.00 less than any other good starter. And there is no additional expense required for maintenance.

And remember that the Kellogg Unit includes the famous Kellogg Power Tire Pump

Endorsed by the foremost engineers; adopted by many of the leading manufacturers as part of the regular equipment on their cars for 1913, and recommended as special equipment by many others; will deliver up to 200 pounds pressure in less than three minutes; is operated on the engine merely by throwing a lever; is thoroughly tested before leaving the factory, and is fully guaranteed for one year.

The Kellogg Unit can be attached to any car

See our exhibit at the Auto Show, and you will specify the Kellogg Unit as a part of the equipment of your next car.

KELLOGG MFG. CO., 10 CIRCLE ST. ROCHESTER, N. Y.

New York Office: 1733 Broadway   Chicago Office: 1108 Michigan Ave.   San Francisco Office: 444 Market St.

Kellogg compressors were used by McFarlan in 1912 and 1913 (*Motor Age*, Dec. 11, 1913).

The McFarlan building and the motor department in 1912 (*Self Starting McFarlan Six*, Catalog 31, 1912).

New York, where three cars were on display, each with a different chassis. The *Buffalo Evening News* was quoted as saying, "The self-starting McFarlan Six is one of the exhibits at the big show. Buffalonians and residents of Western New York have displayed considerable interest in McFarlan Six cars and the 1913 models evidently are destined to be quite numerous here abouts."[80]

A number of new agencies had been landed early in the year offering a wide market for sales. New dealers included the Jos. B. Deibler Motor Car Company in Chicago,

Russell Bros. in Kenosha, Wisconsin, O.R. Crutcher in Lexington, Kentucky, Louis F. Benton Company in Los Angeles, Green Bay Motor Car Company in Madison, Wisconsin, S.M. Foote in Middletown, Connecticut, N.A. Racine in Montreal, Canada, Swartz & Company in New Orleans, C.B. Swan in Old Town, Maine, Gerlinger Motor Car Company in Portland, Oregon, Carthage Motor Car Company in Rochester, New York, and the Coller-Reitz Motor Car Company in St. Louis.[81] That was an impressive list of new dealers until one recognizes that most of the businesses held multiple franchises selling more than just McFarlans. The company did not have the capacity to provide each dealer with many vehicles, and it was not at all difficult to obtain a franchise. One gentleman in Montana purchased two McFarlans so he could get the dealership and the discount that went with it.[82]

For 1913, McFarlan considered themselves to be at the forefront by equipping all models with Vesta Dynamo electric lighting along with the compressed air self-starter. No longer was it necessary to stop the car to light the acetylene headlights and kerosene side and tail lamps when darkness approached. Instead, just turn the switch for instant illumination. All body styles except the Roadster had seven lights including two interior rear compartment courtesy lights. Also supplied was a speedometer with gradometer. The latter provided bragging rights for the driver who managed to climb the steepest grade. An electric horn was also provided, as were two tool boxes, one on each fender's splash plate.[83] It was common practice to attach one or more tool boxes to the running boards in order to have the necessary equipment available for roadside repairs, but the containers sometimes hampered entry and egress. Attaching the tool carriers to the fenders left the running boards unobstructed, but may have limited the quantity of tools available when repairs had to be made.

Possibly the most confusing model year for McFarlan was 1913, as they offered three lines of cars, Series "S," "T" and "M." The Little Six became the Series "S," the Big Six became the Series "M" and the Series "T" was new, priced between the other two.[84] Series "S" and "T" used the same 124 inch wheelbase whereas the Series "M" was 4 inches longer. The engines for each series varied in size and horsepower rating as might be expected. What was truly astounding was that the engine for each model was of a different design, and each came from a different manufacturer. The number of interchangeable mechanical parts between the three series was nil. McFarlan seemed to be searching for their preferred power train combination, but chose to make the customer their "test goat" for judging reliability and durability instead of having an adequate program of testing and evaluating performance themselves.

The price leader, the Series "S," listed at $2,300 and was available as a 2-passenger Standard Roadster, Turtle Back Roadster, Standard Coupe, Turtle Back Coupe, a 4-passenger touring or a 5-passenger touring. The engine was by Herschell-Spillman, a T-head design with cylinders cast in blocks of three.[85] The bore and stroke were 4 by 5 inches providing a horsepower rating of 40–45. The valves were enclosed and the engine hung from three points instead of the previous four. The clutch was a multiple disc type that ran in oil. The transmission was mounted on the rear axle with gears that were said to be impossible to strip.

For 1913, McFarlan fielded three series, each using an engine manufactured by a different company. Few parts were interchangeable (*Motor*, Nov. 1912).

SIX-PASSENGER McFARLAN "SIX"—MODEL 27, SERIES T.

Fully equipped — equipment including 100 per cent. efficient Air Self-Starter with Kellog pump. T-Head Motor, 4 x 6, cast en bloc, developing 67 H. P. (See complete specifications on another page.)

A HIGH-CLASS "SIX" AT THE PRICE OF A GOOD "FOUR."

McFarlan Motor Car Company
Connersville, Indiana

The new offering for 1913 was the Series T, which boasted a T-head engine displacing 452 cubic inches (*Introducing the Makers of the McFarlan 6*, 1913).

    The Series "T" engine was a T-head type with cylinders cast en bloc with bore and stroke of 4 by 6 inches, displacing 452 cubic inches and developing 50 horsepower. Four main bearings carried the crankshaft that had a diameter of 2 inches. An unusual feature was the flywheel that was formed in such a manner as to act as a fan. The flywheel fan was in addition to the usual fan that was mounted on the front of the engine behind the radiator.[86] This engine had been built by the Light Inspection Car Company of nearby Hagerstown, Indiana, later known as Teetor-Hartley. The company name was changed to recognize the Teetor brothers, John and Charles, and their friend Charles Hartley, who owned the business and developed the engine. Except for the engine and a heavier clutch, the Series "T" used the same running gear as the Series "S," including the rear axle mounted transmission. Both "S" and "T" series had 21 gallon gas tanks mounted at the rear of the body. Body styles offered on the series "T" were the same as those available on the Series "S" with the addition of a Vestibuled Limousine. Prices started at $2,500.

    The Series "M" listed at $2,750 and was carried on the larger 128 inch wheelbase. The Wainwright-built engine that developed 55–60 horsepower was advertised as the

Model 34

A ROADSTER that is as comfortable to ride in as any touring car. Seats are tilted so passengers' position is natural, while at the same time they are more secure at high speed. There is plenty of power to handle higher than ordinary gearing, which is optional on this model, making a very fast car if desired. A double bucket seat "Speedster" model is furnished as an option under this number. This has the high, sloping cowl and true stream lines. A pointed radiator, which adds to the extremely lively appearance of these models, is optional on either.

Model 34T, $2,500.00   Model 35T, Speedster, $2,500.00

The Model 34 came as either a roadster or a speedster. The speedster had double bucket seats and extra high gearing. A V-shaped pointed radiator could be ordered on either model (*Self Starting McFarlan Six*, Catalog 32, 1913).

most powerful engine for its size in the world. In its 1913 literature, the company claimed that this series was offered in answer to the demand for a high powered, high speed, overhead valve job. "The motor is a development of our racing motor," the brochure text stated, "and is the one that carries the McFarlan flag whenever it appears on the track. In speedway races this model has made seventeen miles to the gallon of gasoline for two hundred miles." It was actually the Brownell engine that held that record. "It is capable of a speed of 95 miles per hour under racing conditions."[87] The engine, clutch and transmission formed a unit. An unusual feature was the crankcase that extended the length of the power unit. The same oil lubricated the engine and the transmission.[88] The gas tank on the series "M" was of 17 gallon capacity and was mounted under the front seat. Bodies offered were the Standard Roadster, 4, 5 or 7-passenger tourings and the Vestibuled Limousine. All models came with 37" × 4½" tires.[89]

The self-starter continued to be a well-advertised feature using the Kellogg compressor. McFarlan claimed their system was the first that used a separate air compressor to supply the air. Company literature explained that most compressed air starters got the required pressure from the expansion of exhaust gasses. The McFarlan starter supplied "pure" air at 150 pounds pressure at all times, not oil saturated exhaust gasses. When the button in the dash just below the air gauge was pressed, air under pressure was admitted into the cylinders and the engine would turn over and keep spinning until it fired on its own. One change made in the system included moving the water pump to a position in front of the compressor. The air pump was driven by shaft directly from the water pump.[90]

There is no evidence that McFarlan cars were any more sought after by crooks than any other make. All makes were vulnerable to the thief with sticky fingers. One 1913 McFarlan, an expensive model, was taken without permission from in front of a hotel in Anderson, Indiana. It was reported that a pardoned convict had been seen driving the car away at high speed and the police couldn't catch it. The next morning, law enforcement from the area met with residents of the village of Everton, asking them to be on the lookout. There was speculation that the car was being taken into the hills of Franklin County to be hidden. It was noted that the McFarlan factory people would assist the owner in recovering his car. Just how the company intended to help in that effort is not clear.[91]

As motorized vehicles became more common, the movement to improve the condition of roads escalated. Various organizations were formed throughout the country calling for better roads. Among the best known efforts was the Lincoln Highway Association. They provided some funding for road building through individual and business contributions, but government agencies were stuck with the bulk of the cost. Searching for ways to obtain the needed revenue to finance road construction, virtually every state picked up the practice of requiring motorists to purchase a license plate in order to operate a motor vehicle within their domain. A problem developed when some states insisted that tourists purchase a license for their automobile even though they lived elsewhere, but visited more than once or twice a year. Maryland claimed to have guards at their borders who would take motorists' names, then check to see how often they visited, with the intention of collecting license fees. The problem was addressed when a bill was introduced in the United States House of Representatives in June of 1913. It provided that motorists of any self-propelled vehicle using public highways in interstate commerce be required to have only one license. The plate of one state was to be recognized by all states in the union.[92] With that source of revenue being limited, states were once again searching for ways to fund road improvements until they hit upon the idea of taxing gasoline. With that ingenious system, revenues were collected by local businesses and submitted to the state treasuries where the money was presumably used for building or improving roads.

The Series T Motor

Left Side Series T Motor

The motor in the McFarlan Series T models has been developed along lines suggested by the best and most intelligent automobile motor practice of late years. The bloc casting and extremely short over-all length of it make an exceedingly stiff motor and one entirely free from bearing trouble and little, annoying knocks.

Cylinder dimensions are 4 x 6 inches, affording the most approved bore-stroke ratio. A long-stroke motor is a better puller at all speeds than any other type, and in this T Series motor the best type of long-stroke motor is exemplified. It has more main bearing surface than the average five or seven bearing motor. Four main bearings are used. The magneto and water pump bearings are double row annular balls.

The extremely clean appearance of the motor is in line with the best ideas. At the same time, the means used in securing the clean appearance also make the motor dust-proof and absolutely noiseless.

Right Side Series T Motor

Page Fifteen

The Series T engine was produced by the Light Inspection Car Company of Hagerstown, Indiana. The flywheel casting had fanlike blades that moved air to help cool the engine (*Self Starting McFarlan Six*, Catalog 32, 1913).

In the fall of 1913, it became apparent that McFarlan had fallen into serious financial trouble. Automobile production had stopped and the factory was essentially shut down. Several automobile makers were facing similar problems as credit restrictions forced manufacturers into insolvency. One of the better known of these firms was the Pope Manufacturing Company of Hartford, Connecticut, but American Motors of Indianapolis and Cutting Motor Car Company of Jackson, Michigan, also went into receivership. Although McFarlan had been in business in Connersville for 57 years, it was in serious financial trouble to the point that restructuring was required to save the company.[93]

McFarlan's production for the year was fewer than 200 automobiles, which meant limited cash intake. The company had spent a significant sum by participating in the Indiana to the Pacific Tour earlier in the year. Failure to adopt a standardized power train meant buying in small quantities and paying premium prices to parts suppliers. Company officials had also failed to separate the automobile operation from the carriage company. Advertisements for carriages regularly listed their manufacturer as the McFarlan Motor Car Company, but the carriage builder was actually still the McFarlan Carriage Company. Horse-drawn vehicle sales had come to a standstill, so that part of the business had become a financial burden on the whole operation. Adding to the problem was the sales arrangement under which McFarlan cars were distributed through a separate sales organization. That concern skimmed a portion of the profits that were already limited by such small production.

Management had recognized the impending failure of the carriage company and took steps to remain in business by incorporating into the McFarlan Motor Company and conducting business completely separate from the previous organization. On September 24, 1913, Alfred Harry McFarlan was named president and Burton M. Barrows, vice president and sales manager of the new concern. The company was assuming the responsibility of not only the manufacturing, but also the sales of their products. The new concern was organized and incorporated with an authorized capitalization of $100,000. As large an operation as the McFarlan Carriage Company had been in the past, it had never been incorporated, but had been wholly owned by the McFarlan family and a few trusted associates. The newly formed McFarlan Motor Company broke that tradition, but only for a small number of select stockholders. As soon as the paperwork was finalized, a contract was negotiated for engines and other parts so they could begin assembling vehicles again.[94]

Plans were to liquidate the affairs of the McFarlan Carriage Company at an early date.[95] Meanwhile, a petition had been filed with the United States district court in Indianapolis asking that the concern be adjudged bankrupt and that a receiver be appointed. The petition was filed by the Scheidel-Thompson Mfg. Co., the Indiana Lamp Company, and the Ansted Spring and Axle Company. The latter two companies were located in Connersville and were owned by Edward W. Ansted.[96] Later that month it was reported that R.N. Elliott, who had been appointed a trustee of the bankrupt McFarlan Carriage Company, had filed a petition asking for authority to sell the real estate belonging to the company.[97] The request was heard by H.C. Sheridan, the referee, on Nov. 3.

Indeed, the property was put up for sale and was eventually sold on December 31,

2. Six Cylinder Cars Exclusively

[Facsimile of handwritten Articles of Incorporation of the McFarlan Motor Company, dated September 24, 1913, signed by Alfred H. McFarlan, Burton M. Barrows, Arthur Dixon, Edward W. Cotton, and J. Werle Vincent, all of Connersville, Indiana.]

Having foreseen the impending bankruptcy of the McFarlan Carriage Company, management formed a new corporation in order to continue automobile production.

1913, to E.W. Ansted, one of McFarlan's major creditors.[98] What a blow this would have been to the deceased John B. McFarlan who had built the factory 26 years earlier. The McFarlan family, who worked for and whose fortunes came from the carriage factory, seemed to have turned their backs with little concern when resources were needed to keep the factory from being sold. The sale of this property put the McFarlan Motor Company at an additional disadvantage. Instead of owning their own facility, they were required to pay rent in order to continue in business.

Why the McFarlan family didn't step in and purchase the factory that J.B. had built is a mystery. They had as many or more resources as anyone in Connersville. Just two years earlier, the family controlled property in the four corporations they owned valued at $246,120, not including their bank holdings and other stocks. Property taxes they paid made up nearly one sixth of the city budget. When the carriage business folded, there seemed to be little interest beyond Harry McFarlan to continue the business that carried the family name.[99]

As the company resumed production, apparently some lessons had been learned after the confusing power train lineup in 1913. For 1914 McFarlan scrapped the previous year's offerings except for the Series "T," opting to continue only its most successful model, with improvements. The engine powering the Series "T" was the same as the previous year with bore and stroke of 4 by 6 inches.

Production did get on track in good order and by late November of 1913, several Series "T" automobiles were on their way to distributors. Three cars were shipped to agents in Los Angeles, three more went to Waterloo, Iowa, one to Houston, Texas and three even went out of the country to a dealer anxiously awaiting them in Calgary, Alberta, Canada.[100]

In what seemed to be a common practice with McFarlan, well into the model year, a new series was added. McFarlan claimed that it did not follow a yearly change cycle as did most of the industry, but would make changes only when they were needed. The new Series "X" was identical to the "T" except for the engine, which had a bore and stroke of 4½ by 6 inches making a whopping 572.5 cubic inch displacement. The larger engine provided more power, but both were of nearly identical design and both were produced by Teetor-Hartley of Hagerstown, Indiana. Each power plant had cylinders cast en bloc with T head design, and a circulating splash oiling system. The bottom of each connecting rod was indented to scoop and throw oil as the engine turned, thus providing lubrication for the pistons and rods. An oil pump forced lubricant to the main bearings. On the right-hand side of the engine were the Stromberg G3 carburetor and the Mea magneto. The centrifugal water pump, electric generator and air pump were located on the left-hand side.[101]

Gasoline was carried in a 22 gallon cylindrical tank made of seamless steel that was mounted at the rear of the body. Fuel was fed to the engine by a small cam action fuel pump mounted on the engine. A Stromberg double-jet carburetor was used. Electrical equipment consisted of a Mea magneto to provide spark for the ignition plus a Deaco electric lighting system. The size of the brake drums (rear wheels only) was increased to 16 inches in diameter with bands 2½ inches wide giving 1 inch of braking surface for every

2. *Six Cylinder Cars Exclusively* 91

Model 61.

Model 61 T, with 4″ x 6″ Motor.   Model 61 X, with 4½″ x 6″ Motor.

The Handiest Roadster ever built. Will carry equipment enough to go across the continent without replenishing. Has regular gasoline tank in rear of frame, holding 22 gallons and auxiliary tank back of seats holding 18 gallons. Auxiliary tank will be built with separate oil compartment at slight extra cost. There is a trunk inside the spare tires. High gearing, making a very fast car, is optional on this model.

Extra tires not regular equipment.

Model 61 T, $2590.00   Model 61 X, $2900.00

For 1914, the Model 61 was offered in two series, Model T and Model X (*McFarlan Six*, Catalog 33, 1914).

8½ pounds of weight. Rear springs were changed from full elliptic to ¾ elliptic. The springs were underslung with the bottom leaf being 56 inches long. A full set of Truffault Hartford shock absorbers was included as standard equipment.

Styling was very much like the previous year, but was cleaner as the hood merged into the sloping cowl eliminating the cowl lights on touring cars and roadsters. In a new method of securing the top on open models, the top was strapped to the windshield when in closed position. Collins "one-minute" curtains were folded inside the top for convenient storage and easy access.[102]

Another refinement for the year was in the pneumatic starting system. It was improved with a more efficient compressor and a larger air tank. An all metal four-cylinder Lipman pump supplied the 10 by 40 inch seamless tank with air pressure up to 300 pounds. Supposedly, a pressure of 250 pounds would spin the motor at a rate of 200 rpm for up to 85 seconds. The increased volume of the tank helped when engines did not start quickly.

A convenience item introduced partway through the model year was the Gray Pneumatic Gearshift, invented by Edward E. Gray of Plano, Illinois. It was expected to make driving easier by changing gears with the aid of compressed air. In addition, the Gray system allowed for a clear floorboard in the front compartment. The gear shift lever was

Model 64 T, with 4" x 6" Motor.　　　**Model 64, Six Passengers.**　　　Model 63 X, with 4½" x 6" Motor.

The most popular model in the McFarlan line, and deservedly so. Not requiring extreme width at the rear, most beautiful lines are possible, and the McFarlan treatment of these possibilities ranks with the most artistic. It is forty inches between the seats in the tonneau. The rear seat is forty-three inches wide and twenty-two inches deep. The auxiliary seats are large and comfortable and have springs in their cushions. A most satisfactory car in every particular. Since this picture was taken the style of auxiliary seats has been changed. They now fold down against the back of the front seat and are the same style seats as those shown in the limousine interior on page 17.

Extra tires are not regular equipment.

Model 64 T, $2590.00　　　　　　　　　　　　　　　　　　　　　　　　　　　Model 64 X, $2900.00

Model 69, Seven Passengers.

Model 69 T, with 4" x 6" Motor.　　　　　　　　　　　　　　　　　　　　Model 69 X, with 4½" x 5" Motor.

Very few limousines approach the tone exemplified in this model. It is original. The interior grades with that of any car, no matter what the price, in appointments. Because of the comparatively short wheelbase it is an ideal town car, and the spring suspension is such that it is as comfortable for touring as it is possible to build. The rear compartment is sixty-five inches long, over all. The auxiliary seats are large and comfortable. Color and material for trimming are optional. There are lights under the rear doors. Eleven lighting fixtures in all.

Model 69 T, $4000.00　　　　　　　　　　　　　　　　　　　　　　　　　　　Model 69 X, $4310.00

replaced by controls on the steering wheel and a foot pedal took the place of the emergency brake lever.[103] A similar system of gear changing was being marketed by Cutler Hammer, but it was electric powered. In order to change gears with the Gray system, the motorist moved a small indicator similar to the throttle, in the center of the steering wheel, to the desired gear. Gear shifting could be done silently and as rapidly as the operator could move the indicator and depress the clutch. Shifting up or down as desired could be accomplished via air under pressure so long as the engine was running to power the compressor.[104]

McFarlan was one of the few companies to offer this convenience, which was short lived because the company would soon adopt electric self-starting, eliminating the need for the air storage tank and large pump. Reliability problems also developed with the Gray system, which had hit the market before all of the wrinkles had been worked out. Additional problems were experienced when driving over rough roads because the fittings did not remain airtight with constant vibration.

McFarlan continued using the transmission that was attached to the differential, forming a type of transaxle.[105] Several manufacturers in the industry were using a similar type of transmission rear-axle combination during those years.

The touring car that was displayed at the Chicago Auto Show was light brown in color and had clean lines. The wheelbase had been increased from 124 to 128 inches providing additional space in the engine compartment, but because the hood was longer, it was fitted with three fasteners on each side, instead of the usual two, to prevent rattling.[106] Other innovations were the attachment of the horn to the right headlamp bracket, and the battery box being mounted under the front foot board.[107]

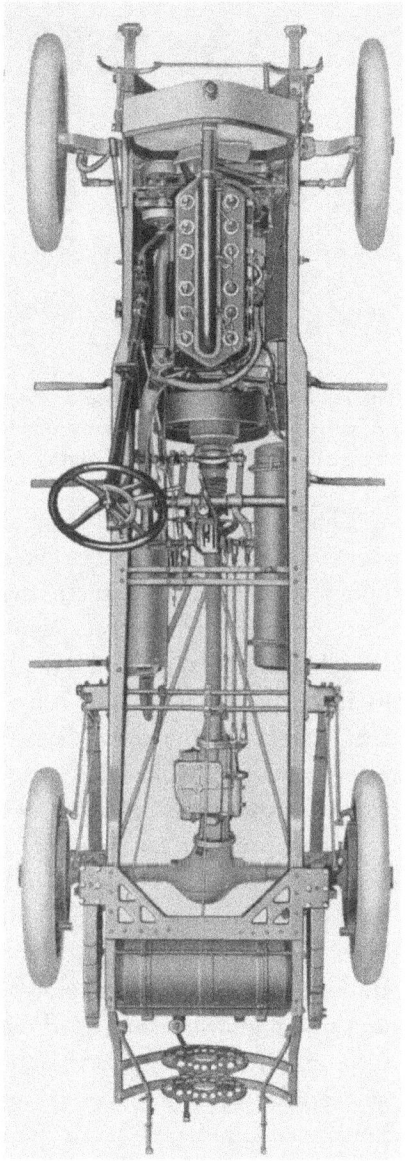

In 1914, McFarlan built a common chassis for models T and X. The long tank attached to the right frame member was the air tank. Note the long rear springs and the transmission attached to the differential (*McFarlan Six*, Catalog 33, 1914).

Opposite, top: The six passenger Model 64 was offered on either the T or X chassis (*McFarlan Six*, Catalog 33, 1914). *Bottom:* The 1914 Model 69. The Limousine interior had all of the comforts one could desire. Eleven lights provided illumination where desired (*McFarlan Six*, Catalog 33, 1914).

The engines for both the T and X series were manufactured by Teetor-Hartley, formerly the Light Inspection Car Company of Hagerstown, Indiana. Most mechanical parts were interchangeable (*McFarlan Six*, Catalog 33, 1914).

The most controversial change for McFarlan in 1914 was the relocation of the steering wheel to the left-hand side of the car. During this time period, the automobile related topic that could generate the hottest arguments was the proper location of the steering wheel, gearshift and emergency brake levers. The earliest cars generally were steered from the right-hand side, a practice that followed the custom of sitting on the right side while driving horse drawn vehicles. Most car makers had also initially placed the gearshift and emergency brake controls to the right of the driver, usually on the outside of the car. The reason given for this location was that most people were right-handed, and thus could handle the controls easier if they were located to the right of the driver.

Several smaller cars began placing the steering wheel on the left-hand side during the period of 1907–1909, and when Henry Ford adopted that system on his popular Model T, other manufacturers began to follow suit. When driving in towns or cities where the driver needed to watch out for oncoming traffic, or when making left-hand turns, the advantage of left steer was obvious; however, driving in the country gave credence to the right steer argument as it helped the driver stay clear of the edge of the road where a side ditch was often muddy. Many larger cars held on to right steer longer because they were more often used in the open country. Pierce-Arrow was the last American automobile company to join the rest of the industry with left steering, as they held out until the 1921 models were introduced. As early as 1912, Pierce-Arrow made their stand clear with the following statement: "The fact that right-side steer has become standard practice all over the world indicates that this is the natural position for driving." In spite of the position taken by the prestigious Pierce, more and more companies joined the left steer practice. McFarlan and most other makes had already relocated the gearshift and other controls toward the center of the car where they remained to the right of the driver.[108]

Body styles offered for 1914 were the open touring and roadster, each selling for $2,590. McFarlan did offer a closed model, the 7-passenger limousine. This land yacht rode on 37 by 5 inch tires and sold for $4,000.[109] Closed cars were generally less popular because they were considerably heavier and were not as maneuverable on poor roads. Their higher prices also meant that fewer customers could afford to purchase them.

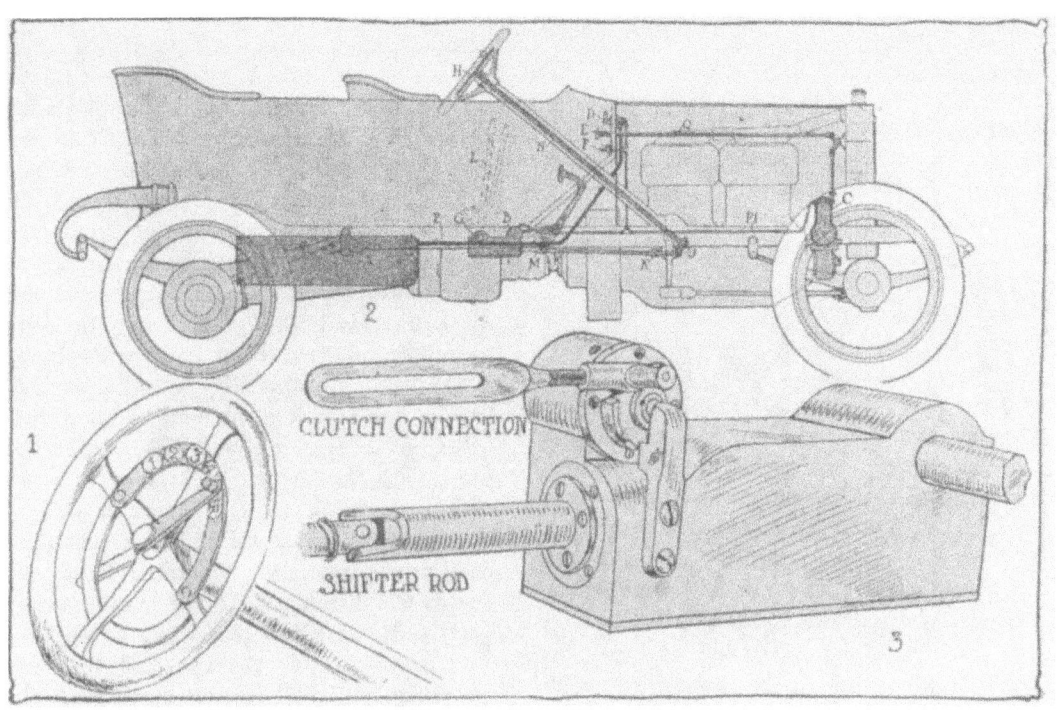

An early attempt to take away the drudgery of shifting gears was the Gray Pneumatic Gearshift (*Motor Age*, June 19, 1913).

Agitated citizens raised concerns about the carelessness shown by some test drivers. These complaints weren't directed solely at McFarlan, but included all of the local manufacturers.[110] Most McFarlan chassis were road tested before the body was installed to make sure the quality standards had been met. One regular test route was north from Connersville on the Milton Pike, a generally straight unimproved road leading toward Cambridge City. A test driver would sit in a bucket type seat mounted to the frame and drive at a speed faster than most thought necessary. One such test run ended tragically when the test car turned turtle in the ditch, killing the driver instantly.[111] Knowles Barbin, age 50, a tester for McFarlan, was reportedly

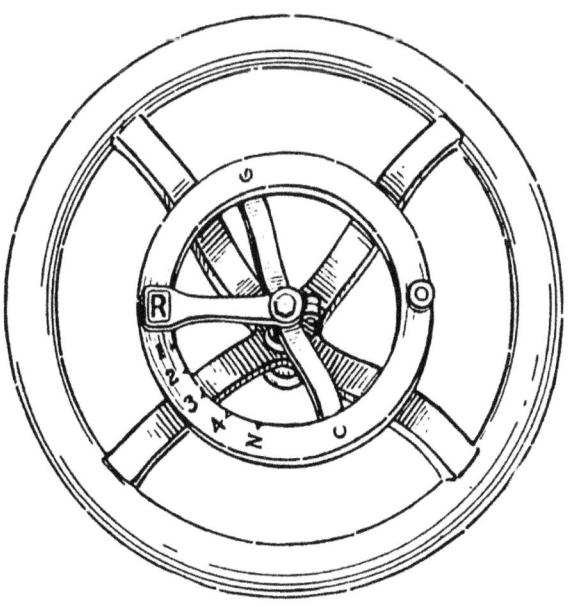

The controls of the Gray Pneumatic Gear Shifter as they were positioned on a McFarlan steering wheel (*Automobile Trade Journal*, Feb. 1914).

The driver's controls and instruments were located conveniently and easy to use in the 1914 McFarlan Models T and X (*McFarlan Six*, Catalog 33, 1914). Note the accelerator pedal located between the clutch and brake pedals.

driving at a high rate of speed on the Milton Pike near Beesons Station when he lost control and the car turned over on him.[112] Another time, a similar type of accident severely injured the youthful test driver.

McFarlan was not only recognized as a producer of quality automobiles, but they also built professional vehicles including ambulances, funeral cars and fire apparatus. The use of horses by the Connersville Fire Department continued into 1915 when they were replaced with McFarlan fire trucks, and two local funeral homes used McFarlans to give the final ride to the cemetery in a vehicle of undisputed distinction. On at least one occasion McFarlan built a truck that was used to do road work in Fayette County, Indiana.

As they prepared for the 1915 season, McFarlan announced there were open territories in Kansas City, Missouri, Atlanta, Georgia and Texas.[113] These were significant openings because those agencies had been very successful dealing in McFarlan carriages several years earlier. Continued were the series "T" and "X" with styling changes that included a longer and lower profile. The cowl was flat instead of tapered, thus making an unbroken line from the radiator to the back of the body. Large vents were placed in the top of the hood to help dissipate the heat from the engine and the side vents were placed at an angle instead of being vertical. McFarlan was now becoming quite a large vehicle with another increase in wheelbase from 128 to 132 inches. In the process of lengthening the running gear, the longer frame permitted the body to be set lower. Also, the upholstery did not project above the bodyline at any point which gave a sleeker appearance. A small cowl was added at the back of the front seat, providing space for a compact locker in which to keep valuables. Extra seats, sometimes called taxi seats, folded down under the locker when not in use. Interior dimensions were spacious as the distance from the back of the front seat to the front of the back seat measured a generous 40 inches with the extra seats folded.[114] Even with the longer wheelbase, most models showed a 300-pound reduction in weight, in large part due to changes in body construction where the wood framework was nearly two-thirds lighter than before. Some adjustments in chassis construction also reduced weight.[115] The marque was moving into the upper middle range price range with the series "T" open models starting at $2,590 to $4,000 for the Limousine, and, for the series "X," $2,900 for the touring to $4,310 for the limousine.

McFarlan boasted some of the most powerful passenger cars in the industry for 1915, powered still by engines from Teetor-Hartley of Hagerstown, Indiana. The series "T" featured a T-Head of 452 c.i.d. with a bore and stroke of 4 inches by 6 inches that developed 67 horsepower. The model "X" engine retained its mammoth 572.5 c.i.d. engine with a bore and stroke of 4½ inches by 6 inches and a claimed horsepower rating of 90. Lubrication for both engines used the splash system and many parts were interchangeable between engines.[116]

The compressed air system of cranking the engine had proved less than satisfactory. Although it worked fine under ideal conditions, maintaining the amount of air pressure necessary required that all fittings were sealed perfectly. Most driving, especially on rough country roads, was far from ideal. Too much bouncing would shake fittings loose in the

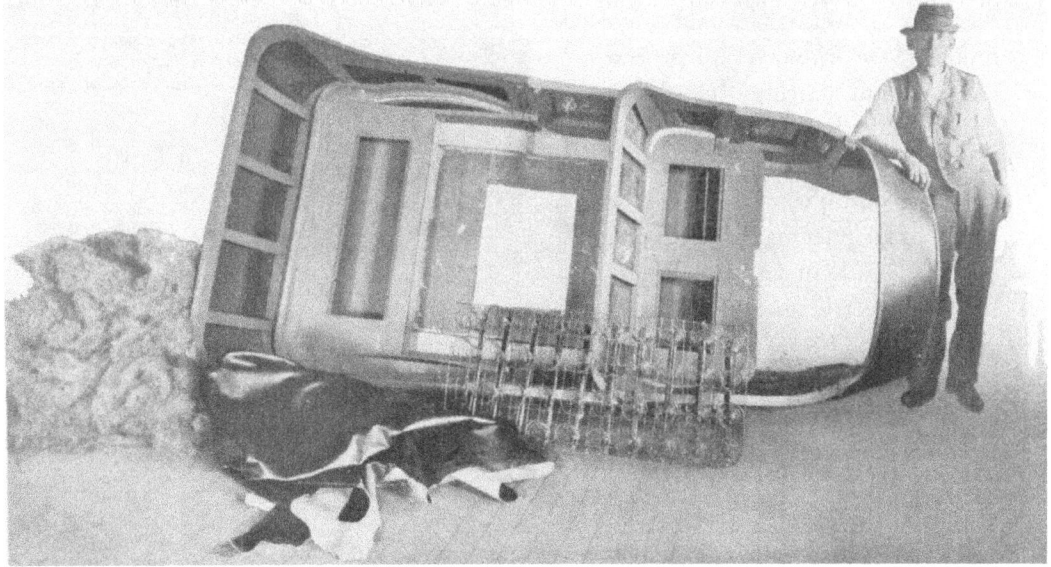

Shorty Moore, foreman of the trimming and top department with 27 years experience at his trade, shows the cushion springs and upholstering materials that went into making a McFarlan (*McFarlan Six*, Catalog 33, 1914).

Automobile testers often showed excessive speed and careless driving. This test chassis "turned turtle" on the Milton Pike, killing the driver (courtesy Wayne Goetz).

complicated and bulky system causing air leakage that could leave the driver without starting assistance. Even sitting overnight would often result in low air reserve, but several days without starting almost certainly required use of the crank to bring the engine to life. Therefore, for 1915, customers were given a choice of the pneumatic system or a considerably lighter weight Westinghouse electric starter at no extra charge.

Westinghouse already supplied the generator for the lighting system that now included a dimmer for the headlights. The carburetor was a Stromberg Model G with vacuum

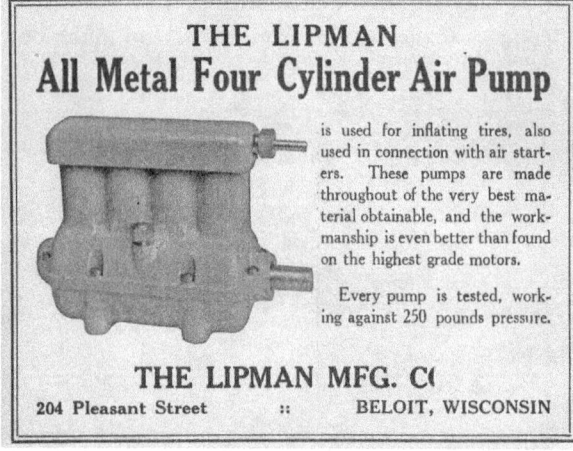

In an attempt to improve the reliability of the compressed air starting system, McFarlan introduced a heavier duty Lipman air pump (*Automobile Trade Journal*, Jan. 1914).

fuel feed from the 20 gallon rear mounted tank. A big change that year was replacing the multiple disc clutch that ran in oil for the 16 inch leather-faced cone clutch with twelve flat adjustable springs under the leather. In addition to making adjustments and repairs much simpler, the new clutch weighed several pounds less. Two other changes in the

For 1915, McFarlan offered the choice of either the new Westinghouse electric starter or the compressed air unit, as this ad indicates in the fine print at bottom. The choice for electric was overwhelming, so the compressed air unit was phased out (*The Automobile*, August 20, 1914).

Series T, 4 x 6 Motor, 60 Horse Power, $2830.   Model 104, Four Passenger Submarine   Series X, 4 1-2 x 6 Motor, 90 Horse Power, $3140.

The McFarlan Four Passenger Submarine offers more grace of design, more ingenuity of construction, without sacrificing its utility than has ever before been offered in one model. The front compartment has a cushion 41 inches in width and 19 inches in depth. The tonneau compartment is identical in size with the front compartment. The passengers in the tonneau are brought very close to the passengers in the front compartment without sacrifice of leg room. A portion of the space under front seats has been utilized to give this very pleasing arrangement. The closed baggage carrying space in the rear of the car not only adds grace of line to the car and carries out the stream line effect, but also avoids the vacuum and accompanying loss of power created by the flat-type designs. A tonneau cover made of top material converts this model into an ideal turtle back roadster in less than a minute. Wind resistance has been eliminated, and the result is the most complete and useful four passenger touring boat ever offered. We recommend it especially for ocean to ocean tours.

The McFarlan tire rack cannot be improved upon. It provides for the carrying of two mounted and fully inflated 36 x 4½ Silvertown tires and Firestone rims. The loosening of one buckle releases both tires; the tightening of one buckle holds them so securely that they cannot chafe or drop off. The whole effect is symmetrical and ornamental.

McFarlan Tire Carrier

An unusual body style introduced mid-year was the Model 104 4-passenger Submarine. Body panels were of hand hammered aluminum; the rear bustle contained a trunk compartment said to offer protection from water and dust, and the radiator was V shaped (*McFarlan Six*, 1916).

chassis added to weight reduction. The middle frame crossmember had been made lighter and the top portion of the ¾ elliptic rear springs was shortened. Retained was the three-speed transmission mounted on a short subframe that attached to the rear axle. The axle ratio of 3.58 to 1 permitted the operator to attain substantial speed while still providing adequate power to meet expected needs.[117] Steering was on the left-hand side with center

A McFarlan fords a river in Alberta, Canada, in a 1916 ad. Large wheels afforded excellent ground clearance (*McFarlan Six*, 1916).

gearshift that had been relocated close to the seat, so there was room to pass through from one side of the front compartment to the other. This automobile rode on 36 × 4½ inch tires mounted on Firestone demountable rims offering adequate ground clearance as road conditions dictated.[118]

The need for dimmers for headlights had not been evident just a few years earlier. Automobiles were rarely used after dark when lights burned carbide or acetylene, but electric lights proved to be much more reliable and provided brighter illumination that tended to be blinding when looking at them. As a means of increasing safety on streets at night, cities began passing ordinances requiring light dimmers on automobiles. Indianapolis, Chicago and other large cities were first to adopt such laws, but other metropolitan areas soon followed.[119] McFarlan responded, as did most other manufacturers, by including light dimmers as standard equipment.

McFarlan's 1915 advertising was not timid, touting "the only tried and proven medium-priced six on the American market."[120] This claim, of course, failed to consider other marques such as Marmon, Buick, Oldsmobile, Hudson, Studebaker and several others that were well established in the field.

An unusual body style was introduced mid-year with a most unlikely identification: the McFarlan Submarine. The name choice was surprising in view of the world situation at the time. Most of Europe was embroiled in the "Great War," a conflict in which the United States claimed neutrality while in reality heavily supporting the Allies, Great Britain and France. The most lethal weapon on the open seas at that stage of the war was the German submarine. It had definitely captured the imagination of people interested in the newest weapons, but brought great fear as it was being used effectively by Germany in unrestricted submarine warfare, principally against ships belonging to Great Britain, France and countries friendly to them. One month prior to McFarlan's launching their Submarine, a German sub had sunk the British ship *Lusitania*, taking the lives of 1,198 persons, of which 197 were U.S. citizens. Using the Submarine name seems even more unsuitable for a family business that was founded by an immigrant from England.

The rear compartment of the Model 107 Seven Passenger Touring, available in both the T and X series, came with luxury appointments including extra seats that folded into the cowl (*McFarlan Six*, 1916).

McFarlan had been a manufacturing institution in Connersville for nearly 60 years, offering employment to generations of local citizens (courtesy Fayette County Historical Museum).

However poor the choice of name, the Submarine was an interesting body style— a close-coupled dual cowl open car seating four passengers. Body panels were of hand hammered aluminum. Its features included a bustle-back built-in trunk to keep luggage or picnic baskets dust and rain free. This was one of the earliest built-in trunks on an American passenger car. The side panels were a bit lower for a sporty flair, and rear seat passengers were given added foot room under the front seats. Passengers were pampered by seat cushions and backs that were deep and luxurious. Wire wheels and a pointed radiator added to the sporty motif.[121]

A major event in 1916 that involved the entire community, actually the entire state of Indiana, was the centennial celebration of the Hoosier state. An historical pageant of significant proportion was organized involving hundreds of children and adults in the Connersville area. As might have been expected from a prominent community leader, Harry McFarlan served as a member of the committee for the auto parade. McFarlan automobiles were one of the locally made vehicles to take part in this major celebration.

For 1916, McFarlan continued offering two sixes, series "T" and "X." The running gear and body for both series were identical with each using T head engines that had cylinders cast en bloc. The power plants were the same in every way except for the piston bore. The smaller "T" engine had a bore and stroke of 4 inches by 6 inches whereas the

We Are Pleased To Announce The Continuation For Another Twelve Months Of Our Series T and X Chassis

A large number of refinements have been incorporated which have resulted in greatly increased Power, Speed and Comfort. These Series will be fitted regularly with Six and Seven passenger touring, Four passenger Submarine or touring roadster body types.

It is needless to say that the equipment includes every convenience known to the motoring public.

The Standard colors formerly furnished will be retained for quick shipment. On individual orders, when time is given, personal ideas of the owner as to upholstering and general color scheme, will be followed without additional charge.

We have urged you to avail yourselves of these special privileges.

60 Horse-power, Series T, $2680.00
90 Horse-power, Series X, $2990.00

Individual bodies specially designed and built to order by our Custom Body Department.

McFARLAN MOTOR COMPANY, Connersville, Ind.
Address Desk "A"

In writing to advertisers please mention THE HORSELESS AGE.

For 1916 the T and X series both continued (*The Horseless Age*, August 15, 1915).

This Model 111 Town Car built on the series X chassis with an unusual basket weave finish offered prestige for a $4000 price tag. McFarlan was one of the very first manufacturers to use side-mounted spare tires; this model also sported wire wheels and a trunk. Interior appointments included a black walnut panel on the front of the enclosed passenger compartment with McFarlan designed vanity cases and an additional courtesy light (*McFarlan Six*, Catalog 35, 1916).

"X" boasted 4½ inches by 6 inches and 90 h.p.[122] Teetor-Hartley continued to be the supplier, but now the T head had aluminum pistons plus other lighter-weight moving parts, permitting increased engine speed. Higher rpms were made possible by using four large main bearings, the center ones being 2⅜ inches in diameter and the end bearings 2⅛ inches. In addition to the splash lubrication system, an oil pump was driven off of the exhaust camshaft. The electric starter by Westinghouse eliminated the troublesome pneumatic system entirely. While making the move to the more reliable electric power source, the starter unit was relocated from the left to the right side of the engine and was activated through the flywheel instead of using a series of gears to the crankshaft as had been done in the past. Both the starter and the generator were mounted lower, making it easier to remove the valve covers for service. Westinghouse also supplied the generator and lighting system. The water pump, which was formerly cast integrally with the crankcase, was now mounted separately for easier repair or replacement. The use of a cone clutch was continued, but the pressed steel unit was replaced with a lighter weight aluminum unit.[123]

Another change that made the McFarlan more serviceable was moving the transmission away from the rear axle and mounting it on a subframe toward the middle of the main frame along with the engine. Gears were 3½ percent nickeled steel, and the diameter of the squared shaft was increased to 1⅝ inches. Transmission gears were carried on annular bearings.[124] Part of the weight reduction came from using a full floating differential and rear axle that was made of pressed steel, replacing the heavier malleable casting used previously. Its gear ratio was dropped to 3.07:1, providing surprising economy plus plentiful speed wherever road conditions permitted.[125]

One of the most striking innovations for 1916 was the use of cantilever springs, similar

Built in Series X Only **Model 113, Coupe** *90 Horse Power, $3600*
The coupe is the ideal town car for those who prefer to do their own driving. This model is designed to accommodate three passengers with the greatest ease. Special attention is called to the accessibility of the compartment under the rear deck. It can be reached without the usual contact with the dust and grime of the roads.

Built on the X series chassis was this Model 113 Coupe. Note the curved glass corner windows up front (*McFarlan Six*, Catalog 35, 1916).

to those used on the English Rolls-Royce. The rear spring consisted of 14 leaves, the unit being 58 inches long and 3 inches wide and shackled at both ends. This massive spring was not arched, as was most common, but under normal load was quite straight and was claimed to give remarkable riding qualities. The frame was strengthened in order to accommodate the unusual setup.

In general appearance, the 1916 car was similar to previous models. The radiator was somewhat higher and the side panels of the body had been raised giving a more streamlined appearance while the passengers were carried lower. The company kept certain standard body types in stock for prompt delivery, including the recently introduced Submarine, a two-passenger roadster, a dual cowl open car, and five and seven passenger tourings and sedans.

McFarlan was also entering the more exclusive custom market. Although virtually all bodies were designed and built in the McFarlan plant, a custom body department had been established from which purchasers could order alterations in design, color and upholstering materials to suit their fancy.[126] The ability of this small producer of automobiles to cater to customers' desires placed them among the exclusive marques. This also gave them a recognition that they had not previously known. As more and more custom work was requested, McFarlan's image blossomed into a prestige vehicle with prices that soon reflected their achieved status.

For the 1916 model year, prices took a modest $90 increase, partially reflecting increased demand for war materials. European countries that were involved in the conflict and were friends of the United States provided an active market for American manufacturers who were happy to oblige by supplying all kinds of goods.

Built in Series X Only Model 117, Berline *90 Horse Power, $4300*

The Model 117 Berline with its 90 horsepower Teetor-Hartley engine listed for $4,300 and was available on the series X chassis only (*McFarlan Six*, Catalog 35, 1916).

Any manufacturer would gladly receive testimonials that expressed owner satisfaction. One such letter from William Faversham, a well known Broadway actor, was published in an ad that appeared in the February 1917 issue of *The Theatre*. He wrote,

> Last Saturday night Mrs. Faversham and I left the theatre at 11:30 to motor down to our place at Lloyd's Neck. We did some tall plowing through virgin drifts of snow, I tell you! It was a sight but the car behaved beautifully. On her high speed she threw up such a tremendous lot of snow it didn't seem to be safe, so we slowed her down to low speed, and then she went through in the most extraordinary manner you ever saw. With the exception of the drifts of snow which she threw to one side, we might as well have been on a smooth road. We really enjoyed the adventure. There was a house party where we were Sunday night. Two of the party motored down in the daytime and had taken different roads to ours to avoid all the snow. They did it in about three hours to three and a quarter. They didn't expect I would come in the car — they thought I would come on the train, and in the morning when they saw my car in the garage they were rather surprised. At dinner, on my plate was a boutonniere, with the following poem:
>
>> "Oh Favvy, you're a sweet one
>> And you always were a darlin'.
>> But I love you more than ever
>> Now I've rode in your McFarlan."[127]

For 1917, McFarlan changed model identifications and dropped the series "T," concentrating on a single engine. The series "X" was relabeled the Model 90, reflecting the horsepower rating. The car was lowered so that the top of the body panels on open cars was only 48 inches from the ground, yet the ground clearance remained unchanged. Passengers were carried lower although the backs of the seats were raised above the body

Above: The major improvement for 1916 was moving the transmission forward so it was part of the clutch and engine unit (*The Automobile Journal*, August 25, 1915). *Left:* Cantilever rear springs, similar to those being used by Rolls-Royce, made their appearance for one season only. They were 3 inches wide with 14 leaves (*The American Chauffeur*, Nov. 1915).

panels to permit the use of heavier upholstery. The auxiliary seats, when not being used, folded into a cabinet built into the rear compartment cowl. A central compartment in the cabinet could hold two quart thermos bottles to keep lemonade cool, coffee hot, or provide beverages of choice for the occupants. The steering wheel was designed so that it could be tilted out of the way to facilitate entering and exiting the vehicle. On cold days, the wheel could be heated to give the driver additional comfort.[128] All of the electrical wiring was centralized in a control box located on the steering column. Thus, when changing from an open body to a closed type body, as was sometimes done for use in the colder seasons, it was necessary to pull out only two connectors from the box.

McFarlan continued their experimentation with new products in one of the cars displayed on the show circuit, equipping it with a Vesta centrifugal magnetic transmission. McFarlan had purchased Vesta's electric headlamps for several years. The Vesta self-shifter did away with the generator, starter, clutch, flywheel and transmission, replacing them with a flywheel dynamo, planetary gearset with low, high and reverse positions, and controller. The armature of the Vesta unit was powered by the engine. At low speeds, the coupling between the engine and gearset was electromagnetic. At higher speeds, the dynamo's brushes doubled as a centrifugal clutch locking the unit into direct drive.[129] One had only to press the buttons, and speeds were changed electrically. The system was

For 1917, McFarlan proclaimed "a new standard." The Series T and X designations were dropped. One powertrain was offered, identified as the 90, standing of course for the engine horsepower rating (*Philadelphia Metropolitan Opera*, April 17, 1917).

produced under Vesta patents. The listed price on the particular car, as equipped, was $4,500. There was no indication as to whether or not the car was ever sold or what happened to it after the shows ended.[130]

As it became more and more evident that the U.S. would become directly involved with the war in Europe, prices increased a substantial $210 during the 1917 model year, making them even more a car for the wealthy. One advertisement bluntly stated that the McFarlan was primarily a conveyance for cultured people. The implication may have been that to be wealthy also meant that one was cultured. Company literature listed the type-127 seven-passenger touring with wood spoke wheels for $3,200, followed by the type-122 five-passenger touring with wire wheels for $3,400. The customer could opt for a type-136 seven-passenger touring sedan at $4,300, or the top-of-the-line type-154 Knickerbocker Cabriolet at $5,000.[131] Also offered were a coupe for $4,000 and a Landaulet for $4,600.[132] A trend-setting practice started that year by mounting spare wheels and tires for some models on the running board ahead of the front doors. This was done especially when optional wire wheels were chosen. For the next 20 years, this method of mounting spare tires on the side of the cowl, or in fender wells, became quite popular and was offered by most manufacturers as either standard or optional equipment.

In what had become almost a biennial tradition, the wheelbase was again stretched 4 inches to a lengthy 136 inches. The cone clutch adopted a couple of years earlier was replaced with a three-plate dry disc unit. The torque tube driveline was changed to an open drive shaft. Suspension changes were made both front and rear. The front springs became semi-elliptic, measuring 40 inches in length. At the rear, the 56 inch cantilever springs introduced the previous year gave way to 62 inch underslung semi-elliptic units. The company now promoted its "McFarlan cradle type" suspension.[133] The Teetor-Hartley 4½ by 6 inch bore and stroke 572½ c.i.d. engine continued with some changes. Spark plugs moved into the head immediately over the center of the combustion chamber, and the valves were inclined toward the center providing more efficient operation. The combustion chamber volume was decreased, raising compression from 60 to 70 pounds. New camshaft action opened the intake valves more quickly making the engine more responsive. A button on the steering column control box actuated the starter.[134] The frame was entirely new, drawn in at the front to permit a shorter turning radius. Midway back the frame became 40 inches wide supporting the body directly under the sills.

One special occasion that allowed McFarlan to showcase their handsome new offerings was a large parade held in Indianapolis on October 12, 1916, for the cause of promoting good roads. President Woodrow Wilson was in town to give a speech and was one of the observers. For this prominent event, automobile manufacturers and dealers were invited to parade their wares in front of an expected 50,000 viewers.[135]

The United States entered the Great War on April 6, 1917. Increased demand was placed on goods and services with the war effort taking first priority. More than 1,000 Fayette County boys and young men entered the armed services. All of the local manufacturing companies felt the loss, and lots of job-switching took place as companies offered higher wages or some type of perk to draw workers. Such problems were common throughout the country. Agents would show up from larger cities promising better wages in Dayton, Indianapolis or Cincinnati. One solution was to hire women and girls to fill some jobs. More help came when the Department of Labor made it illegal to recruit laborers away from other businesses.[136] Hired help was still at a premium throughout the war, and for several months after it ended.

Local companies did serve the war effort well, just as the community had demonstrated their patriotism through war bond purchases, leading the nation in meeting their quota. There was also a profit motive for each company, including McFarlan, and company management sought government contracts with lucrative payouts for products that were needed for the

After price increases late in the 1917 model year, all open touring types were listed at $3500. Wire wheels were an extra cost option (*Motor*, August 1917).

The type 134 Knickerbocker Cabriolet premiered in 1917, priced at a hefty $5,000 (*McFarlan Six, By This Sign—*, 1917)

war effort. In the case of McFarlan, their skilled woodworkers were kept busy turning out 6,000 wooden tool boxes. Also made under government contract were waterproof cushions stuffed with kapok to help soften hard benches and to serve as life preservers for American servicemen on troop ships.[137] Other products the local company produced included leather cushions used in ambulances and on ships, officers' folding tables, metal ammunition boxes, platting boards, handling trucks for sea planes, and Jacob's staffs.[138] As the war effort escalated, manufacturers were encouraged to convert their plants to 100 percent war work. An edict came from Washington that the changeover was to be completed by January 1, 1919, to avoid possible government intervention.[139] Six months after the conflict ended, McFarlan was still assembling several thousand waterproof steel cases to be used by Army engineers.[140] That job had been contracted during wartime and was not cancelled, though many of the contracts had been set aside after hostilities ended.

McFarlan's quality of workmanship during their wartime production received high praises. One local newspaper noted, "The McFarlan Motor Company, during its course of activities for the government, established a record that was not surpassed, perhaps not equaled, by any manufacturing concern in the United States." The article went on to say that government inspectors became thoroughly satisfied with their visits to the factory and not one article was returned to the company for correction.[141]

Intended to be chauffeur driven was this Touring Sedan without front compartment windows or passenger door (*McFarlan Six, By This Sign —*, 1917).

Shipping of finished cars by rail had been a significant problem in the past, but it was usually seasonal. During the fall harvest season, moving grain and shipping coal in preparation for winter often took priority, but with a war being fought, rail transportation could be counted on only when cars were available. Several auto manufacturers started a system of "mass drive-aways" as a means to keep deliveries current. McFarlan didn't have nearly as serious a problem because their volume was so much lower, about one car a day. However, by the spring of 1918, they were driving cars to dealers when possible. The company had found that they could drive a new vehicle through to Philadelphia, Boston, New York City, or other cities on the Atlantic coast more satisfactorily than to wait for railcars to become available. Therefore, McFarlan cars were leaving this eastern Indiana city in what was called a slow procession bound for metropolitan points. They arrived looking less new and glistening, but the company claimed they were better than the cars sold new with zero miles. The company declared, "A practical test of the vehicle from Indiana to, say Boston, was in itself worth much to the purchaser." Presumably the car would operate better after being broken in, even over the terrible roads that were traversed. This method of delivering new cars was an example of the resourcefulness needed to operate successfully during that period.[142]

The 1917 McFarlan was longer and lower. With the wheelbase extended to 136 inches, suspension changes permitted the car to ride 4 inches closer to the ground (*The Automobile*, June 15, 1916).

Even as the Great War continued and the United States was openly involved, McFarlan introduced new models for the 1918 season. Because of increased material costs, prices took a hefty $400 increase effective April 6, 1918. The new offerings had significant mechanical and styling changes. Several new body styles appeared, some of which were given names to add distinction. As if to express support for the Allies, the Submarine was renamed the Destroyer. With the more patriotic ring it listed, after prices were adjusted, for $4,150. The Pasadena was a 5-passenger touring with sidemounts and California top for $3,900; the Knickerbocker Cabriolet, the top-of-the-line town car, listed at $5,650; the Philadelphia Berline or the Continental Landaulet could be had for $5,300; and the sloping straight front sedan or sloping "V" front sedan listed at $5,000.[143] The newly introduced sloping front sedans indicated factory designers had begun to recognize the need for some improvements in air flow. The public apparently wasn't ready for such styling because, after a few years, McFarlan dropped this style in favor of the more traditional square look.

The most important changes were to the engine. The same size power plant, now called Teetor-McFarlan, was continued, but an additional set of spark plugs was added, giving two plugs per cylinder, with two separate ignition systems, each of which was controlled by an ignition switch. One switch controlled the plugs fired by the Westinghouse battery and distributor, while the other turned on or off the system connected to the high-tension magneto. Both could be used at the same time or either one would work individually. The reasoning for this extravagance was protection should one of the systems fail. The continual reinforcement of McFarlan's position as a quality machine was enhanced by including Warner lenses in the headlights, a gasoline spray primer for cold weather starting, an engine driven tire pump, shock absorbers all around, an eight day clock in the dash and a cigar lighter. Closed cars offered even more luxury with silk window curtains and roller window shades, pillows, hassocks, vanity cases, smoking requisites and other niceties. The tire size was 35 by 6 inches, running on wood spoke artillery type wheels as standard equipment, or Houk No. 6 wire wheels as an extra cost option.[144]

For the past several years, McFarlan engines had been supplied by Teetor-Hartley of nearby Hagerstown, Indiana. This family owned company was established in 1896 and had been managed mainly by members of the Teeter family. In 1900, the company name became the Light Inspection Car Company because they were manufacturing a lightweight bicycle type vehicle used for inspecting railroad tracks. Later on they began making automobile parts and eventually complete engines that that were sold to several manufacturers including McFarlan. The company name was changed in 1913 to Teetor-Hartley Motor Company.[145]

Something happened in early April of 1918 that caused the McFarlan Company to rethink who their engine supplier should be. A controlling interest in the Teetor-Hartley Engine Works was sold to Frank and George Ansted, who were in control of the Lexington Motor Company, an automobile manufacturing concern that was also located in Connersville, Indiana.[146] The Ansteds' purchase was not supposed to affect McFarlan in any way; however, the new owners were most interested in designing and producing a new power plant for the Lexington automobile. Although they promised other companies would have production as time and space permitted, McFarlan decided to seek a new supplier. Within two years, an engine of their own design was being manufactured by a different company. This change was probably a good move because a major part of the Ansted purchase was done by promissory note and within three years, the Teetor family attempted to repossess the company because of lack of payment on the balance due.

Top: The steering wheel would tilt for easy entry or exit and could be heated for cold weather driving — welcome perks for the chauffeur. *Bottom:* The extra taxi or jump seats could be folded into the cowl and hidden by the doors (both photographs, *Motor Age*, June 8, 1916).

Just two days after the armistice was signed on November 11, 1918, the War Commodi-

Above: McFarlan kept their skilled craftsmen busy building 6,000 wooden tool boxes like this one for the armed services. *Below:* During the war McFarlan also built several thousand metal surveyor's cases for Army engineers (both photographs by author).

ties Board issued a notice that McFarlan and other automobile manufacturers could return to production on a 50 to 60 percent basis as quickly as they could procure materials. One Connersville newspaper noted that "to the local companies, which turned from their own lines of industry to war work merely at the bidding of the Government, it will be literally like going home to go back to their former paths."[147]

Within a few weeks of cessation of fighting, permission was given to resume regular manufacturing as materials became available. McFarlan welcomed the opportunity to return to full production, which meant no more than one car a day at most. By the spring of 1919 a new dealer, the

George Ansted purchased 500 shares of preferred stock in the McFarlan Motor Corporation at $10 each on August 16, 1918.

Updyke Automobile Company at 1001 North Meridian St., Indianapolis, had taken on the franchise for this limited production prestige vehicle. Updyke's new line offered either the Daniels Eight or the McFarlan Six, believing that the demands for their particular motorcars were varied, though exacting, and included beauty, comfort, convenience, sureness, ease of control, efficiency and durability, and that these two marques would meet the demands of the most exacting buyers.[148]

In the fall of 1919, rumors were circulating that the McFarlan Motor Company was planning to expand its operation. Although in fact McFarlan had no size increase in mind, it was planning a good business move of a different nature. For nearly six years, the company had not owned the building where its craftsmen built fine automobiles, as it had been purchased by Edward Ansted after the McFarlan Carriage Company had gone into bankruptcy. Only the east wing of the four-story building was used for automobile manufacturing. The west wing had been rented out to various other companies. In November of 1919, McFarlan was able to complete negotiations for the purchase of the property, thus returning its ownership to the family that had built it some 42 years earlier.[149]

A few months later, another minor change caused some uneasiness for a time when the McFarlan Motor Company dissolved its charter as a Connersville, Indiana, corporation.

The 4-Passenger Destroyer with boattail body (*Automobile Trade Journal*, Nov. 1917).

All of the stock of that company was already held by the McFarlan Motor Corporation, whose charter was filed in Delaware. The Delaware corporation offered more flexibility in that it also permitted the building of aircraft and other products, if the company so desired. After its wartime production of a variety of items for the government, there was some thought that the company might investigate entering other markets.[150] Soon after that adjustment of paper, the company began listing itself as McFarlan Motor Corporation.

For 1919 and 1920, McFarlan fielded an assortment of models including the model 122 2–4 passenger roadster at $4,800, 124 4-passenger Destroyer touring at $5,050, 125 4-passenger Sport with six wire wheels at $5,000, 126 6-passenger touring at $4,800, 127 7-passenger touring at $4,800, 131 Town Car at $5,900, 134 7-passenger Knickerbocker Cabriolet at $6,550, 135 Sport Sedan at $6,100, 136 sloping V or straight front sedan at $5,900, 137 Philadelphia Berline at $6,200, 138 Limousine at $5,950 and 141 Continental Landaulet at $6,200.[151] Two popular accessories from the period that lasted into the mid–1920s were Westinghouse air shocks and spotlights. The big shocks, resembling artillery shells, could be aired up to stiffen the ride and aid in cornering, or some air could be let out for a softer ride.

THE McFARLAN NINETY

TOURING ROADSTER
Type 122
Two, Three and Four Passenger

THE McFARLAN NINETY

CONTINENTAL LANDAULET
Type 141

The Sloping "V" Front Sedan showed signs of concern for better air flow while still offering excellent ventilation (*McFarlan Six, "By This Sign,"* 1918).

Although the automotive trade magazines listed the changes each year for every manufacturer, and McFarlan accepted the free publicity, the company didn't consider it necessary to do yearly model adjustments. Instead, they took the position that they would make changes as the need arose, regardless of the time of year that might occur. Those changes did often coincide with other manufacturers' new model introductions. McFarlan made no changes, however, from 1919 to 1920.[152] They still participated in the most prestigious automobile show held in New York City, which was geared toward promoting each year's new models. One NYC newspaper noted, "There is another roadster made in Indiana which should appeal and it is a big fellow. It is at the McFarlan booth and sits well beside a big touring sedan."[153] Another large exhibition was held at New Orleans where McFarlan showed three cars. The roadster and the sedan each received a blue ribbon award and the Sportster won the grand prize trophy.[154] Smaller cities also staged shows that sometimes drew the company's attention, such as the one held at Indianapolis in

Opposite, top: The Type 122 Touring Roadster was available in two-, three- and four-passenger configurations. *Bottom:* The Type 141 Continental Landaulet (both photographs, *McFarlan Six, "By This Sign,"* 1918).

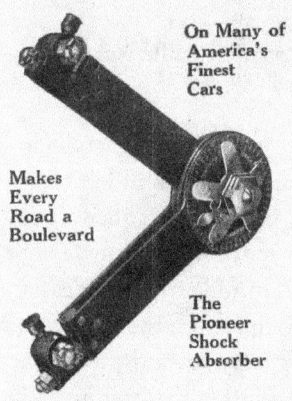

McFarlan had been a longtime user of Hartford shock absorbers (*The Journal of the Society of Automotive Engineers*, July 1918).

Above: Sport model McFarlan designed and built for C. C. French. It is credited with ninety horsepower and looks the part. Among its interesting features is the method of carrying the spare disk wheel free of the fender.

A "sport model McFarlan" designed and built for C.C. French. Note the unusual rear windshield with extension windwings (*Motor Life*, Jan. 1920).

March of 1920, where three large McFarlan cars were on display. The Motor Mardi Gras was held in the Manufacturers Building at the State Fair grounds and closed with carnival festivities designed to include the entire family with show activities.[155]

McFarlan's very limited production might suggest that their sales would be totally within the United States. That was not the case. Because the marque had become one on the most exclusive cars in the world, they were hard to get and the company kept few cars in stock ready for delivery. Virtually every car was sold before it was completed and most were sold before they were started. McFarlan automobiles were owned by Spanish royalty. Others had come into favor with the wealthiest classes of Chile and Cuba.[156]

One of the McFarlans that went overseas ended up in Sweden. August Huzell and his son, Eski, owned a hardware store in Karlstad, the provincial capital of the province of Varmland, located approximately halfway between Stockholm, Sweden, and Oslo, Norway. Eskil came to the United States in 1919 or early 1920 and, almost certainly, visited Connersville. He ordered five Lexington Minute Man Sixes and one McFarlan Town Car. All of the cars were delivered to Karlstad in the spring of 1920 and the McFarlan was registered in May of that year with Mr. Eskil Huzell as owner. He kept the car until 1925 when he apparently disposed of it and the car was taken out of the register. The fate of this car is unknown; however, a McFarlan which may or may not have been the Huzell car was later registered in a province south of Varmland. No more McFarlans are known to have been registered in Sweden.[157]

By 1920, McFarlan sported one of the most powerful engines of any American automobile, so it seemed like a sure bet when Mr. Frank Hatch, a McFarlan owner, made a challenge. He had heard of a record breaking run from New York City to Montreal, Canada, that had been made in a Franklin automobile. He was convinced that he

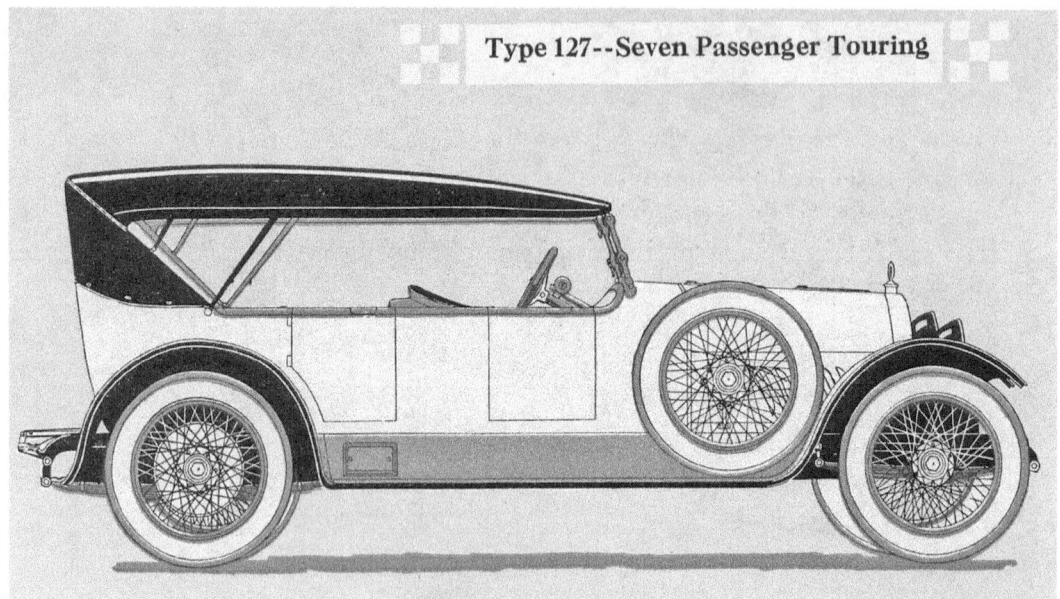

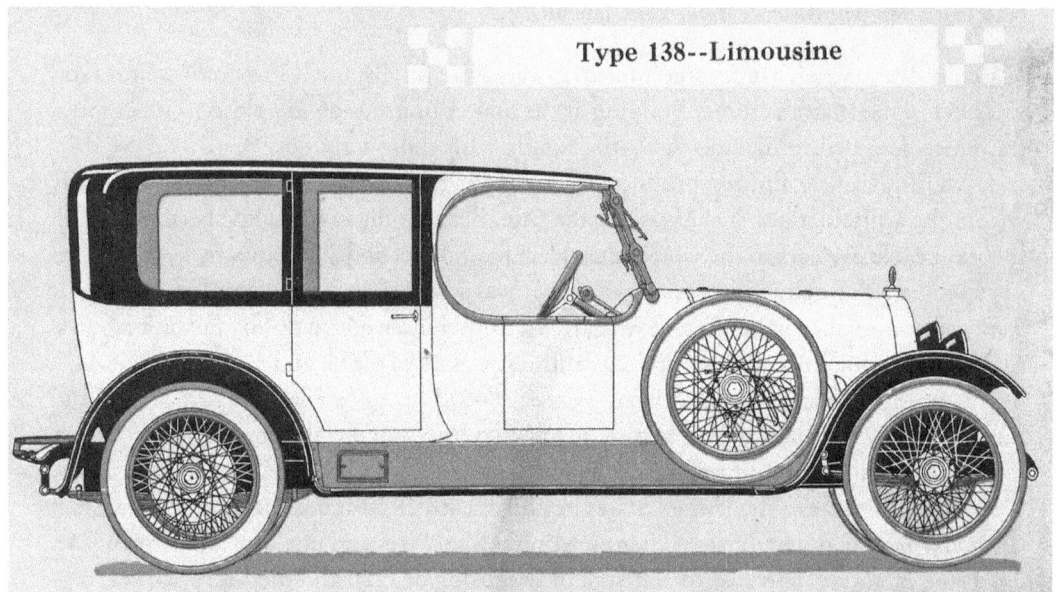

Top: The 1919–1920 Type 127 Seven Passenger Touring with optional wire wheels. *Bottom:* The 1919–1920 Type 138 Limousine's three-piece windshield and side curtains, when installed, protected the driver from the most severe weather (both images, *McFarlan Ninety*, Book 41).

could wipe a Franklin off the map in a one-way run between the two cities. Franklin was an air-cooled automobile with considerably less power than the "Big Mac," and Hatch was so sure of himself that he put up $2,500, which Art Schlobohm, the Franklin dealer, matched. The $5,000 was placed in escrow for the winner. The Franklin was to be driven by Johnny Banks, who had piloted the air-cooled car when it broke the record. That

Above: "Beauty of line and finish characterize the exterior" of this 1919–1920 McFarlan sedan with steel disk wheels (courtesy Antique Automobile Club of America Library, Hershey, PA). *Right:* Interior appointments in 1919–1920 included plush cushions and hardwood cases with toilet accessories for "the convenience of feminine passengers" (*McFarlan Ninety*, Book 41).

didn't bother Hatch because he knew his McFarlan, with 90 horsepower, could easily outrun the 50-horsepower Franklin 9-B.

The contest started from 245th Street and Broadway in New York City at midnight on June 30, 1920. By toss of a coin, it was decided that the Franklin would leave first, followed one hour later by Hatch in his McFarlan. Each car had, as a passenger, an observer selected by the opponent.[158] On good straight roads the huge truck-like McFarlan could outrun most any opponent, but the journey to Montreal was anything but good. Once out of New York City, the roads were typical of the day: unpaved and very rough. The Franklin, with only 50 horsepower, but much less weight and far better handling, easily ran away from its

McFarlan Motor Company
BUILDERS OF SIX CYLINDER
AUTOMOBILES EXCLUSIVELY

Connersville, Indiana

April
Twenty-first,
1920

Commercial Union Assurance Co.
53 John Street,
New York, N. Y.

Gentlemen: ATTENTION: WM. M. BALLARD.

In reply to your letter of April 15th., will say that we have mailed you our catalogue for 1920 cars. Also our price list.

We do not run on yearly models and the 1919 cars were identical with the 1920. No change. We have also included in the catalogue that we have mailed you a price list and instruction book.

We trust that this will be everything you want.

Sincerely yours,
McFARLAN MOTOR CO.

-- Vice President --

BMB:K

McFarlan made no changes between 1919 and 1920, but a totally new automobile would be introduced for the 1921 season.

challenger, arriving in Montreal hours ahead of its more powerful opponent to collect the prize money.[159]

McFarlan engines were no longer built by Teetor-Hartley after 1920. Although the company was located at nearby Hagerstown, Indiana, and had built the power plants to McFarlan's specifications, a completely new automobile had been designed and would be powered by the new Twin Valve Six.

3

McFarlan at the Brickyard and on Tour

Every new automobile manufacturer sought ways of getting the attention of prospective customers and proving the reliability of their particular product. One way of meeting both objectives was to compete successfully in racing events. The better known the event, the more influence it could carry with the buying public. Very early on, McFarlan claimed to have absolutely no interest in speed contests. A January 1910 ad assured prospective owners that they were relieved of the expense of company built racing cars and professional drivers that were of no value or significance to the average buyer. The ad went on: "You are vitally interested, not in records, but in what the car will do in your hands, and we have designed and built, keeping constantly in mind the man who drives his own car."[1] That all changed within just a few months when McFarlan actively participated in factory sponsored racing and experienced a moderate amount of success. McFarlan was quite fortunate to be located in fairly close proximity to the brand new and very promising Indianapolis Motor Speedway. Racing events were just beginning to be held at the 2½ mile oval and the speedway was experiencing birthing pains at about the same time that the first McFarlan automobiles wheezed into life.

The Indianapolis Speedway was incorporated on Feb. 9, 1909, by Carl Fisher, Arthur Newby, James Allison and Frank H. Wheeler of Wheeler and Schebler. A three-day meet initiated the track tragically in mid–August of 1909, ending with loss of life and a devastated macadam surfaced track. Rumor had it that the American Automobile Association would not sanction further events there, so the track's promoters got together with the National Paving Brick Manufacturers Association in September, and in just 63 days, the Indianapolis Speedway was reborn into what became know as "The Brickyard." On Dec. 17, Indiana Governor Thomas R. Marshall, assisted by his private secretary, Mark Thistlewaite, ceremonially laid the last of the 3,200,000 bricks on the speedway track. The final brick was gold-plated and weighed fifty-two pounds. After a few grandiose words, the track was reopened and the first car to hit the new hard surface was an Indianapolis-built Empire 20, chosen because the track owners had a controlling interest in the Empire Car Company.[2]

Several racing events initiated the newly resurfaced track during the summer of 1910, and on Labor Day weekend a series of contests were held to mark the closing of motor car competition at the speedway for the season. Races were held on Saturday, Septem-

W.J. Barndollar in car number 23 and Fred Clemmens in number 24 were ready to race on the newly resurfaced track at the Indianapolis Speedway, Labor Day weekend 1910 (McFarlan Six catalog 1911).

ber 3, and on Labor Day, September 5. An Indianapolis newspaper noted that the McFarlan Motor Company would be entering the racing game at the Indianapolis speedway. The company entry form indicated they would mark their debut by a plunge for all the good things in the prize list. In other words, they were willing to compete in any contest for any prize they could get, an ambitious undertaking for an untested marque. This event was noted as being the "richest race on the Labor Day list," as it offered a total of $2,400 in prizes.[3]

McFarlan had two entries, both of which were early 1911 models. Number 23 was driven by W.J. Barndollar, who had built his reputation as a driver for Frayer-Miller and Lozier; number 24 was driven by Fred Clemens, who was from Indianapolis and new to racing.[4] Cars were assigned a number in the order in which their entry was received. When McFarlan decided to enter into competition, they did so using paid drivers who were supposed to be at least somewhat experienced.

Saturday started out cloudy with the threat of rain, but the weather cleared making a pleasant day for spectators and participants. For security purposes, military guards were stationed at various places throughout the grounds. Activities were kicked off officially mid-morning by the Maxwell-Briscoe band from New Castle, Indiana. The day's races included a five-miler for cars of 231 to 300 cubic inches displacement. In this race, Marmons finished first and fourth, Falcars placed second and third, and McFarlans, with the 248 cubic inch Brownell engines, driven by Clemens and Barndollar, came in seventh and eighth respectively. In a five mile free-for-all handicap race, a Cole was first, a Matheson second, Clemens' McFarlan third and Barndollar fifteenth. The highlight of Saturday's racing program was the Remy Grand Brassard 100 Mile race. In that event, out of eleven starters, Nationals won first and second places, followed by a Speedwell in third and a Midland fourth. Clemens, in his McFarlan, placed fifth with a time of 1 hour, 31 minutes and 42.44 seconds. Barndollar placed seventh.

Among the drivers lined up waiting to race during the 1910 Labor Day weekend event are Clemmens, nicknamed "Skinny," in number 24 and Barndollar in number 23, immersed in fumes while waiting for the starting gun (Indianapolis Motor Speedway Museum).

Labor Day events went off as planned even though a heavy downpour of rain occurred shortly before the first event was to take place. The weather, however, soon cleared and remained favorable through most of the afternoon, leaving the track cool and in excellent condition. The early rain reduced attendance, but there were still approximately 18,000 spectators on the bleachers and in the grandstand when the Maxwell-Briscoe and Overland bands stopped playing and starter Fred Wagner got events underway at about 1:15 P.M. A number of Connersville fans were on hand and were treated to an exciting day. In the five mile race for cars of 231 to 300 cubic inches displacement, Barndollar came in fourth and Clemens fifth behind a Marmon and two Falcars, but the real success for McFarlan was in the five mile free-for-all handicap where Barndollar placed first, followed by a Firestone-Columbus, then Clemens, who claimed third place.[5]

The premier event for the weekend was the 200 mile race for cars with a piston displacement of 600 cubic inches or less and with a minimum weight of 2,300 pounds. Both McFarlans were entered in the race even though their engine size was less than half the maximum size permitted. At 3:30 P.M., the twelve contestants were sent on their way when starter Fred Wagner fired his revolver into the air. At 30 miles into the race, the No. 8 National, No. 32 Marmon and No. 24 McFarlan were fighting for the lead with the National two lengths in front. The lead changed between the Marmon and the National whenever one of them had to stop for fuel or tire changes; however, after 75 miles, the National led for the rest of the race. The Marmon dropped out at 170 miles. As the race progressed, the bright sunshine left and a threatening cloudburst enveloped the track in such darkness that the starter and timers had much difficulty in bringing the race to a successful close. Barndollar, piloting the McFarlan number 23, gradually moved up in the field, even passing number 24, as he drove without stopping for fuel or a tire change. He covered the 200 miles in 3 hours, 3 minutes, 29.12 seconds and came in third behind two Nationals and received $300 in prize money. Clemens was

Bert Adams, a native of Connersville, became the chief test driver for McFarlan. He also drove in the City of Atlanta races in November 1910 and planned to be in the first 500 mile race at Indianapolis in 1911, though he dropped out before that event (Indianapolis Motor Speedway Museum).

on his final lap when the race was halted because of the threatening weather. He was awarded a fifth place finish.[6] This had been an outstanding showing for a company that had been building cars for less than a year and had just gotten its first taste of competition. After the events had finished, a gentleman by the name of Disbrow, who was in the racing business, asked if he could take one of the McFarlan cars to St. Paul, Minnesota, at his own expense where he wanted to enter it in a 24-hour run. Company representatives appreciated his interest but declined the offer.[7]

Both drivers, Barndollar and Clemens, reported after the races that their cars were in as good a condition as when they started, and both cars went through each race without even a change of tires.[8] Of the twelve cars that started the race, only five finished, two of which were McFarlans. Number 23 was the only car that did not stop during the 200 miles. Number 24 stopped but once, and that was just to refill the oil tank. There was no mechanical work done on either car the entire time they were at the Labor Day events.[9]

Labor Day Summaries

Five Mile Free-for-All Handicap				200 Miler — 600 c.i.d. or Less			
No.	Make	Driver	Time	No.	Make	Driver	Time
23	McFarlan	Barndollar	5:08.32	9	National	Aitken	2:47:54.74
30	Firestone-Col.	Frayer	5:09.65	7	National	Livinstone	2:53:26.30
24	McFarlan	Clemens	5:13.65	23	McFarlan	Barndollar	3:03:29.13
6	Cole	Edmunds	5:14.00	18	National	Greiner	3:05:56.85
25	Parry	Hughes	5:14.30	24	McFarlan	Clemens	flagged off
5	Speedwell	Clemens	5:19.00	28	Black-Crow	Stimson	out on 78th lap
33	Cole	Endicott	5:19.35	10	Marmon	Dawson	dropped out
14	Matheson	Basle	5:19.68	32	Marmon	Harroun	dropped out
18	National	Greiner	5:23.20	5	Speedwell	Clemens	dropped out
11	National	Merz	5:28.40	16	Falcar	Gainaw	dropped out
19	Herreshoff	Emmons	5:33.37	14	Matheson	Basle	dropped out
16	Falcar	Gainaw	5:35.42	29	Midland	Ireland	dropped out
37	Staver	Kiefer	5:37.37				
28	Black-Crow	Stinson	5:37.90				
34	Cino	Fritsch	5:40.93				
29	Midland	Ireland	5:41.35				
21	Herreshoff	Smith	dropped out[10]				

Another 1910 event in which McFarlan had moderate success was the City of Atlanta races scheduled to be run November 4 and 5 at the Atlanta, Georgia, speedway. In the Labor Day event, both McFarlans were driven by so-called professional drivers, but at Atlanta, Bert Adams and Stanley Kepler, were employed by McFarlan. A third driver, Fred Clemens from Indianapolis, was considered to be professional, as he had driven earlier at the Indianapolis Speedway.

Adams was listed as a newcomer to automobile racing; but was well respected in his hometown as a master mechanic. He had been in business in Connersville, running a garage along with two other partners, but sold his interests in 1909 with the intention of

The City of Atlanta races were run November 4–7, 1910, with two McFarlans participating (*Catalogue of McFarlan Six Cylinder Automobiles*, 1911).

A Simplex and two McFarlans in the City of Atlanta race in November 1910 (*The Automobile*, Nov. 10, 1910).

going to work for Stoddard-Dayton.[11] Instead, the 19-year-old Adams ended up employed at McFarlan where he became their chief test driver and occasionally competed in racing. Stanley Kepler had come to Connersville in 1909 to help Harry McFarlan and his team get automobile production started.

Although Clemens made the trip to Atlanta, he was apparently recovering from an illness so Kepler shared driving responsibilities. Neither Adams nor Kepler had had racing experience, but both were considered to be expert drivers and good competitors.[12] The McFarlans had two serious handicaps placed upon them: they weighed less than the minimum weight requirement, so 400 pounds of ballast was added, and with their small 248 cubic inch engine displacement, there was little hope to successfully compete against machines with much larger power plants.

On Friday, November 6, a 100 mile race was held to claim the Coca-Cola trophy. It was noted to be for stock chassis with engine sizes from 301 to 450 cubic inches. Both McFarlans were entered in this race even though their engines didn't meet even the minimum requirements. A Falcar came in first, followed by Wescott, Marmon, Pope-Hartford, Falcar, and the two McFarlans bringing up the rear. It was considered remarkable that all of the cars that finished the race maintained an average speed of over 60 miles an hour, a speed never before attained in a 100 mile speedway contest for that class of cars.[13] The longest race of the day was a 200-miler for stock chassis cars with 451 to 600 c.i.d. The McFarlans with 248 c.i.d. engines competed after special permission was granted. Of the 11 cars that started that event, seven finished in the following order: Marmon, Lozier, Lozier, Falcar, Falcar, Simplex 50 and Clemens' McFarlan. Adams dropped out after 39 miles with a broken tappet mechanism. The number 23 McFarlan ran the entire race without a stop, but did not finish in the money.[14]

The highlight of the weekend was a 250 mile race that was to have been run on Saturday, but was rescheduled to Monday, November 8, because of inclement weather. Adams did quite well, coming in sixth place for $100 prize money.[15] Adams' performance in that

Bert Adams at the wheel of McFarlan number 23. He relinquished his position to Mel Marquette as Indianapolis race day approached in 1911 (Indianapolis Motor Speedway Museum).

race drew comment in an article in *Motor Age*. One of the most interesting pieces of work of the entire race was furnished by driver Bert Adams and the No. 24 McFarlan. Adams stopped but once in the 89 laps to replenish his oil tank, which was very small, holding only about eight gallons. The McFarlan didn't show sensational speed but demonstrated real consistency. The Marquette Buick, the Lozier and Adams' McFarlan were the only cars in the race that had no mechanical trouble of any nature.[16]

City of Atlanta Races

Coca-Cola Trophy 100 Mile

No.	Make	Driver	Time (min.)
12	F. A. L.	Geinau	86:17.5
26	Wescott	Knight	86:32.1
28	Marmon	Dawson	87:27.3
17	Pope-Hartford	Basle	90.07
27	F. A. L.	Pierce	93.47
24	McFarlan	Adams	98.51
23	McFarlan	Kepler	100.34
14	F. A. L.	Hughes	out at 80mi.
11	Marmon	Heineman	out at 80mi.

Grand Prize 250 Mile Free-for-All

No.	Make	Driver	Time (min.)
6	Lozier	Horan	206:15
40	Buick Marquette	Burman	207:21
44	Simplex	Matson	209:09
36	Simplex	Beardsley	217.20
5	Lozier	Mulford	235.45
24	McFarlan	Adams	241.08
34	Halladay	Harrell	251.22
43	Firestone-Col.	McKinstry	out at 208mi.
21	Marmon	Harroun	out at 208mi.
28	Marmon	Dawson	out at 184mi.
3	Fiat	Stoddard	out at 76mi.[17]

In the first 500 mile race at Indianapolis, May 30, 1911, McFarlan number 23 leads the pack going into the first turn (*Automobile Trade Journal*, Dec. 1, 1924).

A letter sent by the McFarlan Motor Company to James A. Brown, president of the Consolidated Vehicle Company in California, gave McFarlan's view of the Indianapolis and Atlanta races. "While we won only one first and one second, we were fourth in the twelve-mile class race, and sixth and seventh out of twelve starters in the 100 mile race and third and fifth in the 250 mile race. This race, as you know, was for cars away above our class, for which we had to get special permission to enter and also carried extra weight to qualify, giving us the smallest motor and the greatest weight in proportion to our piston displacement. In the 100 mile race we went through without a stop, the only car to do so, and finished fifth out of the sixteen who started, against two Loziers, two Simplexes and a 100 horsepower Buick Marquette. As you can see, we were in a class with cars selling at least $2,000 more than ours, beating eleven others of the highest priced cars made in this country."[18]

Beginning in 1911, the Indianapolis event was promoted as a 500-mile race with an unheard of purse of $25,000, of which the winner was to get $10,000 and second place, $5,000. The first "500" was held on Decoration Day, May 30, with forty cars participating. On race day, enthusiastic spectators came from every direction. Railroads ran extra trains; 12 interurban lines feeding into the Indianapolis Traction Terminal unloaded fans at the rate of 12,000 an hour. All 35,000 Speedway seats had already been sold out, but by the end of the day, speedway president Carl Fisher estimated that 90,000 spectators had attended. The *Indianapolis News* reported the worst automobile traffic jam in the city's history and garages did a land-office business repairing machines, fixing tires and filling gas tanks.

Included in the list of cars entered in the race were (one each) Apperson, Cole, Cutting, Fiat, Firestone-Columbus, Inter-State, Knox, Mercedes, Simplex, Stutz, Amplex, Mercer, Pope-Hartford, Alco, Velie, and Wescott; (two each) Lozier, Buick, McFarlan, Marmon, and Benz; and (three each) National, Case, Falcar and Jackson.[19] The McFarlan Number 22, driven by Clemens, had an engine with bore of 3⅝ inches and stroke of 4 inches for a displacement of 248 cubic inches, the smallest engine in the race. McFarlan Number 23, which was to have been driven by Adams, sported the new Wainwright engine with a bore and stroke of 4 by 5 inches for a displacement of 377 cubic inches, 100 less than the winning Marmon.[20] Both Bert Adams and Fred Clemens were well known to Connersville fans.

Clemens was young in the racing game, but had had experience at the Indianapolis Speedway in the Labor Day event in 1910 as well as limited driving in one of the Atlanta, Georgia, races that fall. Adams, originally listed as the driver of Number 23 McFarlan, had driven at the Atlanta Motor Speedway in the fall of 1910, but otherwise was not known in the racing fraternity.[21] As the time approached for racing, apparently Adams had second thoughts, so Mel Marquette took his place in the driver's seat.

Melvin Marquette was born in a log cabin in 1884 to George and Cora Marquette. The family lived in the country near Mooresville, a few miles southwest of Indianapolis. Raised on a farm, Melvin decided that was not the kind of life for him so he pursued higher education, graduating from Purdue University in West Lafayette, Indiana, in 1906. Whether or not he received inspiration at Purdue to build and fly heavier-than-air machines is not known for sure, but Mel designed and helped build his own airplane at a time when few people had ever seen one. He first flew his plane in 1909, taking off from the newly built Indianapolis Speedway. Marquette had initially intended the aircraft to be used as a sideshow attraction at carnivals, but he did fly it a few times.

At some point, Harry McFarlan and Marquette had become friends.[22] The friendship worked for the benefit of both men, because in 1911, when McFarlan needed someone to quickly step in and pilot one of their race cars, Mel Marquette became the logical choice. He was willing to take the risk, was quite versatile both as an aviator and in handling a variety of machines and was not considered to be completely new to racing. Despite the fact that he had been the victim of several accidents, both in race cars and in airplanes, he had continued to follow both lines of sport. When Adams stepped aside, Marquette was hired to drive McFarlan Number 23 in the first 500 mile race.

In order to eliminate the slowest entrants, each car had to qualify for the race. Qualifications were held one or two days prior to the actual race. To prove a car's capability, it had to run at least 75 miles per hour for one fourth of a mile on the brick track, probably being timed on the main straightaway by stop watches.[23] One method used to increase speeds as much as 4 miles an hour was to apply grease to the surface of the track. A large tank wagon containing the slippery goo was pulled by a truck to coat the brick surface. Originally, 46 cars had been entered in the 1911 event, but Gibbons' Velie, Clemens' McFarlan, and Jenkins' Cole were unable to muster the required speed to qualify. The

Falcars had problems obtaining needed parts and one of the Lozier drivers had an accident and couldn't participate. That left 40 starters for the race.²⁴

The problem of scoring 40 speeding automobiles was to be handled by 100 men using four Burroughs adding machines, two Columbia Dictaphones, a Warner Harograph and four Telautgraph machines that would duplicate handwriting from the scoring stands to 12 places on the grounds. The race was started using a "pace lap" rather than a standing start as was common at that time.²⁵ On the left of the front row was Carl G. Fisher, president of the Speedway Company, in his Stoddard-Dayton roadster, acting as pacemaker. When the starting signal was given the cars moved out, keeping

Phillip Marquette, one of Melvin Marquette's sons, holds a photograph of the airplane flown by Mel in 1909 at the Indianapolis Speedway (photograph by author).

good alignment at approximately 40 miles per hour. The pace lap went off perfectly, making an impressive spectacle. The speeding cars accelerated for flat-out competition as Mr. Fisher pulled over to the left, the track official waved the starting flag and an aerial bomb announced that the race was underway.²⁶ Marquette's McFarlan was in the lead going into the first turn.

Although there was an accident causing a fatality early in the race, the scoring process went well until the 240 mile mark when a spectacular accident occurred on the main stretch. Joe Jagersberger's Case broke a steering knuckle and suddenly swerved, throwing his mechanic, C.L. Anderson, onto the track. Harry Knight, driving a Wescott, came upon this accident at 86 miles per hour. He swerved to miss the dazed mechanic, but in doing so, he crashed into the pits, first hitting Herb Lytle's Apperson that was getting a change of tires, then turning end over end in the air and dropping upon Caleb Bragg's Fiat, which was being repaired. The impact was so great that it moved the structure of the pits. Both Knight and his mechanic, John Glover, had serious injuries. Knight, a popular driver, would again compete unsuccessfully at Indianapolis in 1912, driving a Lexington. He was killed in an accident on July 4, 1913, while racing at Columbus, Ohio. In that race, he was thrown from his racecar after blowing a tire and was run over by another contestant.

The spectacular Jagersberger accident sent the judges scurrying from their posts in fear for their own lives and to give their account of the situation. While they were away from their posts, Ralph Mulford in his Lozier and Bruce-Brown's Fiat found a small opening in the wreckage and slipped through, followed by the rest of the field. The rest of the race was accident free and with one lap to go, according to Mulford, the Lozier was flagged

Melvin Marquette at the wheel of the McFarlan number 23 (Indianapolis Motor Speedway Museum).

first, the Fiat second and Harroun in a Marmon, third. The Fiat dropped out during the last lap with a broken spark lever; the Lozier completed the lap and then took extra laps, just to be sure, but when Mulford stopped, Harroun was receiving the recognition of having won the race. Mulford was sure that he should have been the winner, so both he and Lozier protested and a review was promised.[27]

An account given by *The Automobile* magazine stated that considerable doubt had been expressed among the automobile fraternity as to the accuracy of any times that may have been given out because it was known that the wire through which the wheels of the racing cars sent the recording impulses had broken at least twice, causing the timing and scoring to be based upon the observations of the timing officials. The magazine, however, did not disagree with the final outcome of the race.[28] By the next morning, all lap and scoring charts had been destroyed and the Marmon Wasp remained the recognized winner.

Marquette and his McFarlan ran the entire race and made a respectable showing in that he was still running at the end of the contest. However, after the first ten places had been determined, the rest of the contestants, including Marquette, were flagged off of the track and the race was declared officially over.

The grease wagon and spreader laid down a layer of goo that sometimes helped increase track speeds up to four miles per hour (Indianapolis Motor Speedway Museum).

The following year, 1912, there were two Indy 500 contestants from Connersville. McFarlan competed again and rival auto maker Lexington also had an entry. The elimination trials, or time trials, were run on May 27 under the direction of starter Fred J. Wagner. By the time race day came, 24 cars had qualified, including both of the Connersville entries. The Lexington with driver Harry Knight ran a qualification lap with a time of 1 minute 58.54 seconds for a 76 mph average, and the McFarlan Number 23, with Mel Marquette as driver for the second year, qualified at 1 minute 53.26 seconds for an average speed of 79.5 mph.[29]

Marquette appeared to be the very driver who might bring a victory for the company. The *Indianapolis Star* newspaper stated boldly that Marquette was "one of the most versatile men in the handling of motors in the United States."[30] In practice at the speedway, Marquette showed the possibility of reaching speeds of 100 miles per hour on the straight stretches. His McFarlan was powered by a larger 6-cylinder Wainwright built engine with 4¼ inch bore and 5 inch stroke for 477 cubic inch displacement.[31] Those who were rooting for the McFarlan were encouraged when Marquette easily met the qualification standards by running the required distance at nearly an 80 mph average.[32] Other qualifiers

Mel Marquette, driving, and Ray Fowler, riding mechanic, in McFarlan number 23 (Indianapolis Motor Speedway Museum).

included three Stutz cars, three Nationals, two Mercedes, two Cases, and two Loziers; fielding one each were Fiat, Lexington, Simplex, White, Cutting, Firestone-Columbus, Marquette Buick, Schacht, Knox, Mercer and Opel.

Ray Harroun had retired from racing so there was sure to be a new winner for the 500. Spirits were exceptionally high in Connersville with two companies preparing for the big race. Both the steam rail line and the interurban traction line added extra runs to accommodate the mass of fans that were hoping to see one of the local entries bring home the victory. Fans were arriving in Indianapolis, not only from this east central Indiana community, but from near and far. Special trains brought in as many as 150 Pullman cars with parties from Chicago, St. Louis, Dayton and other cities as speedway officials anticipated that possibly 80,000 people would pay admission for this major event.[33]

The 1912 race was free from controversy in declaring a winner; however, it still had a surprise finish. Ralph DePalma, driving a Mercedes, set the pace and led almost the entire race. After 450 miles, he was more than 12 miles ahead of his nearest competitor. But with just five miles to go, DePalma's Mercedes suddenly lost power and began slowing

Left: After running well for 63 laps, the right rear tire blew and the retaining wall became the resting place for McFarlan number 23. ***Right:*** In order to gain additional speed, the wood spokes were covered with a metal disk. The impact of the accident dislodged the disks on three of the wheels (both photographs courtesy Phillip Marquette).

down leaving a trail of oil behind. The unthinkable happened as a connecting rod had broken and had punctured a hole in the crankcase. Though still in first place, the Mercedes quit altogether, stopping on the fourth turn of the 199th lap. DePalma and his riding mechanic attempted to push his car over the finish line in a desperate effort to salvage the victory. When DePalma's predicament was noticed, Joe Dawson, running well behind in second place, was signaled to cut loose, and he passed the non-running Mercedes on the main straightaway of the final lap to win the race. After Dawson took the checkered flag, he drove two additional laps to forestall any question as to the distance he had run after the previous year's controversy.[34]

Several hundred fans from Connersville were in the great throng of spectators as the cars roared around the brick-surfaced 2½ mile oval. Their high spirits were soon dampened and then turned to disappointment as both local cars left the race. The Lexington with Harry Knight driving was the first participant to drop out. On the eighth lap, the engine locked up, ending his hopes. The McFarlan ran a good deal longer, having completed 63 laps for a total of 157 miles when, rounding the stretch at the north end of the speedway, the right rear tire blew. Driver Mel Marquette was unable to control the car and it climbed the concrete retaining wall at the entrance to the home stretch. After sliding for at least 100 feet, the McFarlan struck a telegraph pole, splintering it upon impact. Marquette was able to stay in his seat, but riding mechanic Ray Fowler, a popular Connersville test driver, was thrown onto a pile of sand, receiving several minor cuts and bruises. Marquette was awarded 25th place. Although the high hopes of that eastern Indiana community were dashed, the Connersville contingent could take pleasure that none of their participants received life-threatening injuries in what could have been a very serious accident.[35]

Mary Fowler Robinson, the 98-year-old daughter of Ray and Edna Fowler, related to this author the events of that day, which were talked of periodically within her family. Mary noted that she herself was at the race, in a way — but she wasn't born until about six months later. Her mother saw the accident happen and knew that her husband had been ejected from the car. The time it took her to get to the first-aid tent resulted in some

Above: The end of the racing career for McFarlan (author's collection). *Below:* Mary Fowler Robinson holds a photograph of the pass that admitted her father, Ray Fowler, to the speedway grounds (photograph by author).

very scary moments until she approached him and he called out to her. Only then did she learn that her husband had escaped serious injury. Mary said that she understood that her dad had been badly bruised and had some scrapes, but was fortunate to escape with his life.[36]

The accident at the speedway ended McFarlan's involvement with factory sponsored racing, but an interest in speedway events continued among some McFarlan fans. In late May of 1914, 15 businessmen from Buffalo, New York, stopped in Connersville on their way to attend the annual 500 mile race. The men were riding in three McFarlan automobiles and were known as the "McFarlan Six Club." The guests were shown through the big factory on Mount Street and several other local sights before enjoying a banquet given in their honor. Early the next morning, the visitors from Buffalo left for Indianapolis, accompanied by two additional Big Sixes filled with company personnel, all of whom were spectators at the Memorial Day race.[37]

A few weeks following Marquette's accident at the Speedway, the McFarlan Motor Company participated in another less dangerous activity to keep in the public eye and to promote their own as well as other Hoosier built products. Instead of competing with other companies, an event was designed to encourage cooperative efforts. The Indiana Automobile Manufacturers Association sponsored a four-state tour, inviting Indiana-made vehicles to participate as a promotion for their products, to prove their reliability, to encourage tourism and to spotlight the need for good roads, all while receiving publicity in newspapers and trade magazines. Dealers along the tour route that handled the various Indiana-built vehicles were notified when to expect the entourage and were encouraged to have prospective customers in attendance to witness the performance of the machine of their interest.

The first of these outings, the Four-States Tour, was to traverse parts of Indiana, Ohio, West Virginia and Kentucky, covering nearly 1,300 miles. The caravan assembled at University Square in Indianapolis and left on Tuesday morning, July 9, 1912.[38] Originally, plans called for 28 vehicles to be in the party including four that were of a commercial nature. The 21 vehicles that actually participated represented fifteen Indiana manufacturing companies and included one each from American, Cole, Great Western, Lexington, Marion, Marmon, Parry, Premier and Pathfinder, two each from De Tamble, Maxwell, and McFarlan and three Haynes cars. Commercial vehicles included a Nyberg truck, the Premier Schooner and a Whitesides truck. W.D. Edenburn, official route maker, rode in the Great Western. He carried a large amount of confetti to spread along the way marking the route, especially at crossroads or turns since there were few road signs to give directions. The Marion carried Ray Leeman, the checker, while the secretary rode in the Lexington. The Schooner was their emergency vehicle while the Nyberg truck transported a pipe organ and the Whitesides truck, a piano, to provide entertainment at stops. The Premier car and the Pathfinder each sported ten-tone Gabriel horns.

Roads in the metropolitan area were excellent, but as the parade of participants journeyed away from the Capital City, conditions deteriorated. Stops the first day included Kokomo, Peru, Wabash and the overnight at Fort Wayne. The farther away from Indianapolis the tour progressed, the less desirable the roads became. Indiana pikes generally had a gravel surface, but grading was needed to smooth washboard surfaces and eliminate holes. Three days of traveling Ohio's dirt roads left tourists with rough, corrugated faces. At least the weather was dry or mud would have been a more serious problem to deal with. All of the manufacturers seemed to feel that the tour was effective in generating sales and good will, and the next tour would be even longer.[39]

With two McFarlan cars participating and running the 1,300 mile route efficiently, company officials could have expected to receive a great deal of publicity. Instead, little attention was given this small manufacturer. The *Indianapolis Sun* newspaper was quite complimentary, noting that because no accidents had befallen McFarlan which would have earned them a place in the news column and because of the quiet and ease with

The McFarlan Big Six participated in the Indiana-Pacific Tour during the summer of 1913 (courtesy Jim Wicker).

which the two cars covered the route of the Four-States tour, they had not caught the public's attention. McFarlan was not even lucky enough to draw the position of pacemaker. That position carried the honor of being at the front of the parade for a day, and those who were chosen to be the leader publicized their favored position. Special appreciation was given for McFarlan's air compressor and tank that gave them pneumatic self-starting convenience while providing others relief from using a hand pump after encountering a tire failure.[40] McFarlan received little benefit from this event other than the good will they built among other participants. Driving responsibilities were shared by Bert Adams and Harry and Herbert McFarlan. Herbert was Harry's cousin and was in charge of company arrangements; he was a rather quiet, unassuming person who preferred to be out of the public eye. Most participating companies looked for ways to attract the attention of the press and thus promote their effort. McFarlan, with two cars that performed flawlessly, went largely unnoticed by the public or press.

In September, the company sent a Big Six to the northeast to participate in an endurance tour sponsored by the Buffalo, New York, Automobile Club. It lasted four days and covered a distance of 800 miles through western New York and eastern Pennsylvania. The contest was known as a class E grade III reliability tour. The tour would start from and return to Buffalo, making a loop and taking a different route each day. One object of the contest was to finish the competition without having any penalty points assessed against the vehicle. Points could be given for anything that had to be done to keep the car in operating condition from the time the tour left Buffalo in the morning until it returned in the evening.

From left to right, Herbert McFarlan, Harry McFarlan and Bert Adams (courtesy Jim Wicker).

Some of the makes represented in addition to the McFarlan Six were Amplex, K-R-I-T, Hupmobile, Maxwell, R.C.H., Warren-Detroit, Premier, Pierce-Arrow and Paige-Detroit. A Studebaker 30 was the official pilot car, leaving one hour before the others to allow time to mark the route.[41] The pacemaker's car was a Premier and the chairman rode in a Pierce-Arrow.

The first day out, participants drove through a downpour and it was a muddy grind, with road conditions varying from good, to bad, to indifferent. After they returned to Buffalo that evening, the contest committee reported that all of the entrants completed in good order, with only a few contestants given penalty points for minor infractions. The R.C.H. received three points for having to add water en route, the Maxwell got four points for repairs made and the Hupmobile was assessed eight points for needing to add gasoline twice during the day.[42]

On the second leg of the tour, an unexpected accident occurred which could have had serious consequences. While Winfield Graham was driving, the McFarlan was involved in what was referred to as a minor accident. It was reported that the car "turned turtle." There were no serious injuries to the car's occupants, but for an instant, it looked as if the car would be withdrawn from competition. Instead, it was righted back on its wheels within a minute or two and the engine was restarted. A few repairs had to be made, after which it continued on its journey.[43] In spite of the mishap, the Big Six checked in both at noon and at night ahead of schedule. When the cars returned to Buffalo that evening, the contest committee assessed 10 penalty points against the McFarlan because of the repairs. Penalties were also assessed against the Paige-Detroit and the R.C.H., each receiving three points for repairs. Had it not been for the one incident, the McFarlan would

A number of nights were spent with accommodations that left a little to be desired (courtesy Jim Wicker).

have maintained a perfect score, but would probably have received little recognition. After the event was over, Bert Adams reported that the car had "finished the tour all O.K. (McFarlan) received more publicity than if we had finished with a perfect score."[44]

For 1913, the Indiana Automobile Manufacturers Association planned a much more ambitious event, billed as the Indiana-Pacific Tour. It, like the Four-States Tour of 1912, was not a speed contest, but instead a publicity stunt to direct attention to Indiana-made products. The tour generated so much enthusiasm among manufacturers that some of the factory officials chose to take their families along, not as a part of the tour proper, but accommodated on a special Pullman, planning to rendezvous at various points en route, while tour participants sometimes camped in the rough.[45] Of the twenty vehicles listed as starting the tour, there were two each from Apperson, Marion, Haynes, American, and Henderson and one each from Pilot, Premier, Marmon, Pathfinder, Stutz, Empire (another Connersville product), and McFarlan. There were also three trucks, a Premier, a G & J and a Brown, used to carry extra gasoline, tires and supplies. The Premier truck was actually a prairie schooner body mounted on a Premier car chassis that was used to carry extra tires. Among the 70 passengers was Carl G. Fisher in his Marmon. He was a high profile promoter of the good roads movement in general and the Lincoln Highway in particular. Another passenger of special note was Elwood Haynes, who claimed to have built the first American automobile. A favorite among race fans was Ray Harroun, winner of the 1912 Indianapolis 500, who was driving one of the Hendersons. J.M. Ward, secretary of the association, was in the Premier pilot car, which led the way spreading confetti to mark the route.[46] The McFarlan was piloted by Bert Adams, who had also driven in the city of Atlanta race, with passengers Arthur Dixon and Christopher Cox of Connersville, and Guy C. Core from Indianapolis.[47]

The Indiana-Pacific Tour began in Indianapolis at 2:00 p. m. on July 1, 1913. The caravan lined up along New York Street between Meridian and Pennsylvania streets, in a heavy downpour. Hundreds of spectators sought shelter in nearby businesses while the band played "How Dry I Am."[48] A representative of Governor Ralston presented the tourists with a flag. Cars then left at one-minute intervals. Driving the old National Pike, now U.S. 40, the tour was met in Brazil, Indiana, by civic leaders, then went on to Terre Haute, arriving at 7:30 P.M. A large banquet was held at the Elks Club with speeches and good roads resolutions presented. The group headed north and west the next morning at 7:30, through Paris, Illinois, and on to Springfield, still contending with heavy rain and gumbo mud roads.[49]

From Indianapolis to Terre Haute the party followed the white bands the Hoosier Motor Club had placed on utility poles. From Springfield through Alton, Illinois, to St. Louis there were black and white banded poles, and red, white and blue bands guided them as they traversed Missouri. Across Kansas, the tour followed Golden Belt; farther west, out of Denver, it followed the Midland Trail that was marked with black and gold markers wherever possible. On across the country the parade went. The roads in Utah were just paths except within range of Salt Lake City, then from Lake Tahoe in Nevada into Sacramento, California, the roads were excellent. Tour participants drew lots each night to determine the running order for the next day and no one was to pass the pacemaker. Every evening and two or three or more times

Herbert McFarlan demonstrating the strength of the McFarlan rear fender (courtesy Jim Wicker).

each day the motorists stopped for pleasing diversions of food and drink and talks on the subject of road improvements.

Stops in Illinois included Decatur, Springfield, Carlinville, Alton and Granite City, while St. Louis, Columbia, Boonville and Kansas City did the honors in Missouri. Having Carl Fisher along lent prestige to the tour. It may also have helped motivate the state of Missouri to drag and scrape 100 miles of the St. Louis to Kansas City route.[50] The sunburned, dusty Hoosiers relished a warm bath and a good meal at the end of the day, but sometimes found themselves camping out in tents where modern facilities were not available. A day and a half break in Denver helped give rest and preparation for the long upward climb over the Rocky Mountains through Berthoud Pass with some of the grandest scenery of the trip.[51] When the elevation of 11,305 feet was conquered, the parties stopped long enough to make snowballs in mid–July. It took a full day to make the run of only 104 miles, but all of the cars made the grades in good shape, although some required assistance.[52]

The tour concluded at Los Angeles after 34 days were spent traversing eight states for a total distance of 3,852 miles. Only one car dropped out en route: the Stutz didn't go beyond St. Louis. Extra stress on the trucks took its toll. The Premier prairie schooner broke an axle out in the desert leaving the driver and passenger stranded 80 miles from a town. They spent 18 hours in the rough without food or water before being rescued by a passing motorist. The Brown stripped first gear while pulling underpowered cars up a steep grade in Colorado. Later it experienced broken springs and, after being repaired, had to drive night and day to catch up with the others by tour's end.

In Santa Barbara, California, the G & J truck, driven by Walter Wiedley, was hit by a street car that whirled around a corner without warning. A front wheel was crushed, the radiator damaged and the fenders bent into the body. Repairs were made overnight and the truck finished the tour on schedule. Also in Santa Barbara came the only tragedy of the tour. A Haynes six driven by L.R. Wagner drove out of the Hotel Potter garage as a six-year-old boy stepped backwards in front of the car. He was run over and killed instantly. The Connersville cars received praise for outstanding reliability on the tour. The Empire, by far the smallest car in the run, amazed other participants as it demonstrated its ability to keep up with the big boys all the way, and the McFarlan Six was reported as having had a distressingly tame trip — quite a compliment after a rigorous cross-country journey.[53] The men who made the entire journey in the Number 16 McFarlan were Bert Adams, Arthur Dixon, Chris Cox and Fred Wellman.

L.E. Benton, an automobile man from Los Angeles, rode from there to San Diego with the Connersville crew and was quite complimentary about the car's performance. In a telegram sent to the factory, Benton noted that the company had reason for a great deal of pride as the McFarlan that made the strenuous trip to the Pacific Coast was not a brand new car just out of the factory. It was one of the earliest 1913 models and had seen substantial service prior to the tour. First driven as an experimental test car, it then saw extensive use as a demonstrator at automobile shows. It did hard service in relief between Connersville and Dayton, Ohio, just after the terrible 1913 flood and was also used to carry freight from Indianapolis to Connersville when shipping by rail was too slow.

Although it had already clocked a significant number of miles before the tour, it made the trip of more than 4,000 miles with no mechanical adjustment except for the carburetor.[54]

After a couple of months on the road, the local participants were ready to head back with lots of stories to tell and many eager listeners awaiting their return. McFarlan had a sizeable following on the West Coast, so it wasn't difficult to dispose of the well broken-in vehicle. Little time was wasted catching a train for the return trip home.

4

Professional Vehicles and Bodies Built to Order

Although McFarlan never entered the mass-production segment, the company did broaden its sales potential by offering professional vehicles including ambulances, funeral cars and fire apparatus. Probably the most challenging of these custom creations to build were machines used in fighting fires because the demands on those vehicles were great. They needed to be ready to respond when an alarm sounded, and they were very much in the public's eye as firemen used the beautiful red trucks to bring fires, the most dreaded of all emergencies, under control.

The day of the hand- and horse-drawn fire fighting apparatus was rapidly passing, both in large cities and in smaller communities. Larger metropolitan areas led the way with more modern equipment, but the changeover was anything but simple. Most firemen, being part of the general populace, had little or no experience in driving anything faster than a good horse. Nor did they have the know-how to service or repair motorized vehicles. Therefore, not only was there the substantial cost in purchasing the new equipment, but a financial commitment had to be made for training those involved in how to start the engine, how to safely operate the large machines and the steps of maintaining this new type of fire fighting apparatus. Sometimes training was provided by the company making the sale, but more often, the burden fell upon each community. Various driving and mechanic schools, generally located only in larger cities, charged a fee to prepare fireman and other emergency personnel in using motorized vehicles.

West Chester, Pennsylvania, was one of the communities that suffered severely from fire before local authorities were convinced of the need to equip the fire department with motorized apparatus. As in most communities considering such a move, opponents to the changeover to motorized vehicles claimed that increased costs would wreck the cities' budgets. Indeed, it did cost considerably more to purchase a self-propelled fire truck than one drawn by horses. However, operating costs proved to be much less with trucks. Pawtucket, Rhode Island, had 11 pieces of horse-drawn fire apparatus and 22 horses in 1910. During that year it cost a total of $3,617.13 for forage and shoeing. After motorizing the department, the amount paid for gasoline, oil, alcohol and grease was $190.95 for one year. This, of course, did not include repair parts that would be needed as the trucks got older.

Aside from monetary considerations, the motorized equipment far surpassed the horse-drawn fire wagon by saving precious moments getting to and from fires. Valuable time was saved at the very onset of a run. Where it had been necessary to release the horses from their stalls and harness them to their respective wagons, with the motorized equipment the operator quickly climbed to the driver's seat while the engine was being started, then sped from the station. The minutes gained may well have saved lives and property.[1]

An additional factor that probably didn't, in itself, sway many fire departments to the advantages of motor driven apparatus was the issue of space gained in the fire house. By eliminating horses, their fodder and other equipment necessary for their care, more than enough space would be gained to house additional fire fighting equipment if needed. More importantly, the quarters for the firemen would also be much more sanitary and definitely freer of unpleasant odors by not having the animals housed in the same building or an adjoining structure.

An unusual story came out of Skaneateles, New York, regarding the usefulness of a motor fire truck. The community had passed up purchasing a 75 horsepower fire truck because many had believed that a motor vehicle could not maneuver the deep snowfalls that they sometimes encountered. A heavy snow in early March also brought the dreaded sound of the fire alarm. About 30 men tried, without success, dragging one of the hose-carts toward the burning home. In desperation, they turned to the nearby Dodge Brothers dealer who had a new sedan on display. He quickly started the 35 horsepower car, drove through the drifts to the hose-cart and pulled it to the scene of the fire. He then went back to the station, hooked up to the hook and ladder wagon and trundled it to the fire. The motorized vehicle proved itself beyond a doubt on that occasion.[2]

Until 1914 the Connersville Fire Department had considered horse-drawn fire wagons the most logical way to give fire protection to the city. Recognizing the need for an equipment upgrade, Fire Chief O.S. Riggs approached the city fathers in 1913 to install an electric light on each fire wagon. The practice, up to that time, had been to light the eight coal oil lamps on each wagon before beginning a run, only to have them blow out with the dash out into the outdoor air. The City Council recognized the need and responded positively. A battery powered light that was larger than those on an automobile was installed on each of the three horse-drawn wagons by B.F. McCready. Every fireman was also provided with a flashlight to aid in his work.[3] This effort showed a real concern from the city fathers and significantly improved the safety of the firemen, the equipment and onlookers when emergency runs were made after dark.

Soon after the improved lighting was installed, a new city administration of the opposite political party took charge and a new fire chief took the reins January 1, 1914. The new chief, Hassett, recognized the progress made by the previous administration but decided it was a good time to challenge the new city fathers to do the previous administration one better and really go modern. He wasted little time in approaching the City Council with a plan to replace one wagon and a team of horses with a motor truck. Chief Hassett reasoned that horses soon grew unfit for emergency service because of the strain put upon them with fire runs. The hose wagon also needed to be repaired or replaced. Since both expenses were to be dealt with soon, a motor truck could fill the purpose

In the fall of 1914, Connersville, Indiana, purchased its first motorized fire wagon — a McFarlan, of course! (author's collection).

better. Hassett also explained it would cost less than half as much for maintenance of a motor vehicle compared to the cost of feeding the team of horses, and the purchase could be handled through a well respected local firm.[4]

Within a month, a contract had been drawn up with the McFarlan Motor Company to provide a combination hose and chemical truck powered by a 90 horsepower T-head engine. The truck would have a powerful search light on top and up to eight men could be carried on the vehicle, thus allowing for the full crew to arrive at the same time.[5]

On November 27, 1914, the McFarlan motor fire wagon was delivered for station No. 1, also known as Central Station. It was described as being a beautiful model, bright red in color with black and gold trim, resembling the trucks used in large cities. It carried all of the latest improvements including an automatic hose reel, ladder racks, a siren whistle, the search light and a compressed air self starter. This convenience was supposed to guarantee that the engine would start within 30 seconds, even in the coldest weather. It was also noted that the machine would be kept near a steam radiator. City Council members and Mayor Phillip Braun looked the truck over and it was given a test over the worst streets in town, even climbing the 5th Street serpentine hill with the old hose wagon being pulled behind without any problem. The purpose of pulling the hose wagon was to have additional hose and ladders when needed. Each man at station Number 1 was to be taught to drive, but the regular chauffeur was expected to be Harry Meyers, a new member of the department. The motor truck eliminated the need for one team of horses at the station. They were offered for sale within a few weeks.[6]

Payment for the impressive new fire truck, reported to have cost $3,500, wasn't quite as easy to come up with as had been expected. The Council agreed to pay $400 initially. Another $400 installment would be made in June of 1915. There were also two notes for $1,700 each with 6 percent interest to be paid later.[7]

City fathers were so impressed with their new truck that on March 8, 1915, a motor hook-and-ladder wagon was added at a cost of $3,000. This was essentially a tractor-trailer combination with only the tractor part of the vehicle being new, and it was of McFarlan manufacture. The trailer part of the hook and ladder rig used the old hose wagon with the front wheels removed. It was fastened to the truck using a fifth-wheel type connector. There was some concern expressed as to whether or not the trailer's large wooden rear wheels would hold up under higher speeds, but tests in a run as fast as 50 miles per hour on Western Avenue gave no indication of any problem, so the second fire truck was added.[8]

On April 5, 1915, a third vehicle, a motor truck identical to the first one, arrived for station No. 2 at a cost of $3,500. Again, a deferred payment plan was arranged. Over a period of just eight months, Chief Hassett had convinced the Connersville city fathers to eliminate their reliance on horse power and create a thoroughly modern motorized department. The Council had made what seemed to be the logical choice by purchasing the new equipment from McFarlan Motor Company, a respected local concern. The value of all of the fire department equipment in 1915 was listed at $16,121.[9]

Although the public was enthralled by the shiny new vehicles with their whistle sirens, they still missed seeing the familiar horses that they admired and many knew by name. One chap, who used to grab a ride on the hook and ladder wagon as it turned the corner of Court Street and Central, when on a run, wondered what had happened to the fire department horses. These spirited animals were appreciated throughout town as citizens watched them respond to the call of "fire! fire!" Rosin and Fred were the first to go. They no longer stretched their necks and made a record for speed; now they were pulling a hearse in Liberty, Indiana, the county seat to the east of Fayette County. Jim and Dan were the next to be replaced by the motor wagons. They were kept for a couple of months to make sure the newfangled equipment worked before being sold to the Conner and

By late spring 1915, the Connersville Fire Department could boast of having gone completely modern with the latest equipment (courtesy Rick Free of the Connersville Fire Department).

Sherry stables. Teddy and Brownie, from the upper station, were the last to be replaced. They ended up being sent to France to serve the Allies as officers' mounts in the war zone.[10]

A great amount of pride and a rush of adrenalin was provided local people as they watched the bright red trucks heading out on an emergency run. It was every bit as exciting as when fire wagons were pulled by fast horses. People on the street had to get accustomed to clearing the way more quickly for the faster vehicles. The increased speed of the motorized fire wagons enabled them to arrive at the scene sooner, but there were also additional dangers. An accident that occurred with one of the recently acquired trucks may have been attributed to the added momentum that came with heavier equipment and higher speeds. The truck from station Number 2 was damaged when it struck a tree at the corner of 6th Street and Eastern Avenue while en route to a fire. The machine, being driven by Clem Hibbs, had reportedly been going at great speed, but had slowed to make the turn. As the heavy truck swung around the corner, the rear wheels skidded allowing the back part of the machine to come into contact with a tree. The ladders were torn from their hooks and the rear part of the truck was damaged. Repairs were required, so the McFarlan was returned to the local factory. Fortunately, there were no injuries and Clem Hibbs was not judged to be at fault.[11]

In another incident, Harry Williams, a fireman at the same station, Number 2, received injuries when he was thrown from the hose wagon as it whipped around the corner at 9th and Western Avenue, on a run to the Davis Brothers shop. Although his injuries were not life threatening, Williams had a hard landing and sustained numerous bruises requiring medical attention. There was no mention as to whether or not speed was a factor in this accident, nor was the driver named, but the machine had skidded as it made the turn, indicating excessive speed.[12]

A third and more serious accident occurred in July of 1919, also involving the equipment housed at Station No. 2. The fire apparatus being driven by Dora Beaver collided with a small touring car driven by Harry Cottom while responding to a fire alarm at midday with the bell clanging and siren sounding. Mr. Cottom drove onto Central Avenue from 6th Street while the heavy truck, responding to an emergency, should have had the right-of-way. The little car, no match for the truck, sustained broken wheels and a smashed windshield, and the driver was thrown to the street. Cottom received cuts, bruises and back pain and was attended to by a physician. The McFarlan fire truck also had to have considerable repairs. The large wooden bumper rail on the front snapped as if it were a matchstick, one headlight got caved in and the front axle was bent back under the engine. Although the truck was more than four years old, it was still repaired at the factory where it had been built.[13] This accident had some people sitting up and taking notice that the truck had sustained more damage than might have been expected and that it might not have been built as sturdily as necessary for a vehicle of that weight.

About four months later, there was cause for further alarm when two fire trucks were out of commission at the same time. One hose truck and the hook and ladder tractor unit were both broken down. The pinion gears had locked up on the hose truck after a run and the rig had to be towed to the McFarlan factory where mechanics worked on it all night. It was decided that the gears were just not strong enough to hold up under heavy use. At that point, the oldest truck was five years old. It was noted that the differential had gone bad in the ladder wagon seven times, in the newer hose wagon five times and in the oldest truck four times. The oldest truck had also broken down twice during that month.[14] The specifications for the fire apparatus are not known for certain, but McFarlan automobiles used what is now known as a transaxle with the transmission being attached to the rear axle unit. Regardless of the setup used in the trucks, it just was not stout enough to withstand the strains of propelling the heavy fire equipment.

The Public Safety Committee of the City Council investigated the matter and noted that the truck's rear axles were not strong enough and that something should be done about it. Persons who were supposed to be in the know advised that the axles could be replaced without the cost being appalling.[15] Although a fix could have and should have been carried out immediately when the problem was identified, a permanent solution might have involved considerable expense. Because of McFarlan's transmission and differential combination, a proper fix would require replacement of everything from the clutch to the rear axle with commercial grade units.

The Council was slow to make decisions on what to do with their fire equipment. They always caught flak after a breakdown, but things soon returned to normal. There was a loud outcry to act after a more serious fire on New Year's Day 1920. The house of Frank Purcell, who lived in Edgewood, near station No. 2, caught fire. When the alarm came in, the men at the nearby firehouse climbed aboard and started the truck, but as it rolled into the street, it broke down. Several precious minutes were lost until equipment from the Central Station arrived too late to save the structure or its contents.[16] Again, pressure was applied to purchase better equipment. Even the Rotary Club pledged their support to work with whatever group was necessary to fund new trucks.[17] The City Council expressed concern but decided they needed to get permission from the State Board of Accounts to float a bond issue. They apparently did not seriously consider rebuilding one truck at a time with a more substantial driveline.

Problems and frustrations continued with the fire equipment as a newspaper headline in March 1920 proclaimed, "Weak Kneed Truck Gives Down Again." While responding to a fire at Dr. N.G. Wills' home, the truck from station No. 2 again experienced a locked differential at the corner of 8th and Summit. Fortunately, equipment from the Central Station had reached the scene and was able to provide assistance.[18]

Still another breakdown occurred in December of 1920, on the way to a fire at the home of Mrs. Malinda Bertsh near 9th and Grand Avenue. The hose truck quit while en route and had to be towed back to the station. A chimney fire had spread to the roof, but other equipment arrived quickly and extinguished it using chemicals. A bond issue was being negotiated at the time, so there was hope for improvement to come.[19]

The City Council did take positive action in March of 1921 by ordering an Ahrens-Fox pumper at the cost of $12,500.[20] All three McFarlan trucks were kept in service after the new pumper arrived, but two of them were replaced just over a year later when a second Ahrens-Fox pumper and a Reo Speed Wagon chassis were purchased.[21] Both of the hose wagon chassis were sold when the new equipment arrived, but the beds were kept. One was mounted on the Reo chassis and the other was put in storage for future use. The hook and ladder tractor trailer unit was retained until 1925 and continued to be used when needed.[22] A spectacular fire at the First National Bank building in January 1924 pressed into use the McFarlan tractor pulling the hook and ladder trailer, still trundling along on its large wooden wheels. It provided additional equipment that was necessary in fighting that major blaze.

The arrival of new fire fighting equipment did bring a sigh of relief, but problems still occurred from time to time. One rather serious accident happened at 20th and Grand Avenue when the Reo hose wagon, while on a run, swerved to miss a car that drove into its path. The truck, driven by John Smith, struck the curb, capsized and smashed against a tree. David Moore, Ralph Clark and Smith were ejected from the truck, all suffering serious injuries that required hospitalization, and the truck was damaged severely.[23] But this time, it was McFarlan to the rescue. When the troublesome McFarlan hose trucks were replaced, their beds were kept. The one installed on the Reo was destroyed in the accident. After the accident, the spare McFarlan hose truck bed was removed from storage and Herman Broedling was engaged to fit the body and chassis together. He did the job so effectively, it looked as if it had been factory installed.[24]

When all was said and done, the locally made fire equipment did perform reasonably well. The average life expectancy of a car in those days was just over five years, but these vehicles, even with all of the repairs required, lasted a minimum of eight years and were then sold to be used for other purposes. Also, the McFarlan pumpers had cost the city only about one fourth of the $12,500 that each of the Ahrens-Fox trucks cost. Had the City Council tackled the differential gear problem when it was first identified, additional years of service would probably have been realized.

McFarlan Motor Company also built at least one truck for general hauling. In the April 1918 Fayette County (Indiana) Commissioners meeting, bids were received for the purchase of a 3½ ton motor truck for use on county highways. Bids had previously been filed in the office of the Auditor with the following results:

Company	Truck Type		Price
Karl L. Hanson	Diamond T	f.o.b. factory	$4,290.00
Bessemer Motor Truck Co.	Model E	f.o.b. factory	3,660.00
Indianapolis Truck Sales Co.	Little Giant	f.o.b. factory	4,442.00
O. Armleader Co.	Model KW	f.o.b. factory	4,326.00
Inland Motor Sales Corp.	Federal	f.o.b. Connersville	3,900.00
Dora W. Sherry	Master	f.o.b. Connersville	4,568.50
Cadillac Auto Truck Co.	Acme	f.o.b. factory	3,609.12
Quincy T. Lyons	Republic	f.o.b. Connersville	3,750.00
Auburn Sales Co.	Dart	f.o.b. Connersville	3,975.00
Service Truck Sales Co.	Model 275	f.o.b. Wabash, Ind.	4,085.00
McFarlan Motor Co.	Model 35	f.o.b. Connersville	3,528.00

The commissioners, having examined each of the bids, awarded the contract to the lowest bidder, McFarlan Motor Company.[25] It made no difference that McFarlan had never before built a 3½ ton truck, but since the company was located in Fayette County, there may have been extra incentive to promote local industry. About six months later in late November, the shiny new McFarlan 3½ ton dump truck was delivered. The county

For several years during the 1920s and 1930s, some Maxim fire trucks used the McFarlan Twin Valve 572.5 c.i.d. engine. Note the similarity in the shape of the radiator shell with that of the McFarlan.

commissioners claimed it was to be used in graveling and dragging roads or hauling the grader. The purchase price was justified because it would replace many men and teams of horses and would thus save taxpayers money. Manpower was at a premium as many able-bodied males were serving overseas in World War I. The McFarlan truck was the first and possibly the only one of its kind produced by that company. It was powered by the Teetor-McFarlan 90 horsepower dual ignition engine and the transmission was attached directly to the engine and clutch. The bed was made of steel with the capacity of hauling up to three yards of gravel. Heil & Company, of Milwaukee, Wisconsin, manufactured the self-dumping body. When the body was raised, the tailgate would automatically drop to facilitate unloading.[26]

The ill-fated McFarlan fire engines were not the last involvement the company had with fire fighting equipment. The TV series engine that was introduced in mid–1920, with a cubic inch displacement of 572.5 cubic inches putting out 120 horsepower, had brute strength beyond that necessary for powering a luxury automobile. This engine became the source of power for certain models of Maxim fire trucks that were manufactured by the Maxim Motor Company.

The Maxim Motor Company, located in Middleborough, Massachusetts, had humble beginnings as an auto repair shop run by Carlton W. Maxim and his son, Ernest. Their business grew as they became recognized for their ability to repair most any machine they encountered. In 1914, the town of Middleborough decided to purchase a motorized hose car. The Maxim father and son team proposed that they build one to fit the needs of the fire department, and within 60 days, they had the job completed. From that beginning, the Maxim Motor Company, which manufactured many different models of fire apparatus, was developed. The company remained a family owned business until it was purchased by the Seagrave Manufacturing Company in 1956.[27]

In addition to their fire apparatus business, Maxim sold several makes of automobiles and become the New England distributor for McFarlan in the late teens. In 1921, Maxim introduced two new lines of fire apparatus, the smaller "C" model pumper, powered by a 4-cylinder Wisconsin engine, and the larger "M" model with the new McFarlan Twin Valve Six under the hood. Both models had the distinctive Maxim gabled radiator that bore a strong resemblance to the McFarlan automobile radiator.[28]

One of the most creditable accolades for the "Big Mac" engine was given by the Massachusetts Institute of Technology. They showed the Twin Valve Six to be the most efficient power plant on the market for use with pumper trucks of 750 gallons per minute capacity.[29] McFarlan powered fire apparatus were popular throughout the 1920s and into the 1930s.

Other specialty vehicles that the company became involved with were ambulances and hearses. The McFarlan reputation for quality workmanship was becoming known throughout much of the country. By 1915 several businesses sought out the Connersville company to build ambulances and funeral cars. One new emergency vehicle was completed for the undertaking firm of Wright & Updike of Union City, Indiana. That machine had the appearance of a regular limousine in the front, but could be converted into an ambulance or hearse in a few minutes. It was noted as having been splendidly finished throughout.[30]

When the Smith Funeral Home of Connersville decided to modernize their equipment, they did not have to deal with out-of-town strangers. The funeral home was established in 1885 by Thomas L. Smith. His son, Carl C., became a partner in the business in 1892, and had assumed full responsibility for its operation by 1910. Most funeral homes of that period owned their own ambulances but rented a hearse from a livery stable whenever one was needed. When Carl Smith decided his growing business needed more impressive and modern equipment built to his specifications, he contacted another local firm, the McFarlan Motor Company.

Edward W. Cotton, Sr., of McFarlan, negotiated the sale that would update ambulance and hearse service for the Smith Funeral Home and provide a vehicle of striking appearance that would make a favorable impression wherever it was seen. The agreement was to build a combination ambulance hearse. To construct this multi-purpose vehicle the body was to be removed from Smith's horse drawn ambulance running gear, remodeled, and placed on a 1916 McFarlan hearse chassis. The proposal went as follows:

— PROPOSAL TO C.C.SMITH BY MCFARLAN MOTOR COMPANY —
We propose to rebuild your Crane & Breed Ambulance as follows:
We will remove the present roof, build integral with ambulance, with coupe front with two one half glass doors, two glass windows, limousine front wind-shield, dome light in

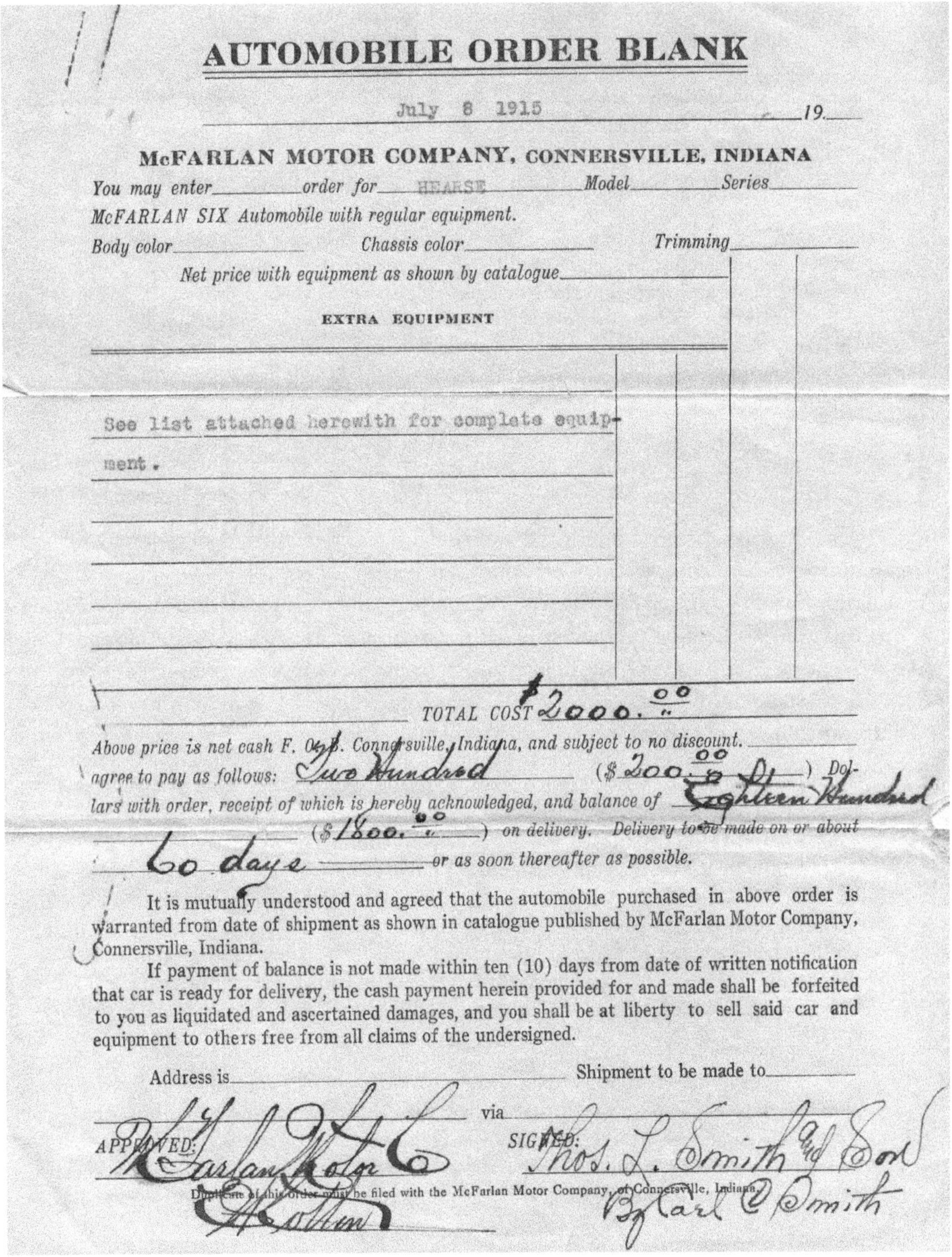

AUTOMOBILE ORDER BLANK

July 8 1915 _____ 19___

McFARLAN MOTOR COMPANY, CONNERSVILLE, INDIANA

You may enter _____ order for __HEARSE__ Model ____ Series ____
McFARLAN SIX Automobile with regular equipment.
Body color _____ Chassis color _____ Trimming _____
    Net price with equipment as shown by catalogue _____

EXTRA EQUIPMENT

See list attached herewith for complete equipment.

TOTAL COST $2000.00

Above price is net cash F. O. B. Connersville, Indiana, and subject to no discount. _____ agree to pay as follows: *Two Hundred* ($200.00) Dollars with order, receipt of which is hereby acknowledged, and balance of *Eighteen Hundred* ($1800.00) on delivery. Delivery to be made on or about *60 days* or as soon thereafter as possible.

    It is mutually understood and agreed that the automobile purchased in above order is warranted from date of shipment as shown in catalogue published by McFarlan Motor Company, Connersville, Indiana.

    If payment of balance is not made within ten (10) days from date of written notification that car is ready for delivery, the cash payment herein provided for and made shall be forfeited to you as liquidated and ascertained damages, and you shall be at liberty to sell said car and equipment to others free from all claims of the undersigned.

Address is _____ Shipment to be made to _____
    _____ via _____
APPROVED: *McFarlan Motor Co* SIGNED: *Thos. L. Smith and Son*
    By Rollin   *By Carl C Smith*

Duplicate of this order must be filed with the McFarlan Motor Company, of Connersville, Indiana.

McFarlan also built quality ambulances and hearses (courtesy Fayette County Historical Museum).

top, trimmed in best grade of leather color to be specified later, and all equipment for funeral directors work.

We will build and fit for Crane & Breed Ambulance, a casket table of our regular McFarlan type with best grade casket hardware, including rollers, pins etc. We will wire hearse body complete, placing two dome lights in the rear compartments, one at the rear and one at the front door.

We will build our latest approved flower racks and sliding flower trucks for use in this vehicle.

We will mount above body on our latest model of ninety H.P. Serial X McFarlan hearse chassis which includes Westinghouse Electric Starter power tire pump for tire inflation. Hartford shock absorbers, Firestone demountable and detachable rims, with 35 × 5 tires, and one extra rim and tire complete, to be placed in tire drawer which we will build under the above described body.

The wheel base on above chassis is 148". The steering is ball bearing, making chassis handle with the utmost ease in the most difficult places.

We agree to paint entire motor vehicle above described in best quality funeral black.

Signed...
McFarlan Motor Company

The Smith Funeral Home listed additional equipment that they required for the combination ambulance hearse. Carl Smith was personally acquainted with those he was dealing with and was quite familiar with the company and their reputation for outstanding quality. Even so, he didn't intend to let friendship interfere with his expectations. One statement on Smith's list of required equipment noted, "everything must be up to the McFarlan standard. Enough said." While demanding top notch workmanship, this communication also illustrates Smith's desire to contain costs by reusing items when practicable.

LAMP EQUIPMENT

Two railroad lanterns nickled complete. Upper half of globe to be painted green with the name Smith etched on the globe. Lanterns to be fitted in brackets and to be placed so as to be easily reached from drivers seat and from the window in the rear of the vestibule compartment. Old side lamps to be replated and fitted with electric lights. If the cost of fitting up these lamps should be equal in price to new lamps, new lamps to be used instead. One dome light in vestibule compartment. Two dome lights in rear compartment. Rear dome light is to be operated from rear door and other lights from switch in vestibule.

REAR COMPARTMENT

Rear doors to have removable draped curtains and also pull curtains. To be fitted with ambulance seats. Use Smith's old cot but fit it with rubber-tired wheels and iron legs. Removable nameplate with the name "SMITH" to be equipped with flower rack, casket table and buzzer on rear door. Tire drawer underneath to be as long as possible, deep enough to accommodate extra tire, truck grips, etc.

PAINTING

Inside painting to be imitation mahogany, outside to be hearse black. Rear steps made to raise and license plate to be fitted to bottom of the step, as vehicle will also be used as an ambulance. To be built on 1916 hearse chassis equipped with 35 × 5 Silvertown cord tires, with extra tire and rim.

Off the Beaten Track by keith marvin

c. 1925 MCFARLAN AMBULANCE---McFarlan of Connorsville, Indiana, primarily a manufacturer of expensive motor cars, produced a small number of ambulances, funeral cars and fire engines on special order. This ambulance, built about 1925, was set on the huge Twin Valve 140" wheelbase chassis which was basis for the passenger car line. With an engine of $572\frac{1}{2}$ cu. in., 24 valves and triple ignition- three plugs firing each cylinder, McFarlan automobiles were highly regarded but seldom seen.

(Photo courtesy Alvit Arnheim and H. Heuroth of Charlottesville Virginia.) McFarlan Hearse (c. 1925- TV Six) From original postcard owned by H. Heuroth of Charlottesville, Virginia.

A mid–1920s McFarlan ambulance (National Automotive History Collection, Detroit Public Library).

The purchase order was signed on July 8, 1915, by Carl C. Smith and Edward W. Cotton, Sr. The agreed upon price was $2,000 with $200 paid up front and the remainder due upon delivery which was expected within 60 days.[31]

The company's involvement with specialized emergency equipment was a natural lead-in to being able to do other types of custom body work. At what point in McFarlan history building custom bodies became a major part of their business is not recorded, but it would seem quite probable that the earliest carriages turned out by J.B. McFarlan were finished according to customers' wishes. As the volume of business increased, so did the standardization of models offered. Even when light-duty horse-drawn vehicle production was reaching its peak, there was some work done to suit specific requests. One example was a handsome wagon that was manufactured in 1890 for Brooks & Tittle, the new proprietors of the Connersville Steam Laundry. This wagon was an excellent means of advertising the new business when on the streets of Connersville as it was used for gathering and delivering laundered goods.[32]

Early in the automotive era, a Connersville concern, Central Manufacturing Company, was recognized as one of the most capable suppliers in the Midwest for wood framed bodies covered with a metal skin. It was not generally known that the McFarlan company was also making similar bodies under contract to various automobile companies. Changing from building bodies for carriages to automobiles had been an easy transition for the concern since they had been in the trade for over half a century.[33] The body building part of the organization was obviously able to turn out their product in greater numbers than the mechanical department that was struggling to produce the McFarlan drivetrain. Therefore, the excess production capacity could provide bodies for other manufacturers such as Auburn, Marmon, Premier and others. These would not have been custom built for the individual, but were made to the company's specifications that intended to install the

Model 124 McFarlan Destroyer design, four-passenger touring

McFarlan had established a custom body department to cater to the whims of persons with the means to have a special design if they wanted. A Kentucky stock farmer commissioned this boattail Destroyer (*Motor Age*, Oct. 4, 1917).

McFarlan was known as a very conservative organization, yet this flamboyant custom built Cabriolet was mounted on a 1921 chassis. Coachwork was done by Kimball for Mr. E.J. Lehmann of Chicago. Unusual features include six fenders, lowering of the radiator to the height of the hood and oval windows (Indiana Historical Society).

already finished body on their own chassis to make a completed automobile ready for market. In 1917, a special custom body department was established to cater to the whims of the most discriminating client as more and more customers had the financial recourses and demanded personalized transportation. During McFarlan's final decade of automobile production, both types of custom work became company mainstays.

One early McFarlan custom creation was a car for candy delivery built for the Geiger Candy Company of Indianapolis. The chassis was not by McFarlan but instead was a lighter duty unit built by another company. The body looked like it was half limousine, half coupe in shape, wrought in white with ornamental glass with rich leather upholstering and appointments indicating it to be a distinctly fancy traveling car. It was sold through the company's Indianapolis agent and was delivered in late 1914.[34]

Another early custom job was made for Ralph Teetor, son of one of the organizers of Teetor-Hartley Motor Company in Hagerstown, Indiana. He wanted a three-passenger roadster, but he preferred a smaller vehicle, so he had a 1915 chassis built mostly of Auburn parts with a smaller Teetor engine. He then had McFarlan build a special body and fenders to his design. The young man described his car as being a beautiful job attracting the attention it deserved. Ralph Teetor was an amazing person who was legally blind from a childhood accident, but was still able to do many things that a person with normal eyesight could do. He used his custom car until 1918, when he sold it and lost track of it.[35]

By 1917, company literature confidently proclaimed "McFarlan coach work is known the world over for its smart appearance, accurate and artistic designing and reliability of construction." The department that had been established to provide custom work encour-

Here is a beautiful car with a special body by McFarlan and appointments in keeping, which makes it truly—an Aristocrat of Motordom—a car in which the owner may take justifiable pride.

Having gone into receivership in 1923, Lexington Motor Company was looking for a way to add prestige and sales to its line. This top-of-the-line Minute Man Six was offered with body by McFarlan beginning with the 1924 models.

aged interested persons to submit sketches of a preferred body style. McFarlan designers could work with combinations for coach painting and upholstery materials to complete the ideas expressed by the most discriminating person.[36]

Trade journals were recognizing McFarlan for their body-building talents as early as 1918. One article noted a special body that had been built for a Kentucky stock farm man. It was a four-passenger Destroyer that had been altered with a boattail rear end. Company officials liked the alterations so well that what began as a special order became the regular body offered on the Destroyer for 1918. Another out-of-the-ordinary body was a seven-passenger touring with an extended Victoria top that had been built for a gentleman from Los Angeles.[37]

A Philadelphia lady who had kidney trouble had her McFarlan modified to meet her needs, with a built-in toilet under the front seat. In another case, a Hollywood personality requested that the car she ordered be upholstered in a blue material that matched her favorite dress.[38] The company cheerfully complied.

At least one pet lover from Cleveland who was financially able had a special request when her car was built. A dog fancier, she specified that her two-passenger roadster be modified with the part immediately behind the seats cushioned to hold her prized canine. The company was glad to oblige, for a sum, of course. In these instances, regular production models were enhanced with special trim desired by customers who were willing to pay a bit extra for something a little out of the ordinary.

McFarlan's custom body building involved meeting the needs of a particular person, and the company did it well, making a strong reputation for themselves. McFarlan also built bodies for various automobile producers, although this work was less known publicly. In these cases, bodies were turned out on a production line, but were finished with the attention to detail for which McFarlan was known. Especially in the 1920s, parts of the factory complex that were not being utilized for automobile production were available for other uses. There were also plenty of skilled workmen available who could receive employment so that both the worker and the company benefited financially.

A sister concern located in Connersville, the Lexington Motor Company, made use of the established McFarlan name to add a bit of prestige to their largest sedans, offering them with McFarlan-built bodies from 1924 until the financially strapped company closed in 1926. The Lexington Minute-Man Six was a well-built automobile that sold in the middle price range. The company was founded in Lexington, Kentucky, in 1908, but moved to Connersville in early 1910. Lexington had had their financial ups and downs, the most recent in 1923, resulting in reorganization. As sales continued to plummet, management sought ways to make their cars more attractive to the buying public. Bodies by McFarlan gave a legitimate selling point, but the company still folded in 1926.

One of the marques that tapped McFarlan for bodies in the early 1920s was Premier, a pioneer automobile company, having been in business since 1903. Its location in Indianapolis, not far from Connersville, may have been a factor in McFarlan's getting the job of supplying bodies, but probably more of an influence than the close proximity was the new company owner, Frederick I. Barrows. Barrows had been connected with the Lexington Motor Company beginning in 1912, rising to the position of vice president and treasurer, but when Lexington went into receivership in April 1923, virtually all upper management personnel were released. Within a month, Barrows had submitted a bid to purchase Premier. The purchase was arranged through the Fletcher Savings and Trust Company of Indianapolis. Barrows was very familiar with McFarlan because his brother, Burton, was McFarlan's vice president, treasurer and plant manager. The Barrows brothers each benefited from the quality image carried by the McFarlan name. Premier gained a bit of prestige by having the respected McFarlan name-tag on their bodies and the big factory on Mount Street kept employees busy supplying bodies for Premier. This arrange-

Premier featured bodies by McFarlan in an attempt to stimulate sales. This body appears to be nearly identical to that offered by Lexington (*Motor*, Sept. 1923).

THE MARMON
SUBURBAN

The Marmon Suburban. As Marmon sales were increasing during the mid–1920s, bodies by McFarlan gave an added touch to a marque already recognized for its quality.

Most Auburn closed bodies were made by Central Manufacturing Company of Connersville, Indiana, but to add a bit of prestige, McFarlan did the finishing trim on upscale models including this 1922 Auburn Beauty Six Sedan. The factory list price of $2,395 made it the most expensive model offered that year (Auburn Cord Duesenberg Automobile Museum, Auburn, Indiana).

ment lasted only about two years until Frederick Barrows changed directions and sold the company.[39]

Being located close to Indianapolis did benefit McFarlan as they provided closed bodies to the Marmon Automobile Company into the mid-twenties. Marmon was experiencing growth during that period and went looking for a body builder that would enhance their sales appeal. McFarlan was glad to come to their rescue.

Another auto company that came calling, also a pioneer in the industry, was Auburn. Burton Barrows, vice president of the Connersville concern, made the optimistic announcement that the contract to supply Auburn with bodies guaranteed capacity output for the McFarlan plant. Auburn's bodies had been built by Connersville's Central Manufacturing Company the past several years. Some of the bodies supplied by McFarlan were still built by Central Manufacturing Company from scratch, then sent to McFarlan in the "white." Paint, upholstery and finishing touches were added and the McFarlan name-tag attached before bodies were shipped to the Auburn, Indiana, assembly plant where they were installed on waiting chassis.

This contract was welcomed by McFarlan, but it was also appreciated at the Auburn

By the mid–1920s, McFarlan was delivering six bodies each day to the Auburn Plant in northern Indiana (*Automobile Trade Journal*, Feb. 1, 1925).

factory. Although one of the pioneer producers of automobiles, the northeastern Indiana company foundered during the sharp 1921–22 recession. A large inventory of unsold Auburn cars clogged their lots and hindered cash intake. At the request of investors who had purchased the Auburn company a few years earlier, Errett Lobban Cord, a successful Chicago automobile salesman, took control and worked his magic by having the unsold vehicles repainted in bright colors and trimmed with nickel plating. The cars sold promptly, injecting much-needed cash into the coffers. As early as 1922, there was an attempt to add more prestige to the Auburn line as company management called upon McFarlan, recognizing their reputation for quality-built, attractive bodies. As sales and production increased, both companies benefited.

By 1925, production at Auburn had picked up to the extent that there was an increased need for McFarlan bodies. One means that McFarlan found to maintain the supply of bodies needed at the Auburn plant was to send a truckload north each day. The result was that a truck loaded with six bodies left the McFarlan factory each morning, traveled through Winchester and on to Portland, which was about halfway to Auburn. There the Connersville driver met another driver headed south with an empty truck. The two switched vehicles, and the second driver took the bodies on to Auburn.[40] This method was considered to be faster than shipping by train and kept inventories low at the Auburn assembly plant, limiting the need for extra storage. The good business relationship between the two Indiana manufacturers continued to grow throughout the 1920s until the McFarlan plant closed.

William C. Durant was well known as a leader in the automobile industry, having been the founder and at two times the president of General Motors and also having been fired twice. After his second removal from General Motors in 1920, Durant attempted to build his own automobile empire. He first concentrated on lower priced vehicles with the

Locomobile model 90 coupe. Note lowness of roof and special windshield construction

Top: In November of 1925, Locomobile contracted with McFarlan to build 1,000 bodies. Soon afterward, McFarlan became the sole supplier for Locomobile bodies (*Automobile Trade Journal,* Dec. 1, 1925). *Left:* Possibly the crowning achievement for the McFarlan custom department was the "Boat Roadster" built on a 1927 Duesenberg Model X chassis (courtesy Peter Heydon).

four-cylinder Star and Durant. He also launched the Flint, a step further up the price ladder. Finally, Durant purchased Locomobile to provide presence in the luxury car field. Durant's ultimate desire was to establish a corporation to rival the one that had given him his walking papers earlier.

Locomobile, also one of the earliest pioneers in the industry, was recognized throughout the country as a luxury marque that even reached into the prestige category when custom bodies were installed on the magnificent model 48. The sharp recession of 1920–1921 had adversely affected Locomobile as it had many other companies. Changes in management had not satisfied creditors and an involuntary petition for bankruptcy was filed January 31, 1922. On October 27 of that same year, company assets were transferred to the Locomobile Company of America, Inc., with the new owner being William C. Durant.[41] In an attempt to maintain Locomobile's image and stimulate sales, a contract was let that called for seven types of custom bodies to be designed by LeBaron and built by different coachbuilders: Brewster, Demarest, Ostruk, Locke and McFarlan.[42] For McFarlan to be placed in the same group of quality coachbuilders as much better known names spoke volumes for the concern. The arrangement worked well and in March of 1925, Locomobile contracted with McFarlan for 1,000 bodies.[43] Within a short time, McFarlan became the sole supplier for Locomobile bodies.[44] The talents of the skilled

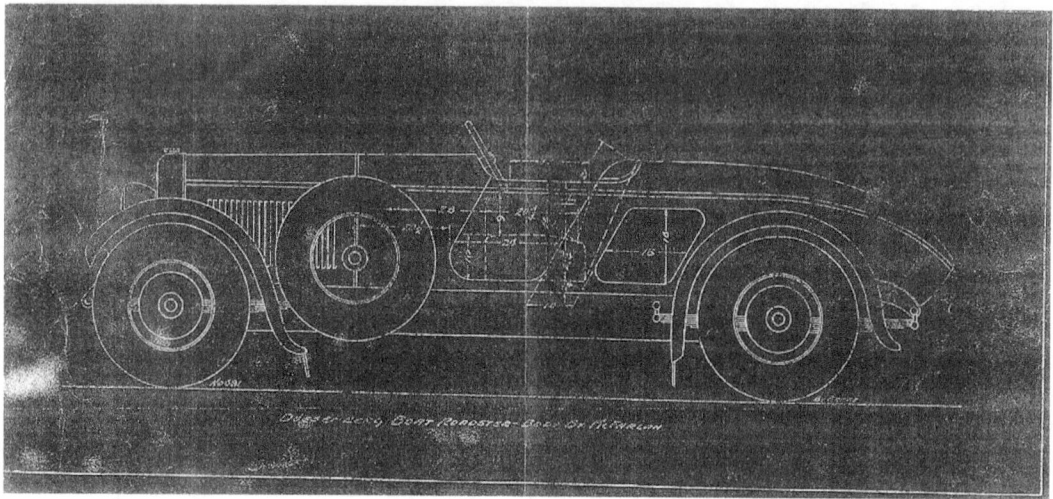

The original drawing submitted by McFarlan used cycle type fenders and no running boards. It was labeled "Duesenberg Boat Roadster — Body by McFarlan" (courtesy Peter Heydon).

craftsmen at the Connersville factory were recognized for providing quality construction while giving attention to detail.

The vast majority of products that left the big factory on Mount Street during the mid– to late 1920s were not complete automobiles, but instead, mainly closed body sedans, coaches and coupes, destined for other factories to add that special touch when mounted on the already prepared chassis to make a complete luxury automobile ready for the customer. There were at least two exceptions to the closed car bodies built by McFarlan, both of which have survived.

Possibly the crowning achievement for the custom body department was a one-off "boat roadster" body designed and built by McFarlan and mounted on a 1927 Duesenberg "Model X" chassis. The McFarlan custom body department would not ordinarily have been perceived as providing the level of prestige associated with Duesenberg, but several factors figured into the choice. Errett Lobban Cord, who had gained control of the Auburn Motor Company by the mid-twenties, aspired to build his own industrial empire. He purchased Duesenberg in the fall of 1926, naming himself as company president. Another company was added to Cord's empire when he acquired the Lycoming Motor Company. McFarlan had been well known to Cord because the firm had been building bodies for top-of-the-line Auburns for several years, eliciting Cord's appreciation for the company's high level of workmanship and design. It didn't hurt that McFarlan became a customer of Lycoming in late 1925, using their engines for the new Eight-in-Line McFarlans. Cord's attachment to McFarlan was further enhanced when he eventually purchased the big brick factory on Mount Street after McFarlan went out of business.

Initial drawings sent to Duesenberg depicted the Boat Roadster with cycle-type fenders and no running boards. The original drawing was labeled "Duesenberg Boat Roadster — Body By McFarlan." Duesenberg management changed the plans to include the sweeping fenders and aluminum running boards as used on other prototype Model

X cars. Later this body became the model and inspiration for the 1928–1936 Auburn Boattail Speedsters (though the much shorter wheelbase of the Auburn resulted in a slightly stunted rear end). The rear fenders were made from stock McFarlan sedan fenders. At first the windshield had a dramatic angle designed to match the front angle of the doors and golf bag compartment, but it had to be altered to look more aerodynamic.

Obviously designed to be used in fair weather only, the boat roadster had no provision for either a top or windshield wipers.[45] This "X" Duesenberg was displayed in the New York Auto Show in November of that year and was later sold to Arnold Kirkeby, a Duesenberg Race Team supporter who was also the owner of Chicago's Drake and Blackstone hotels, as well as the Beverly Wilshire in Beverly Hills, California. This beautifully sculpted

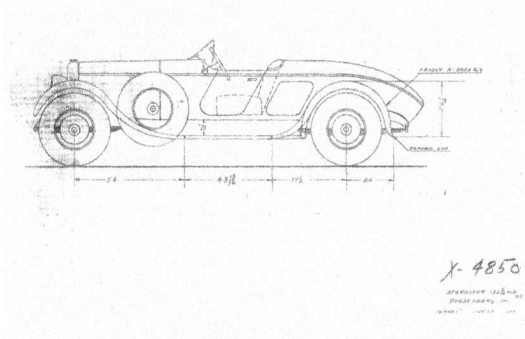

Top: Duesenberg revised the plans to include regular fenders and aluminum running boards. The rear fenders were from a McFarlan sedan (courtesy Peter Heydon). *Bottom:* One of the last bodies to leave the McFarlan plant became a jewel in their crown because it was destined to be mounted on a Duesenberg Model Y chassis (courtesy *Automobile Quarterly*).

and dramatically modeled Boat Roadster has survived to the great appreciation of its many admirers.[46]

In June of 1928, one of the last projects to leave the McFarlan factory was a touring body that was destined for a Duesenberg. It was installed on one of two Model Y Duesenberg chassis built. The other Model Y was fitted with a Derham sedan body. Both of these vehicles were used by the Duesenberg factory during the development of the mighty Model J. The McFarlan bodied Dusie was sold to Augie Duesenberg in 1932 on condition that he destroy the chassis. He slipped a Model A Duesenberg chassis underneath the Y body and sold it to an Indianapolis businessman. It has survived.[47]

5

Why the Stars Came to Connersville

Americans were getting the message that bigger was better, so McFarlan took it one step farther with the assumption that biggest must be best. Although not part of their advertising campaign, that seemed to have been their reasoning as they prepared to launch the new Twin Valve series of luxury automobiles. In just over a decade on the market, the McFarlan had stretched from a medium-sized car with a 120 inch wheelbase to the new 1921 barge-size 140 inches. In the engine, only the number of cylinders, six, had remained the same. The size of the power plant had grown from 248 cubic inches of displacement producing the power of 30 to 40 horses to the monstrous 572.5 c.i.d. that was considered to be the most powerful passenger car engine on the American market at 120 horsepower. McFarlan cars' increase in weight from 2,600 pounds in 1910 to 4,700 pounds for the TV series touring or 5,400 pounds for the majestic Knickerbocker Cabriolet was affected by their increase in size and the much heavier components. Pricewise, there was also significant change. It took just $2,000 to be one of the first to own the new McFarlan Six in 1909. In just over a decade, while mass production substantially lowered the cost of most makes, for the privilege of owning a McFarlan, the price more than doubled for open cars and quadrupled for those opting for the top-of-the-line Town Car.

Through its first decade of production, McFarlan was considered to be a good vehicle, worth the investment, but with little to distinguish it from other cars of similar quality. They had become recognized for outstanding workmanship and custom appointments, but they still looked pretty much like many other makes. Packard was easily recognizable because of the shape of its radiator. Pierce-Arrow sported headlights mounted on the front fenders, and even Franklin, with the Renault type sloping hood or the horse-collar style that followed, could be quickly identified. McFarlan addressed that issue with the TV series and became known for its massive radiator shell, gleaming with German silver and standing tall, well above the hood line. That, along with oversize headlights measuring one foot across, gave it the appearance of brute strength, a car to be reckoned with.

When the McFarlan automobile was at the height of its notoriety, it was sometimes referred to as the American Rolls-Royce. Such a comparison may seem absurd considering McFarlan's obscurity in relation to the world renowned Rolls, but the TV series radiator bore a distinct resemblance to the better known British marque's, and both manufacturers were known for their custom appointments to fit specific customer desires. Even its price

The new McFarlan was an impressive vehicle — a chariot that might sway this young woman's judgment. Illustration by Leslie L. Benson, *The Saturday Evening Post*, Sept. 30, 1922.

suggested Rolls quality as the type 154 Knickerbocker sold for a hefty $9,000 at a time when the highest priced Cadillac limousine was just $5,500.

The new Twin Valve series, introduced mid-year in 1920, used an engine that was built for McFarlan at Jesse Kepler's Dayton, Ohio, machine shop. Jesse's brother, Stanley, had worked for McFarlan as the company was entering the automobile business, but Jesse was credited with turning plans into reality for this massive power plant. It was of McFarlan design with Edward McConegle as consulting engineer. The TV engine had identical displacement to the Teetor-McFarlan it replaced and, in fact, may have been built under license from Teetor-Hartley. One significant difference from the Teetor engine was the cylinder blocks that were cast in threes instead of being a single block. The engine was designed with overkill built in. The TV designation stood for twin valves. There were two sets of valves for each cylinder, 12 intake and 12 exhaust. They were activated by two gear driven camshafts, one on each side of the block. The 24 valves were each 1½ inches in diameter making a large valve area for easy breathing. There were 18 spark plugs for the Twin Valve Six engine, or three plugs per cylinder. The triple ignition was powered by two entirely different systems. A Berling high tension magneto fired two sets of plugs, set at opposite sides of each cylinder. On the intake side was the third set of plugs that

If bigger was better, then being the biggest must have been the best! McFarlan automobiles such as this seven passenger sedan were among the largest passenger cars produced at the time (*McFarlan Six*, 1921).

was fired by the distributor. The engine could be run using the distributor system only, the magneto system only, or both systems firing all 18 plugs simultaneously. Delco provided the ignition and Westinghouse the starter.

Engine cooling was by liquid using a centrifugal pump with cellular radiator core. Along with the oil pump, the hollow crankshaft carried lubricating oil in the ten quart system to all bearings including piston pins and outboard camshaft bearings. The crankshaft diameter at the main bearings was 2⅜ inches. A poppet safety valve in the oil line was installed at the front end as far away from the oil pump as possible to avoid the possibility of any accidental release of pressure before all surfaces were lubricated. The pump was of the conventional gear type located at the lowest part of the sump. Fuel was delivered from the rear-mounted tank by a vacuum system feeding the Stromberg carburetor.[1] The SAE horsepower rating was 117 at a modest 2,000 rpm. Wood spoke artillery wheels were standard, but Houk wire or Disteel disc wheels were popular available options.

The drive line consisted of the disc clutch, Brown-Lipe 3-speed transmission, Spicer universals and a Timken rear axel with bevel gears and a low, for that time, 3.65 to one gear ratio. Other features included semi-elliptic front and rear springs, Gemmer steering gear, 35" × 5" Goodrich tires, Firestone rims, Klaxon horn and Warner speedometer.[2] The clutch was a dry plate multi-disc unit by Borg & Beck. McFarlan had used this unit for the past several years. It required fairly frequent adjustments, especially when the car

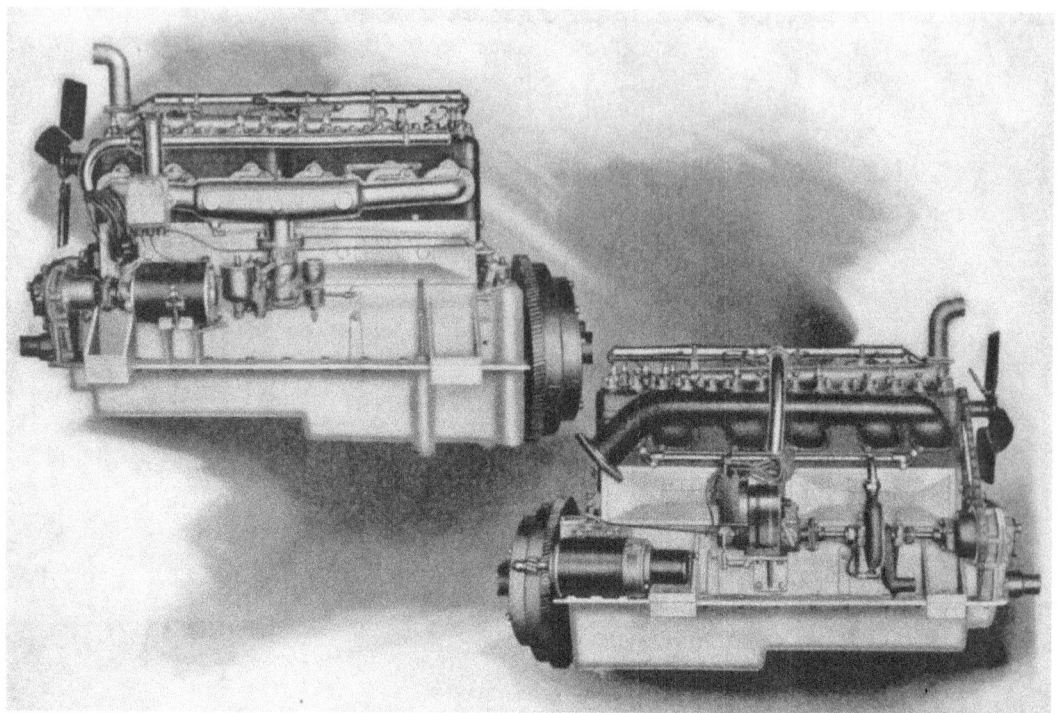

The most powerful engine offered in a U.S. passenger car in 1921 was the McFarlan Twin Valve Six (*The McFarlan Six*, 1921).

was new or when a new unit had been installed. By removing the inspection plate on the upper part of the back of the housing, the clutch unit could be serviced quickly. When both adjustment bolts had been loosened, they were slid to the right to tighten the clutch.[3]

With few exceptions, all McFarlan bodies were constructed in the company's own shop of ash frames covered with hand-formed metal panels welded into a unit. The company was justly proud of their quality. Body styles available on the huge Twin Valve chassis included the four-passenger sport touring, seven-passenger touring, two-passenger coupe, seven-passenger Knickerbocker Cabriolet, sport sedan, touring sedan, suburban sedan, limousine, Continental Landaulet, and the two-passenger roadster with concealed seat for two in the rear, one of the very early rumble seats.[4]

Road testing was a part of the normal production cycle. Each chassis was given an over-the-road run before a body was mounted, but as the new TV Series was being developed, additional tests were conducted running the roads using a bare chassis with makeshift bucket type seats upon which to sit. Some people throughout the area had voiced complaints about company drivers going at breakneck speeds, but testing continued when the company felt the need. One such run a few years earlier had ended tragically. Another run ended almost as badly when the machine driven by 19-year-old Leon Wolverton was in an accident. While driving at a high rate of speed on the gravel surfaced Milton Pike, Wolverton lost control of his test car on the curve in front of the Kyle Stant residence. The out-of-control machine turned over and plunged down a steep embankment. Wolverton's sister, Leora, was a passenger, almost certainly without the knowledge of company officials. She escaped with minor scrapes when thrown clear of the wreckage, but the driver was critically injured when he was pinned underneath and a steel running board support bar penetrated his back to a depth of five inches. The rod had to be sawed off before Wolverton could be extricated. He was then transported to the Connersville hospital where physicians removed the metal, although they had difficulty doing so. His condition was reported as grave, but doctors were encouraged that it had not penetrated the chest area. Wolverton was considered to be a skilled driver but may not have been aware of the sharpness of the curve. Those who had been calling for safer driving by test drivers got some relief after that unfortunate incident.[5]

Even with the hefty weight of these behemoths, having the most powerful engine of any passenger car was sure to bring a challenge as to who could go the fastest. One such match developed in New York where a Twin Valve Six was pitted against a new Pierce-Arrow. The Pierce that competed was hand picked by the dealer who made the challenge. The McFarlan was owned by a private individual, a Mr. Donner. The race was held over a 30 mile stretch of parkway. The Pierce was given a three minute head start but was passed after 20 miles. The McFarlan reached speeds as high as 88 miles per hour and averaged 81.7 for the entire distance. It was an expensive run for the Pierce-Arrow, because before it reached the end of the course, a connecting rod let loose and the engine was ruined.[6] What a difference good roads made in the McFarlan's performance. Apparently this contest was run on a public thoroughfare without official sanction. Surely the cops would have liked to have interceded, but probably couldn't have caught up with either violator.

The introduction of the TV series came at one of the worst possible economic times. The automobile industry was thrown into a tailspin in late summer of 1920. Production had just gotten back to normal after a partial shutdown for World War I when things started falling apart. By mid-year 1920, many banks were refusing to lend money for automobile purchases, and rumors were spreading that the railroads had gained favor with steel companies for allocation of that vital material. Many automobile manufacturers felt the crunch, and some, including the wonderfully engineered Lincoln, a new marque being built by Henry Leland, and well-known companies such as Willys-Overland and Maxwell, would face bankruptcy or reorganization because of this sharp financial downturn. The challenging economic times had little effect on McFarlan because their customers didn't rely on the friendly banker to come through with a loan. Their clientele were tending more and more toward the rich and famous who made a substantial down payment at the time that the car was ordered and handed over the remainder upon delivery. Since most McFarlan cars were custom built and were usually sold before the assembly process began, the company was not caught with a backlog of unsold merchandise that required discount prices in order to liquidate. Actually, McFarlan prices had escalated substantially with the introduction of the TV series and had not been rolled back during the recession.

Being one of the elite marques may have made McFarlans somewhat more vulnerable to thieves who figured they might just as well go for "the best" while they were breaking the law. One such theft seemed for several months to have been the perfect crime. In September of 1920, soon after introduction of the new TV series, a brand new limousine disappeared from the McFarlan dealer in Indianapolis. Both the dealer and law enforcement were dumbfounded because the handsome car had been safely locked away on display in the showroom at closing time, but was missing when personnel arrived for business the next morning. There was no evidence of a break-in, no clues were left behind and searching the area turned up nothing. About five months later in February 1921, a dental equipment salesman went calling upon two new dentists who had set up a practice in Meridian, Missouri. When the salesman entered the office area, he spotted all new dental equipment of the brand that he peddled. Knowing that he had not sold any of the equipment, despite having worked that territory for several years, the salesman contacted the company, who in turn got in touch with the local sheriff. It turned out the dental equipment was stolen, and further investigation revealed that the sticky fingered dentists also had a shiny new McFarlan limousine. When one of the culprits eventually confessed, he explained that he had hidden himself in the Indianapolis showroom at about closing time. Late that night, he opened the doors, slyly removed the car, and closed the building back up. The two aspiring professionals then drove to Missouri.[7]

An unlikely factor in the success of this company as a builder of prestige automobiles was its location in a small Midwestern industrial city far away from the large metropolitan areas where most of the units were sold. Few McFarlan cars were purchased by Indiana residents, and fewer still in the small county of Fayette where these custom built machines were produced. Distributors were located in major cities such as New York, Philadelphia, Boston, Chicago, Los Angeles and San Francisco. These dealers carried McFarlan as a sideline but didn't rely on those occasional sales for survival. Although distributors could handle some specific requests for interested customers, really particular persons often chose to take several days out of their schedules and come to Connersville by train so they could meet with company personnel to express their specific wants, participate in upholstery selection or watch some phase of assembly.

In the late teens and early 1920s, enough people could afford to have their automobile built to fit their wishes that they accepted the inconvenience as a part of the pride of ownership. Train service provided connections to major cities and accommodations were provided locally at reasonable rates — where else but at the McFarlan Hotel. Though not owned by the McFarlan family by this time, it was still the "in place" to stay or be seen in Connersville.

Hollywood personalities who knew the prestige of McFarlan ownership included the famous motion picture producer William D. Taylor, movie stars Roscoe "Fatty" Arbuckle, Dorothy Dalton, Dot Farley, Marie Osborne, Eddie Polo and Wallace "Wally" Reid.[8]

Dorothy Farley was one of the lesser stars, but she played roles in 280 films beginning in the very early silent flicks of 1910 and continuing as talkies and even color became common. Most of her roles were in short comedies. Her lengthy career in the movies lasted for more than 40 years.

Wally Reid was a silent film and stage star with good looks and athletic ability that endeared him to men and women alike. His most popular films were based on auto racing, providing lots of action and attracting large crowds to theaters. *The Roaring Road* and

McFarlan owner Dorothy Farley played many minor movie roles over a period of nearly 50 years (courtesy Antique Automobile Club of America Library, Hershey, PA).

Double Speed brought Reid substantial income while fueling his enthusiasm for fast automobiles. Reid was married and had two children, but for his personal transportation, he preferred McFarlans. He had owned several including a 1921 Twin Valve Six roadster. Reid was one of the film stars known to have visited Connersville. In 1918, he stopped by the factory to check on the delivery date of a new Series 90. In the fall of 1922, he spent

Paramount film star Wallace Reid with his 1921 Twin Valve Six Roadster (author's collection).

an afternoon and evening performing at the Vaudette and Auditorium theaters.[9] Reid almost certainly visited the McFarlan factory at that time, as he had placed an order for a 1923 red Knickerbocker Cabriolet, which was being built for him at the time of his untimely death. This 32-year-old stage and screen star had become addicted to morphine after receiving serious injuries in a train accident. The potent drug had been, at first, used sparingly to control pain, but his reliance on it increased until he was admitted to a sanitarium in Hollywood seeking a cure. He died in January 1923, with his devoted wife at his bedside.

Mary Pickford was another star rumored to have visited the big factory on Mount Street. McFarlan, however, printed a disclaimer about having built a car for Pickford. At least as of March 1920, they said they had not received such an order, but would have been greatly pleased to have been of service.[10] The story had been widely told that Mary Pickford had visited the factory for several days at a time to see that her McFarlan was done right. The rumor was that Miss Pickford endeared herself to the factory workers because she sometimes brought her own sack lunch that had been prepared for her, and sat and ate with the workers. She would have been assured that every detail would be given extra attention by the skilled craftsmen. Pickford was at the height of her popularity and would definitely have been given a warm welcome wherever she went.

Alma Simpson, a well known singer from New York, had climbed the ladder of success and showed it by driving a 1921 McFarlan Sport Touring (National Automotive History Collection, Detroit Public Library).

One story was told about a famous, though unidentified, lady who came to the factory to drive her new McFarlan away. It was a warm day and as she was driving west from town on Rushville Road, air rushing through the cowl vent had a cooling effect on her legs. The drive was delightful as her skirt billowed in the breeze, until a bee entered the car through the open cowl vent and stung her through her bloomers, causing her to run off the road and wreck her new prized possession. After that incident, the company installed a screen inside the cowl vent to keep unwanted insects from intruding.

Roscoe "Fatty" Arbuckle, one of the most popular film comedians of the 1910s was known for his hefty size and his lavish life style. Arbuckle lost much of his following after being arrested and jailed without bond in September 1921. One news release stated that "a formal complaint charging murder was sworn to before police judge Daniel O'Brien against Roscoe (Fatty) Arbuckle, in connection with the death of Miss Virginia Rappe, an attractive motion picture actress." The allegation stemmed from events that occurred at a Labor Day party that Arbuckle, actor Lowell Sherman and film director Fred Fishbach threw at the St. Francis Hotel in San Francisco. Arbuckle was accused of having attacked Miss Rappe during the merrymaking. When it became apparent that Rappe was ill, she was taken to a hospital where she was initially treated for alcoholism. That diagnosis was eventually thought to have been incorrect as the young movie actress died four days later, possibly from an internal rupture that caused peritonitis.[11]

Justice was promised to be handed down quickly as District Attorney Matthew F. Brady was quoted as saying "we have a complete case against Arbuckle." The trial did begin in short order, but resolving the matter proved to be anything but fast. A jury was selected and the trial got under way late in 1921, with the distinct presence of news reporters from around the country recounting every sensational word of testimony. When all evidence of the prosecution and defense had been presented and the jury received the case, it became evident that a verdict could not be reached, as the jury was deadlocked. A second trial soon got under way, and again headlines often carried speculation as to the final outcome. Newspaper men hustled to the telephones, wanting to be first with the news after each witness was heard. Again, the final responsibility lay with the 12 jurists, and again, they could not agree. A third trial, held during the spring of 1922, attracted much less attention. By that time, the charge had been reduced to manslaughter. After the prosecution and defense had each argued their case, the matter was given to the jury for the third time. Within minutes after retiring for deliberation, a verdict of not guilty was returned.[12] Some jurors felt there was absolutely no case against Arbuckle. So strong were the feelings of the jurists that the acquittal was accompanied by a statement of apology signed by all 12 members of the jury and both alternates. They claimed a great injustice had been done to Arbuckle as no real evidence had been presented to warrant the charges.[13] Even though he had eventually been found innocent of the charges, his popularity never returned to what it had been before his arrest. In small town America, where film stars were still on the pedestal as heroes, movie theaters often refused to show Arbuckle films. Such was the case in Connersville where theater management decided it was not in the best interest of their customers to have further exposure to a person having such a tarnished image.[14]

Arbuckle was a true auto aficionado who maintained a small fleet of expensive vehicles, doing much of the mechanical work himself. A Stevens-Duryea, one of the finest and fastest cars of its day, came first. He also had owned a 1914 Alco, a 1917 Rolls-Royce that had been presented to him by producer Joseph Schenck as a contract signing bonus, and a 1919 Pierce-Arrow 66 A-4 with a monstrous 825 cubic inch six-cylinder T head engine.[15] One of the flashiest cars he had owned was a Kissel with low-cut doors that was painted the company's signature chrome yellow and became known as the Gold Bug. Arbuckle would eventually own a custom built McFarlan that he acquired soon after being dismissed from his court escapade. The red 1923 TV Knickerbocker Cabriolet, which survives, was built for Wally Reid, but was purchased by Arbuckle since Reid had died before he could take delivery. This was a car well suited for "Fatty" since he was a hefty person who was able to manhandle the controls and the flashy red color suited his personality quite well.

Monte Blue, whose given name was Gerard Montgomery Blue, was born and raised in Indiana, not far from the McFarlan plant, but probably had little knowledge of the marque until he became a silent film actor. His father was killed in an accident when

Monte Blue and his specially designed McFarlan Twin Valve Town Car (National Automotive History Collection, Detroit Public Library).

Monte was a young child. Blue was raised in the Soldiers and Sailors Orphans Home near Knightstown, Indiana. After stints in a number of different occupations, Monte emigrated to California, where he became a stuntman in the movies. He appeared in the movie *The Grim Game* in 1919 where he did stunts in an airplane for Houdini, who had a fear of flying.[16] Blue acquired a top-of-the-line Twin Valve Six Town Car in the mid–1920s, reflecting his rise from rags to riches.

Film stars were not the only persons of wealth who chose the impressive McFarlan for their own transportation. Politicians and other prominent personalities selected what they considered to be a vehicle representative of their status. The governors of Connecticut and Virginia found reason to flaunt their position by making a McFarlan their car in which to be seen. John H. Trumbull of Connecticut owned a snappy 1926 TV Roadster. Virginia's governor, Elbert Lee Trinkle, purchased a McFarlan Suburban Sedan in 1922. He was a Democrat who held the highest office in that state from 1922 until 1926. Trinkle was the youngest son of a prominent Virginia family. Before being elected governor, he had served two terms in the Virginia Senate.[17]

Even more important, government officials chose to be identified with the prestigious Hoosier made product. The McFarlan Motor Company's Cuban sales agency procured an order from none other than President Menocal, whose taste in motor cars was derived

Virginia governor E. Lee Trinkle and his chauffeur Lee Dempsey with Trinkle's 1922 Twin Valve Suburban Sedan (*Connersville News-Examiner*, Sept. 15, 1922).

and refined from several centuries of luxurious Spanish and Cuban ancestry. His choice of a McFarlan showed appreciation for the status that the marque represented.[18] There would be little doubt about who held the ruling hand when Menocal was being chauffeured about in his chariot.

Another classic McFarlan was shipped to Cuba, ordered by the director of the Cuban lottery. That gentleman was reported to have been a person of distinction on the island and throughout the Latin American world. It is entirely possible his purchase was influenced by the fact that his boss, the president of the republic, had made a similar choice.

The finest testimony to McFarlan's status as a provider of prestige transportation came from Spain early in 1925. An order arrived from Antonio Herida, an agent for the Spanish government, for two splendid McFarlans. Payment was received promptly and in full. When the completed cars were shipped to Madrid, it was noted that the officer who received them was delighted. The initial sale apparently brought such favorable comment that an additional order came by cable for four more McFarlan TV touring cars. This sale was arranged through a Spanish dealer who requested that the cars be sent to Valencia, as soon as possible.[19]

Athletes, too, wanted to flaunt their newly earned wealth by selecting the attention-getting McFarlan for their ride. Among them was the famous boxer Jack Dempsey. Born in Manassa, Colorado, and raised in an atmosphere that fostered toughness, Dempsey

Jack Dempsey was the proud owner of this 1922 Suburban Sedan shown at Welsh's Health Farm (*Connersville News-Examiner*, June 7, 1921).

grew to manhood entering various boxing matches until by 1919, he had defeated Jes Willard to win the world heavyweight championship title and immediate wealth and fame. Between 1923 and 1926, Dempsey had refused to defend his title against Harry Willis, who was black. He did, however, agree to fight Gene Tunney in Chicago on September 22, 1927. Tunney was white and weighed the same as Dempsey. Tunney dominated the fight until, in the seventh round, Dempsey caught Tunney on the jaw three times in succession and sent him to the deck. The referee, Dave Barry, tried to move Dempsey away so he could start the count. Finally he did move to his corner and the count got under way, but Tunney had managed to get up on the count of nine. There were accusations that the referee's count had been extra slow, but by the end of the match, Tunney was declared the winner with Dempsey unable to reclaim the title.[20] Jack Dempsey was the owner of a large 1922 Twin Valve Six Suburban sedan that he had purchased secondhand. He was also photographed sitting in a 1923 TV roadster. Claims have been made that Dempsey owned still other McFarlans. Whether or not these claims are true is not clear, but this marque would have provided the type of sporty luxury car to which the heavyweight boxer might well have been attracted.

In addition to noteworthy personalities who chose McFarlan for ego enhancement,

This 1923 Type 142 roadster would seem a good fit for Jack Dempsey, but ownership has not been verified (author's collection).

other prominent customers wanted the vehicle because it had the most powerful engine in the industry and was thus expected to be able to outrun the local arm of the law. Those involved in such crimes as bootlegging, gambling, prostitution and all sorts of underworld activities sought out prestige transportation for their glamour, but even more because they were built heavily enough to permit installation of armor plate, heavy glass and other amenities as specified by the purchaser.

One such customer, Alfonso Caponi, alias Al Brown, better known as Al Capone, purchased a McFarlan for his wife, Mae, in 1924, and one for his own use in 1926. Capone's personal vehicle was said to have come complete with bulletproof glass, heavy metal shields in the sides and a gun turret that would hold a machine gun. Capone's cars sometimes had provision for such a weapon to be mounted next to the driver. Capone apparently did not visit the factory, but sent one of his henchmen to pick up the car when it was ready. Charles McNaughton, just out of high school and working for McFarlan, remembered being given the assignment to meet "Capone's man" at the railroad station in Richmond, Indiana, and bring him to Connersville to take delivery.[21]

Another story related to the Capone gang was told about Leslie Smith, who, while still in high school, could earn ten dollars plus a return train ticket if he would deliver a

McFarlan to Chicago. He could do the job on a weekend without missing school and it was lots more fun than working in a drug store or delivering papers. Smith remembered having been given a bonus for one particular delivery that went to Frank Nittie, one of Al Capone's henchmen.[22]

One low ranking racketeer with indirect connections to Capone was Frank Hitchcock. Frank dressed well and looked like ready money, even owning a big McFarlan Suburban sedan. Milton Mezzrow, an enterprising jazz musician, told of driving Hitchcock's car from Chicago to Hammond, Indiana, to pick up Millie Smith, an aspiring singer who had caught Frank's eye, but who also had connections with the underworld. Hitchcock played the game with big cars and fancy clothes until his body was found a couple of years later in a ditch on one of those lonely country roads.[23]

Paul Whiteman was one of the last "personalities" to purchase his prized McFarlan. Whiteman was controversially dubbed the King of Jazz during the 1920s. The controversy came about because his band had no members of the Negro race that had dominated the

Paul Whiteman's new McFarlan Twin Valve Custom Touring. The photograph was taken May 27, 1927, outside the Leedy Mfg. Co. at the corner of Palmer and Barth streets in Indianapolis, Indiana. Left to right, Whiteman, McDonald and U.S. Leedy (courtesy Harry J. Cangany, Jr., CLU).

The wonder of the 1923 Chicago Auto Show (*Motor Age*, Feb. 1, 1923).

jazz scene up until that time. Whiteman had an all white band that he had relocated from San Francisco to New York City. There they made recordings for Victor Records which propelled Whiteman and his band to national prominence. In a time when most dance bands consisted of six to 10 men, Whiteman's band numbered as many of 35 members. In 1924, he commissioned George Gershwin's *Rhapsody in Blue*, with Gershwin at the piano. Another of Whiteman's favorites was *Grand Canyon Suite*, by Ferde Grofe. In 1927, the same year he bought a new McFarlan TV touring car, he recorded Hoagy Carmichael singing and playing *Washboard Blues* to the accompaniment of his orchestra.[24]

Among the friends of Whiteman was Ulysses S. Leedy, president of Leedy Manufacturing Company, the world's largest percussion factory, located in Indianapolis, Indiana. Leedy supplied instruments for Whiteman's band and other organizations throughout the world. In the mid–1920s, the Leedy company had bragging rights for having constructed the world's largest drum for Purdue University's marching band. Whiteman visited the Leedy factory soon after taking delivery of his 1927 McFarlan. It didn't appear that the car could haul many of the large drums, but it was good for a promotional stunt.[25]

McFarlan officials boasted that their cars were being sought by a growing clientele

The 1921 Sport Roadster had two auxiliary seats concealed in the rear deck, one of the earliest "rumble seats" (*McFarlan Six*, 1921).

throughout the principal cities of this country and abroad. Net sales had increased by 316 percent during the period from 1917 until 1922. The corporation had net assets of over one million dollars with tangible assets more than four and a half times as great as liabilities. The latter figure was especially important after the sharp recession of 1920–1921. McFarlan production didn't suffer to the degree that other automobile companies' did, partly because of their limited output. The McFarlan car was one of the highest priced and most exclusive automobiles in the country, and it offered outstanding performance from the most powerful engine available in a domestic production car. In 1922, more than 200 men were employed by the factory with an annual payroll in excess of $200,000.[26]

Company officials were well aware of their status that attracted attention wherever fine motorcars were found, so they were especially glad when the opportunity presented itself to produce the most extravagant vehicle known to man. Thus came about the Gold-Plated McFarlan. This car, described as one of the most expensive cars ever built in America up to that time, was a top-of-the-line 1923 Knickerbocker Cabriolet that listed for a hefty $9,000 in regular finish, but with the special bright trim was to sell for $25,000. All exposed trim parts that were normally plated with German silver or nickel were 20 or 24 carat gold plated. These included the radiator shell, Vesta headlamps, cowl, spot, tail and stop lamps, Colonial side lamps, trunk bars, hub caps, winged Motometer, hood hooks, catches and locks, windshield frame and fixtures, Boa constrictor horn, clock, ignition switch and all other instruments, front and rear steps, landau irons, steering

The three-passenger coupe offered sporty "entrance steps" instead of full-length running boards (*McFarlan Six*, 1921).

wheel quadrant and levers, transmitter plate for telephone, various nuts, bolts, screws and washers and even the gasoline tank cap, numbering, in all, 958 separate parts.[27]

The rear passenger compartment was upholstered with imported blue and gold velour of the highest quality. Upholstery in the front compartment required two mirror finish full grain leather hides that were provided by Blanchard Brothers & Lane, tanners, of Newark, New Jersey. This exclusive car was built for display at the Chicago Automobile Show that was held in January 1923. As the individual parts were plated with the valuable metal, security became a problem. Smaller parts were locked in a vault until installed on the car, and even then, some parts had to be duplicated because the originals had somehow disappeared. The car followed the usual McFarlan quality construction. The outside finish was a very dark bluish black, which, with the gold plating, offered a remarkable contrast in color.[28] As was the normal McFarlan custom, this car was built to order. George Buxton of the McFarlan Chicago Company, along with Harry Harris of Harris, Rogers Company, also of the Windy City, sought out prospective customers. By show time, considerable curiosity had developed about the identity of the purchaser. News reporters questioned wealthy personalities connected with chewing gum, baseball, moving pictures and the steel industry, but the expected owner's name was not revealed.[29]

When the special car with glistening gold trimmings had been completely assembled, and before it was shipped to Chicago, local citizens were given an opportunity to visit the factory and drool over its opulence. On a Saturday afternoon in January, the public

California type tops were popular because they offered a fixed top with open air comfort (*McFarlan Six*, 1921).

was allowed to view without charge both the gold plated Knickerbocker Cabriolet and a sporty McFarlan roadster finished in French ivory that was also to be in the show.[30] The Chicago Auto Show was a crowd pleaser. An article in the *Indianapolis Star* noted, "The Chicago automobile show, many say, surpasses the New York show in beauty of display. One interesting factor in the Chicago show is an Indiana-made car, the McFarlan of Connersville. This organization has knocked the eyes out of every visitor with a gold-plated McFarlan car, said to be valued at $25,000."[31] In order to keep sticky fingers at bay, the car was surrounded by a strong brass railing and was watched over by guards, day and night.

The last day of the show was to bring extra excitement when the keys were presented to the lucky owner. The pricey jewel was announced to have been purchased by Harry L. Harris, but in fact Harris had meant to act only in the capacity of a broker, working with the Chicago McFarlan dealer to find a buyer. Apparently the unique show car had not been sold, and Harris was stuck with it until he could find a well-heeled purchaser. Sometime after the show ended the famous gold Knickerbocker Cabriolet was sold to a lady in Oklahoma who chose to flaunt some of the wealth that had come her way through oil. The other two McFarlans exhibited at the show were a 7-passenger touring that went home with E.A. Benson, a musical director, and the French ivory sport roadster that was sold to Edward Moerschbaecher. Both men were from the Chicago area.[32]

One of the men who was employed at the factory for two years was the aforementioned

Top-of-the-line Knickerbocker provided enclosed comfort and privacy for passengers (*McFarlan Six*, 1921).

Charles McNaughton. Just out of high school and needing money to attend college, Mac worked in the smaller factory building where most of the custom jobs were completed. Employed as a draftsman as he was recognized as having artistic ability, he had the job of making a sketch of any custom order so the purchaser could see what was being planned. Then he used the large drawing board, which was part of the factory wall, to make a full size drawing of the car. Next, McNaughton related, "the pattern maker would lay out the wood framing using my drawing, and finally, this big guy, who was from Austria, used a tap hammer to shape the metal. He also hand hammered the fenders to get a rounded shape."[33]

The introduction of the TV series in mid–1920 produced an automobile with distinctive styling that was an attention getter wherever it went. McFarlans of that era, with their resemblance to the famed Rolls-Royce, brought envious stares from the moneyed class just as the company had intended. The low number of vehicles produced plus the attention given to individual customers' wishes allowed the company to justify its advertising slogan, "custom built."

Styling updates were few and subtle. For the years 1921 through 1925, styling was left nearly untouched. One of the most noticeable changes was the adoption of drum style Vesta headlights beginning in 1922. This type of lamp was just coming into vogue and McFarlan was at the forefront of that trend. Another styling change that became available the same year was the reverse slope windshield, described as the Valencia widescreen no glare windshield. It added nothing to aerodynamics and little to aesthetic appeal.

Full-length running boards were eliminated on some models and replaced with aluminum "entrance-steps" to add a sporting flair. The Cabriolet, and other body styles by request, had an unusual feature added, a third set of fenders just behind the front door. Often ridiculed, the extra set of splash aprons helped keep mud off of the rear compartment entrance-step for milady's safety. Fenders were made of flat steel through the 1925 model year with crowned fenders being offered beginning in 1923, but just on the Knickerbocker Cabriolet or by special request. Huge air shocks resembling artillery shells were an option at both front and rear and added to the car's intimidating appearance. Changes in styling were painfully slow and did not keep up with other higher priced cars in the industry. McFarlan would remind critics that they did not intend to be bound by yearly changes, but only made adjustments when they deemed them to be appropriate.

McFarlan benefited from advertising placed by parts suppliers (*Motor*, Feb. 1921).

Many of the fenders and other metal parts were made by McCombs and Sons, a metal fabricating shop also located in Connersville. The heavy metal fenders were hand hammered into shape using the Pettingell hammer machine, the frame of which is still located in the basement of the McCombs and Sons building. The hammering process would have made deafening noise for any persons working or living nearby.[34]

Excerpts from the McCombs and Sons shop ledger give some idea of the volume of business done by McCombs for McFarlan. The following entries are probably from 1923 or 1924.

McFarlan Motor Corporation

June 23	1 pr. Regular rear roadster long aprons	#P.14124	$ 8.00
June 23	10 pr. Regular Splashers	#P.13662	40.00
June 23	1 gas tank	#S.2001	10.00
June 29	10 pair regular fronts (fenders)	#P.13662	60.00
July 7	10 pair of no running board splashers	#P.13663	70.00
July 7	10 pair of rear fenders	#P.13363	60.00
July 15	15 pr front fenders	#P.14265	90.00
July 21	5 left hand only fronts 1920	#S.52108	15.00
Aug. 14	15 pair windshield visors	#14884	3.00
Sept. 11	5 pair reg. Fronts	P.15338	30.00
Sept. 29	4 pair of 1920 splashers	S. 2359	26.00
Oct. 13	Right hand front fender 1922	#S.2414	3.00
Oct. 16	3 pair of jockey Fenders	#P.16008	27.00

This well dressed 1922 McFarlan TV Sport Touring is pictured in front of the Marion County (Indiana) Public Library. This was the first year for the drum type Vesta headlights. One unusual feature on this car was the additional set of fenders in front of the rear doors (Indiana Historical Society).

Jockey fenders were apparently the extra fenders just behind the front door used mainly on the Knickerbocker Cabriolet. Replacement fenders and other metal parts were ordered from McCombs as needed, thus eliminating the necessity of keeping a large inventory of spare parts on hand.[35]

For 1923, McFarlan lowered prices substantially on many models. Most of the automobile manufacturers had done the price rollback about 18 months earlier during the recession of 1920–1921, but McFarlan held firm at that time. The 1923 price leader, if such a term was applicable, was the roadster, which was reduced from $6,300 to $5,400 while the coupe dropped from $7,500 to $6,720. After the price rollback, other styles were priced as follows: Sport Roadster at $5,600, 7-passenger Touring at $5,700, Sport Sedan at $6,600, 4-passenger Touring Sedan $6,720, 7-passenger Touring Sedan $6,810, Town Car or Limousine $6,900, and Suburban Sedan $7,000. Cars intended to be chauffeur driven did not receive the price break, so the Landaulet remained at $8,500 and the 7-passenger Knickerbocker Cabriolet commanded a whopping $9,000. The bare chassis could be had for $4,550. McFarlan cars ranged in weight from 4,600 pounds for the roadster to 5,200 for the 7-passenger Cabriolet.[36]

The huge twin valve engine with 572.5 c.i.d. was cooled by a G & O radiator; the lighting, ignition and starter were Westinghouse. One change in the power plant involved a switch to a Splitdorf double magneto. The clutch was a Merchant & Evans dry plate, and located directly under the front floorboards was the Brown-Lipe transmission with three speeds forward plus reverse. The Timken rear axle used a 3.65 gear ratio. Large 33 × 5 wheels seemed appropriate for the 140 inch wheelbase luxury automobile.[37]

Those who chose to pay the price of the Twin Valve Six did so knowing that their monetary investment would depreciate rapidly. Presumably, the ride was worth it just for the prestige connected with this luxury marque. By the time the car was just three years old, nearly all of the value had depreciated away. A TV roadster purchased new in 1923 for $5,400 was valued in 1926 at $256 to $363, depending on condition, at least a 93 percent drop in value.[38] Other less expensive cars also had a high rate of depreciation because the life expectancy of an automobile was just over five years, but a less expensive vehicle would be worth a similar amount as the McFarlan on a used car lot a few years later.

For several years up until 1924, McFarlan offered only large, expensive, custom built automobiles that were usually chauffeur driven. Industry trends by the mid–1920s had been toward smaller, easier to handle machines that were primarily owner driven. To address the changing market, a new, less expensive automobile was introduced that was powered by a lighter weight engine. It still had six cylinders, as McFarlan had been known for since their beginning, but it was much less complicated. This new series, known as the SV or Single Valve Six, was still considered to be a luxury car and was available as a 3-passenger roadster or 5-passenger phaeton for $2,500, a 4-passenger coupe or sedan for $3,000 or a 7-passenger sedan for $3,100. Within a few months, prices were raised $100

Many of the hand hammered fenders came from McCombs and Sons metal fabricating shop, also located in Connersville. This Pettingell hammer frame is still in the basement of their shop (photograph by author).

across the board on the junior series cars. This McFarlan, with its smaller six cylinder engine, had some formidable competition from well respected marques such as the Cadillac V-8 whose sedan listed for $3,195, Packard's 133 inch wheelbase 8 cylinder sedan for $2,885 or the Peerless 6-70 sedan for $2,765.

The Single Valve series cars weighed more than 1,000 pounds less than the TV series providing for much easier maneuverability. Power was supplied by a Wisconsin model Y engine with bore of $3\frac{3}{8}$ inches and stroke of 5 inches. It used a Delco ignition with Westinghouse generator and starter. The Timken rear axle carried a performance gear ratio of 4.90. Bodies were covered with aluminum just like the TV series, with hand hammered flat steel fenders. The radiator shell was plated with German silver just like the big Macs and a Lorraine driving light was mounted on the windshield. Instead of the monster 140 inch wheelbase of the TV series, the new smaller SV rode on a 127 inch platform.[39] McFarlan literature suggested that it would be a "companion" car maintaining the same high quality standards as the TV series.[40] Presumably, the new SV series was not intended to replace its custom built big brother, but might be a good choice for a second car for the family who had everything.

The company issued the following statement at the time of the SV introduction: "Although of smaller dimensions, the new and lighter McFarlan Six has many of the same characteristics that have made the custom-built McFarlan famous. Its coachwork is also

This Sport Touring came equipped with two extra emergency seats that folded into the rear cowl when not in use. Styling was virtually unchanged from 1922 through 1925 (*The McFarlan Six*).

Top: Built for four passengers on a wheelbase of 140 inches, this TV Touring Sedan sported wire wheels and a rear mounted trunk. *Bottom:* The Sport Sedan for six passengers featured landau irons, a leather top and the Valencia type windshield that was supposed to be glare free. Improving aerodynamics was not an issue with the most powerful engine in the industry (both photographs, *The McFarlan Six*).

The top-of-the-line Knickerbocker Cabriolet was appropriately renamed Town Car in 1924. This car displayed all of the goodies including fender mirrors, spare tire covers, windshield spotlight, coach lamps and trunk. Hand hammered crowned fenders were featured on this series beginning in 1923 (*The McFarlan Six*).

the product of the McFarlan body-shops; the same genuine leather upholstering is used; the same extraordinary care is exercised in the painting of the bodies, while mechanically, the car attains the same high grade degree of excellence."[41] The junior series of cars also maintained a similar appearance to the Twin Valve series.

For customers who chose to spend an extra $150, hydraulic brakes on all four wheels were available on both series of cars beginning with the 1924 models.[42] With their powerful engines that could propel the machines at breakneck speed, improved brakes should have been a must-have option for safety. One of the few changes in the TV series was the renaming of the Knickerbocker Cabriolet as the Town Car. That was more appropriate since the top did not fold as would have been expected on a cabriolet.

For 1925, the big TV series continued with few changes. On the Town Car, a temperature gauge was added to the dashboard instruments, making it much easier for the driver to monitor water temperature than via the thermometer in the radiator mounted Motometer. With the Motometer eliminated, one of the most collectable mascot ornaments ever offered appeared atop the radiator. The ornament featuring a crouched Atlas holding the earth appeared only on the senior series initially. All SV series still used the traditional Motometer to monitor water temperature. A more important improvement for the year, adding considerably to stopping ability, was the fitting of four-wheel hydraulic brakes as standard equipment on all models.

The larger Twin Valve series still offered the roadster at $5,400, the Sport Touring at $5,600, the 7-passenger touring at $5,700, the Coupe or Touring Sedan at $6,720, the

McFarlan was justly proud of the quality of its interior coachwork and offered various seating options (*The McFarlan Six*).

Suburban Sedan at $7,000 or the Town Car at $9,000. Balloon tires were available as a no-cost option to soften the ride and improve handling.[43]

In January, Chicago's Jubilee auto show celebrated 25 years of annually displaying the new models. McFarlan had been a regular participant, and for 1925 they showed three custom built jobs that had been sold even before the show opened. Their Town Car, which had been bought by Joseph J. Trinz, boasted the highest price of any vehicle at the show at $15,000. A type 147 touring car was sold to T.L. Williams for $8,000, well above the $6,720 normal asking price, and a model 75 SV sedan had been sold to F.M. Barnes for $3,900. Since all three buyers lived in the Windy City, they could admire their cars while on display and then drive them home when the show closed.[44]

Closed type bodies were really taking over the market. Industrywide in 1920, there were 245,114 open cars sold compared to 83,864 closed, a ratio of about three to one. By 1924 the figures had changed dramatically with 239,502 open cars selling versus 335,477 closed, the latter accounting for about 58 percent of the market. At McFarlan and other higher priced makes, the percentage of closed cars was even higher.[45] The market demand was demonstrated when McFarlan decided what types of body styles to showcase at the 1925 automobile shows, held in New York City and Chicago. Due to the popularity of the closed body design, their display, though made up of both the TV and SV series, included only one open model.[46]

The year 1925 also provided some unique challenges. Harry McFarlan's health was

Top: Beginning with the 1924 season, McFarlan offered a new Single Valve Six that rode on a 127 inch wheelbase. *Bottom:* The same high quality of workmanship that the TV series cars were known for was continued on the smaller Roadster for two passengers (both images, *The New and Lighter McFarlan Six*).

showing signs of failing. During the winter months, he spent several weeks confined to his home on West 8th Street, recovering from an illness.[47] As the year progressed, Harry's health remained poor, causing him to leave Connersville for the warm, dry air of Arizona. Other family members had already begun wintering in the Southwest. When Harry relocated, his trusted confidant, Burton Barrows, was left in charge. A potentially serious incident occurred in May when a fire started in the vicinity of the dry kiln of the motor room in the big factory building. It was early on a Saturday morning and the fire department responded quickly, averting what could have been a major disaster.[48] The factory stayed quite busy, albeit more in building bodies for other manufacturers than producing their own machines. A night shift was even added in order to keep up with business demands.[49]

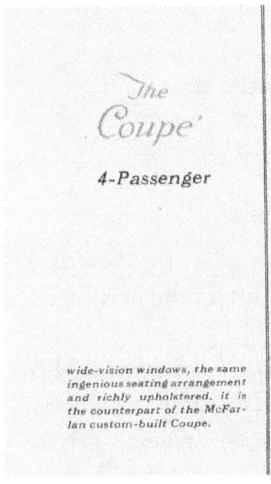

Top: The Single Valve Six Sedan was available for either five or seven passengers. *Bottom:* The Coupe for four passengers and all SV sixes carried the trademark McFarlan radiator shell plated with German silver (both images, *The New and Lighter McFarlan Six*).

As each new year approached, McFarlan management worked to showcase their cars in the major shows. Excerpts from a December 23, 1925, letter to George Sutton, Jr., describe their displays for the 1926 New York City event:

Mr. George W. Sutton, Jr.
6 East 45th Street
New York City, New York
Dear Sir,
   ... It will be a few days before the materials you requested will be available. In the meantime, it has occurred to me that it might possibly be well to give you a brief description of the particular cars we plan to exhibit at the New York Show. At that time there were will be exhibited two cars on our Twin Valve Six chassis and three cars on our Eight-in-Line chassis.

The Twin Valve Six is our DeLuxe model and is powered with a McFarlan designed and manufactured twin valve six cylinder engine which is quite the largest and most powerful engine used in any passenger automobile in this country or abroad. The engine itself develops 120 horsepower and has a piston displacement of 572 inches. All McFarlan cars are custombuilt and this particular job will be a very good example of McFarlan work. There will be a model T.V. 159 five passenger touring sedan, painted cream with black superstructure, with steel wheels and balloon tires and upholstered in cream colored novelty cloth. The model T.V. 177 seven passenger Suburban sedan is painted Egyptian Green with black wire wheels and balloon tires. This job is likewise trimmed with special novelty cloth, the color to harmonize with the paint.

On the eight cylinder line, there will be a model 42 Roadster, painted Bakst Green with orange wood wheels, orange stripe running the entire length of the body and orange underneath the fenders. This job is upholstered in tan Spanish leather and carries a rumble seat and a special compartment built for the purpose of carrying golf bags. The model 75 five passenger sedan, painted Ching Blue with Cooley Blue superstructure, has natural wood wheels and balloon tires. This job is trimmed in blue plush mohair striped with black. The model 74 Brougham, painted Egyptian Green with Brewster Green superstructure, carries green wood wheels and balloon tires and is trimmed in green broad cloth.

There are no striking changes in body types since it has always been McFarlan's policy to make changes as the need arose rather than to make them at any specific time.

Yours very truly,
McFarlan Motor Corporation
R.B. Belknap,
Second Vice President.[50]

It should be noted that there were no Single Valve sixes displayed at the New York show. They had obviously not sold well. The company had high hopes for the new Eight-in-Line as three of the five cars on display were that model.

Public sentiment for more cylinders had finally reached McFarlan management. The company had vowed from the very beginning to make cars with six cylinders only, but by the mid–1920s, 6-cylinder automobiles in the top price bracket just didn't get the attention they once did from prospective customers. Cadillac, Packard, Peerless, Lincoln and many more in the high- or even the mid-price range were using eight or more cylinders and had been doing so for years. McFarlan decided it was time to join the ranks, so a Lycoming Series H engine with a bore of 3 3/16 and stroke of 4½ inches was offered in what was known as the McFarlan Eight-in-Line. The clutch was from Borg and Beck and together with the Warner transmission, was assembled with the engine into a

The Single Valve Six engine was built by Wisconsin and developed 75 horsepower (*Motor Age*, Dec. 6, 1923).

unit power plant. The rear axle was from Timken with a ratio of 5.1 to 1 making for snappy performance, but limiting top-end speed and economy. Chassis lubrication for all-important bearings was done by the time-tested method of oil-cups with wick feed. The wheelbase of 131 inches was in keeping with the luxury car size expected from McFarlan, but the Eight-in-Line cars were considerably shorter and lighter than the Twin Valve series. Prices were competitive with other 8-cylinder luxury cars.[51]

The body types making up the 8-cylinder line were identical in price and equipment with those on the SV6 chassis with the exception of a town car available only with eight cylinders for $4,000. Since the straight eight with 131-inch chassis and the SV6 with 127-inch chassis listed for the same money, the Wisconsin engine cars immediately became obsolete. Open cars were fast fading from popularity, but all manufacturers still offered them. When comparison shopping in 1926, one could find a full range of prices, starting

Some of the 1925 TV series cars sported a mascot of Atlas holding the earth. The one pictured is sitting atop a regular radiator cap on an earlier car (photograph by author).

with the Ford Model T roadster that was available for a mere $260 without electric starter or $345 with. McFarlans in the SV6 line or the new straight eight offered roadsters or the 5-passenger touring for $2,650. Their nearest competitors were the Stearns Knight "S" priced at $2,395 and Dupont "D" at $2,600. Other close competitors were the Packard "6" at $2,585 and Franklin "11A" at $2,635. The senior TV series roadster cost $5,400, well above the Lincoln that listed for $4,000, but far short of the Stevens-Duryea "G" at $8,150. The big TV 7-passenger touring at $5,600 compared favorably with the Locomobile "90" that was priced at $5,500 and Cunningham "V" at $6,150.[52] The introduction of the Eight-in-Line engine made for unusual circumstances because cars with the 6-cylinder TV engine were considerably more expensive than the new 8-cylinder models that many customers viewed as more desirable.

Only a few significant changes were made in the TV series for 1926. Those included

Every available amenity was on this 1925 McFarlan Type 157 TV Special Berline (aka Town Car): rear trunk, fabric roof, six fenders, step plates, coach lamps, spare tire covers and Valencia windshield. This car has survived (*Motor Age*, Jan. 7, 1926).

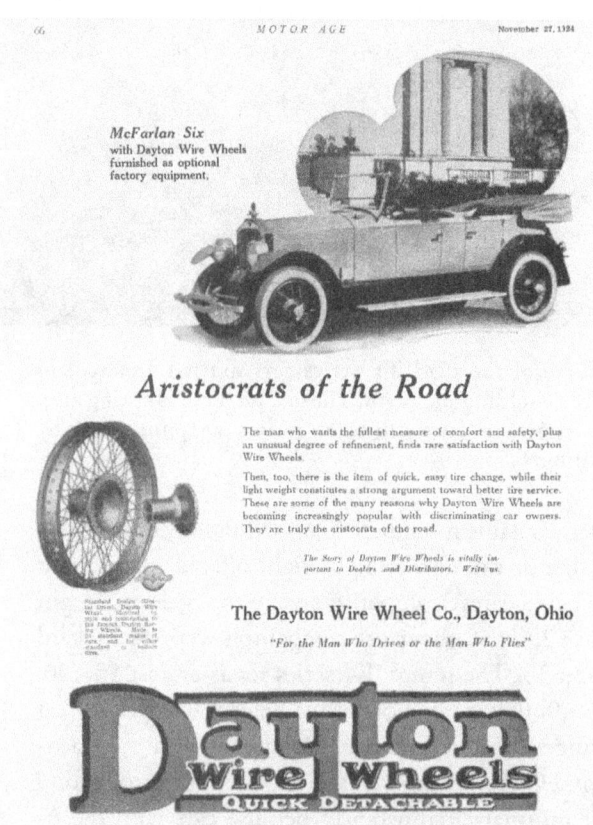

The Dayton Wire Wheel Company was pleased that McFarlan, the "Aristocrat of the Road," had chosen to use their wire wheels (*Motor Age*, Nov. 27, 1924).

replacing the multi-disk clutch with a single plate Borg & Beck unit, adopting DeJon electrical equipment and increasing the battery capacity. The Bowen system of chassis lubrication became standard; thus by pressing a plunger in the driver's compartment, the driver could send lubricant to all moving chassis parts. The vacuum tank was replaced with the autopulse which insured a constant supply of fuel in regulated quantities under pressure. All McFarlans sported the mighty Atlas radiator mascot, and crowned fenders became standard beginning with the 1926 models.

In 1926 the McFarlan organization celebrated 70 years of manufacturing in Connersville. One of the reasons given for the company's continued success was that high expectations had carried down from company management to the workmen. Many employees had been with the organization since their boyhood, while others had followed in the footsteps of their fathers. Tenures of 30 and even 40 years of faithful employment were not uncommon.

A.H. McFarlan still held the position of company president, although he had moved to Arizona and would never return to Connersville. Burton M. Barrows was vice president. Ed W. Cotton, better known as Ned, who had started working for C.E.J. McFarlan making carriages, had risen to the post of company secretary. Tom G. Norris, the factory superintendent, had been with the organization for 30 years, and Charles Reeder, superintendent of the paint department, started with the J.B. McFarlan Carriage Company 44 years earlier in 1882. Other employees in responsible positions included Paul Barrows, custom designer, and Robert B. Belknap, second vice president and advertising manager.[53]

McFarlan was justly proud of the workmanship that went into each car. The frame of the body was made of select second growth ash or elm and, to guard against imperfections, each piece was inspected before being assembled. These woods were chosen over other types that were more prone to splitting or warping under changing weather conditions. All wood joints were mortised and were made doubly firm with glue and countersunk screws. The heavy body sills were made of elm that had been shaped to conform exactly to the contour of the rigid metal chassis frame.

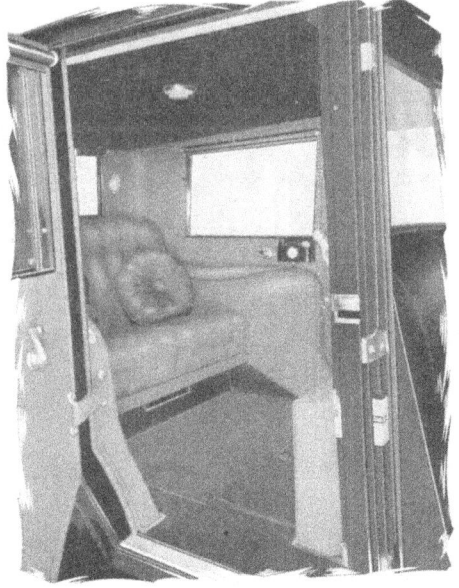

Top: Fitted to a 1926 Twin Valve Six Touring Sedan, the Valencia wide vision, nonglare, ventilating windshield with cast aluminum frame eliminated the necessity of wide front door posts. *Bottom:* Interior hardware and appointments were in keeping with the high quality of the body and chassis construction in the 1926 Twin Valve Six Touring Sedan (both photographs, *After Seventy Years of a "Settled Plan," 1926*).

McFarlan Coach Brougham
Style 879

McFarlan Roadster
Style 842

Top: McFarlan Coach Brougham Style 879. The McFarlan Eight-in-Line had a manageable 131 inch wheelbase. *Bottom:* The McFarlan Roadster Style 842 with rumble seat offered stylish transportation at the entry level price (both photographs, *McFarlan Eight-in-Line*).

All wood parts were saturated in a mixture of linseed oil, turpentine and varnish to protect against moisture and to preserve the wood. The company had used this method for several years, and older bodies that had been returned to the factory for refurbishing proved that the wood had held up well. The wood frame of the body was than covered with one-sixteenth inch thick aluminum to provide a strong lightweight unit that would insure its stability and eliminate rumbling noises. Doors were often a problem on many cars, but on a McFarlan, the edges of the door frames were reinforced with a strip of cold roll steel 1¼ by ⅛ inch securely screwed to the wood frame, and around which the aluminum covering was rolled. On closed bodies, top decks were made of ash rails covered with slats

*Automotive Industries
October 15, 1925*

THE McFARLAN COUPE

Exact Carburetion for McFarlan

The New Schebler Model "S" Carburetor has been adopted as standard equipment for McFarlan automobiles.

The superior performance obtained with this highly refined instrument was carefully verified by the McFarlan Motors Corporation, Connersville, Indiana, in deciding upon its use as standard equipment.

Wheeler-Schebler C rburetor Company
Indianapolis

SCHEBLER
The World's Finest CARBURETORS

Schebler carburetors had been used by many makes of automobiles over the years. The McFarlan name offered a bit of prestige to this supplier (*Automotive Industries*, Oct. 15, 1925).

The M^cFARLAN
Now adopts the Bowen System of Chassis Lubrication as Standard Equipment

McFARLAN TWIN VALVE SIX TOWN CAR

The Bowen System makes the lubrication of the chassis as simple and convenient as stepping on the starter. A push or two once a day on the lubricator button and every chassis bearing is properly and perfectly lubricated—automatically and simultaneously with oil in measured quantities. A drop or a teaspoonful to meet the need of each particular bearing.

BOWEN PRODUCTS CORPORATION
Auburn, New York

of Chassis Lubrication

The Bowen System is not an accessory but a standard equipment part that must be installed before the car leaves the factory

The Bowen System of Chassis Lubrication is fully protected by Letters Patent and Applications pending

Standard equipment on the Twin Valve series McFarlans for 1926 was the Bowen system of chassis lubrication. Pressing a pedal in the driver's compartment sent lubrication to all moving parts on the chassis (*Motor*, April 1926).

one and one half inch wide and set one inch apart. This was then covered with cotton to deaden any rumbling sound, and to provide a smooth surface for the top covering. McFarlan's claim was that the top, when completed, would be solid enough for a dance floor and as waterproof as was possible to make it.

Luxury was extended to the interior of closed cars in particular. Seat backs were wide and elegantly upholstered. A double set of fine-coiled wire springs, each encased in an individual cloth sack and covered with a thick layer of curled hair, provided for comfort. All closed bodies featured conveniently located courtesy lights, both in the top deck and in each rear corner. Lights also operated automatically as either rear door was opened or closed. Chauffeur driven closed cars were also equipped with a dictograph for ease of communication between the driver and the occupants of the rear compartment. Another touch of luxury was provided by the attractive vanity cases and smoking sets that were built-in features.[54] The Valencia windshield design, intended to eliminate glare, was used extensively on closed cars. If it helped reduce glare, it didn't add to the appearance of the vehicle. The painting process was speeded up with the introduction of the new duPont Duco system. The paints and varnishes used formerly had been applied by brush and took up to two weeks to dry. As if the TV series land yachts were not big enough already, a final adjustment to the car's length was made as a bit over an inch was added to the wheelbase, making it 141¼ inches long.[55]

The 1926 and 1927 model years were somewhat reminiscent of 1913 with three different engines in the lineup, each from a different manufacturer, powering three different size chassis. The Lycoming eight offered a great deal more value than the Wisconsin six which was subsequently dropped early in the 1927 season. The three series of cars, each with a different wheelbase, meant that there were about as many body styles offered as there were cars built. The Single Valve 6 series offered the Roadster, Sport Roadster, 5- and 7-passenger Tourings, Coupe, 5- and 7-passenger Sedans, Special Sedan, Brougham, and 5- and 7-passenger Suburban Sedans, all on a 127-inch wheelbase with prices ranging from $2,650 to $3,480. The Eight-in-Line offered 2- and 4-passenger Roadsters, 5- and 7-passenger Tourings, 5- and 7-passenger Sedans, 5- and 7-passenger Suburban Sedans, 4-passenger Coupe, 5-passenger Coach-Brougham and a Town Car, riding on a 131-inch wheelbase with a price range from $2,650 to $4,600. The senior TV series offered the Roadster, 4-passenger Sport Touring, Coupe, 4- and 7-passenger Touring Sedans, 6- and 7-passenger Sedans, Special Sedan, Enclosed Sedan, Suburban Sedan and Town Car, on the mammoth 141¼ inch wheelbase with prices ranging from $5,400 to $9,000.[56]

The company participated in the 1927 New York and Chicago auto shows with Robert Belknap and Paul Barrows present to accept orders. Five cars with special bodies were taken to the East Coast show to win the approval of onlookers. A special engine stand was used to demonstrate the powerful TV power plant. The McFarlan display was considered to be one of the most impressive in the show.[57] McFarlan displayed seven models of the Eight-in-Line and TV series at the Windy City show.[58] In early 1927, R.B. Belknap of McFarlan claimed that all was well — which was perhaps stretching things just a bit.[59]

Sales, especially of the monstrous TV series, were dismal as more and more car owners

McFarlan Twin Valve Six body styles for 1927 included few standard offerings, but custom bodies were still available (*McFarlan 1856–1927 Custom Built*, 1927).

chose to drive for themselves and found a smaller vehicle to be more manageable. Late in the model year, McFarlan announced the addition of a 5-passenger phaeton priced at $3,180 for the 8-cylinder chassis. The Eight-in-Line chassis was lengthened from 131 inches to 136 inches at this time also. On both series, a Bowen central lubrication system became standard. With the press of a foot plunger, lubricant was dispersed under pressure from a central reservoir to lubricate the entire chassis. More importantly and a sign of the times, four models of the TV series were dropped, the 4-passenger coupe and three sedan models.[60] The custom body department was still keeping fairly busy with a variety of jobs. They continued building closed bodies that were used by several quality makers of passenger vehicles including Locomobile, Premier, Auburn and Marmon. Two of the most desirable bodies built that year, a boat roadster and a touring, were completed for Duesenberg and were mounted on their chassis.

In spite of low production, 1928 saw the most significant styling changes in the TV series since its introduction at the beginning of the decade. The sedans had a considerably lower, more modern profile with body styling similar to the Auburn units that McFarlan had been building. A new 4-passenger Town Car was offered for the first time at a substantially lower price of $4600. Also for 1928, Ilco-Ryan-Lite headlamps were featured on the Eight-in-Line and available as an option in place of the Vesta lamps on the TV series. The new illuminating device was manufactured and marketed by the Indiana Lamp Company of Connersville, through an exclusive arrangement with Walter D'Arcy Ryan, Director of the Illuminating Engineering Laboratories of the General Electric Company. The Ilco-Ryan-Lite, easily identified by its very shallow bucket, was a significant improvement in lighting to help make night driving safer.[61]

For the junior series, Lycoming continued to supply the straight eight engine with the 5-main-bearing crankshaft, lubricated by full pressure to all crankshaft and connecting

McFarlan Eight-in-Line body styles for 1927 (*McFarlan 1856–1927 Custom Built*, 1927).

rod bearings. Fuel was delivered via a vacuum feed and the electrical system was by Delco using a Willard battery. McFarlan eights used a large 33 × 6.20 tire size; however, lower pressure balloon tires had replaced the high pressure skins providing a softer ride.[62]

Tragedy struck on the night of March 30, 1928. Burton Barrows had gone back to the factory to investigate the circumstances surrounding the disappearance of a quantity of upholstery. He had made the rounds with night watchman Thomas Norris, and had stayed on the third floor while Norris completed his circuit. At midnight, when the watchman made his rounds again, he didn't find Barrows. He checked and Barrows' car was still where it had been parked earlier, so employees Paul Barrows and Robert Belknap were summoned to help search the building. After scouring the building for two hours, they found Barrows' body at the bottom of the elevator shaft. It was presumed that he had pulled the cord to bring the elevator down from the fourth floor, had failed to step back and was struck on the head as the elevator came down, causing him to be hurled from the third floor to the bottom of the shaft.

Barrows was in the prime of his life at 50 years of age when tragically killed. He had started with McFarlan just out of high school, beginning in sales. From 1904 until 1910, he held the position of manager of the company branch in Kansas City, Missouri. In 1913, Barrows helped organize the McFarlan Motor Corporation and, along with A.H. McFarlan, owned nearly all of the assets. He held the position of first vice president, treasurer and general manager. Since Harry McFarlan had left the city three years earlier, Barrows had

Cars built by McFarlan need no praise ....

THE name McFarlan has an assured position in motordom and in the public's esteem—a position well earned and held by years of conscientious devotion to the task of making a car of distinctive merit.

The public has grown to expect its combination of beautiful lines, comfort, luxurious appointments and a smooth flow of power.

It is not surprising that the McFarlan Motor Corporation should have adopted Lycoming Motors to power its Eight-in-line models. This is in keeping with its policy of giving car owners all and more than the experienced and discriminating motorist expects in power, performance and service.

LYCOMING MANUFACTURING COMPANY
Makers of Fine Fours, Sixes and Eights-in-Line
WILLIAMSPORT, PENNSYLVANIA
Export Department—44 Whitehall Street, New York City
Member of Motor Truck Industries, Inc., of America

LYCOMING
Motors

Lycoming provided the Eight-in-Line engine for McFarlan, and also gave them a bit of complimentary advertising (*Motor Age*, Oct. 28, 1926).

the full responsibility of running the factory.[63] Sadly, no one else had or was given the authority to keep the plant operating, and soon suppliers began seeking payment for materials that had been ordered. Although Harry McFarlan's health improved substantially while in Arizona, he did not return to Connersville.

In late June, Raymond S. Springer was appointed temporary receiver of the McFarlan Motor Corporation. Hyatt Frost, an attorney for the company, said the company was expected to complete a $40,000 order for bodies by the end of July.[64] The company was still a going business, but lacked anyone in the leadership role to pay bills and oversee the operation. Although one of the oldest and most respected concerns in the field, the company would soon cease to exist.

By August of 1928, the factory had come to a standstill. Over the past three years, work had gone on even though Harry McFarlan had left Connersville for Arizona because of health issues. His trusted confidant, Burton Barrows, struggled on, holding things together until he was killed. Two creditors filed a petition for receivership, a move made partly to force the company to declare its intentions.[65] A.H. McFarlan, company president, chose not to return and resume his responsibilities, so the company folded.

McFarlan Motor Corporation next appeared in Kokomo, Indiana. A company by the name of the General Parts Corporation had been formed by a merger of remnants of the Apperson and the Haynes companies, both of Kokomo.[66] They purchased the parts inventories of automobile companies that had gone out of business and sold them piece by piece. Flyers were sent out to McFarlan owners and repair businesses advertising the availability of various repair parts. It seems somewhat ironic that the McFarlan company name ended up in the city that had, more than 40 years earlier, offered free land to J.B. McFarlan if he would build a new factory in that community.

The big factory on Mount Street sat unoccupied from August 1928 until April 1, 1929. On that date, Ellis W. Ryan, a vice president of the Auburn Automobile Company, announced that Auburn had purchased the McFarlan Motor Corporation plant. No definite plan for use of the facility was noted, but expectations were that Auburn's increased production might bring a need for more space.[67] The additional space was put to use for storage of bodies and various other parts and the buildings were used for several years until being razed in about 1939.

Auburn Motor Company had already been involved significantly in Connersville for several years. Their bodies had been built by the Central Manufacturing Company and by McFarlan. As the need for automobile production increased, Auburn had purchased the bankrupt Lexington Motor Car Company and the Ansted Engine plants, located just a few blocks to the north. Preparations for production of complete six-cylinder Auburn closed cars had already started in the old Lexington facility with the first complete car being turned out early in 1929. Auburn automobile production continued in those buildings into 1936. Also, the 1936 and 1937 Cord 810 and 812 automobiles were manufactured in those same buildings.

McFarlan Motor Company was mostly owned by Harry McFarlan, Burton Barrows and a few trusted outsiders. That was probably an advantage in keeping a tight rein on quality control, but it was a tremendous disadvantage when it came to keeping up with the fast changing automotive industry. The massive TV Series cars were head turners in 1920 with Rolls-Royce type radiators and the most powerful engines in any U.S. passenger car, but by midway through the decade, the rest of the industry had moved to smaller, more user friendly vehicles intended to be owner driven, and with more modern styling. Also, the 6-cylinder engine had served McFarlan well, but their tenacity of relying only on the six until 1926 while other manufacturers of medium and top end vehicles had, years earlier, improved performance and added appeal with eight or even twelve cylinders cost McFarlan sales and prestige.

Few McFarlan automobiles found homes in their city of origin, or for that matter, in the state of Indiana, as their major markets were in large cities, especially on the East and West coasts. One elderly gentleman, Don Squires, in 2008 remembered getting an occasional ride to town in an impressive nearly new McFarlan sedan owned by Maynard Erb, who lived north of Connersville, and was a prosperous farmer and businessman. Even so, local owners were the exception rather than the rule.[68]

So, what happened to McFarlan? First of all, it is rather amazing that McFarlan motorized vehicles were ever produced. Harry, the grandson of the company founder, was interested in the automobile business and was given permission to proceed, but the earlier generation of McFarlans, Harry's cousins and uncles, effectively washed their hands of the operation. They took little interest, choosing to invest their financial resources

The 1928 Eight-in-Line Custom Sport Phaeton Model 844 used the newly developed Ilco-Ryan-Lite headlamps (*McFarlan Eight-in-Line*, 1928).

MCFARLAN EIGHT-IN-LINE
Custom Five Passenger Coupe
Model 880

MCFARLAN EIGHT-IN-LINE
Custom Seven Passenger Sedan
Model 886

Top: An unusual body style was this Custom Five Passenger Coupe, Model 880. The wheelbase on the 8-cylinder cars had been lengthened to 136 inches. *Bottom:* An ideal family car was the Eight-in-Line Model 886 Custom Seven Passenger Suburban Sedan. The illustrations were done by E. Pierre Wainwright, a local artist and illustrator (both images, *McFarlan Eight-in-Line*, 1928).

One of the last of the big Twin Valve Sixes was truly a handsome automobile with up-to-date styling—too little, too late (courtesy Keith Marvin).

elsewhere. Harry had limited mechanical knowledge and was therefore dependent on others for advice.

It took several years to settle on a particular engine manufacturer. Even McFarlan's introductory catalog for the TV Series in 1920 acknowledged, "The first few years of this experience covered work with many different types of sixes, including various locations of the valves, sizes of displacement and types of cylinder blocks."[69] Even more time was taken getting past experimental gadgets such as compressed air starters, pneumatic gear shifting devices and cantilever springs.

Product promotion went gangbusters early on by entering competition and advertising in nationally circulated magazines such as *The Saturday Evening Post, McClure's* and others. McFarlan's ads plus racing successes brought far more demand for automobiles than the company was in any way prepared to meet. Production was low and company management chose to keep it that way. By the late teens advertising was all but discontinued, except for high quality catalogs aimed at those able to afford such a vehicle, and small, non-illustrated ads in trade magazines. McFarlan vehicles weren't even advertised in the city where they were manufactured except on rare occasions. Then, as noted earlier, the rest of the industry left this high-quality prestige marque in the proverbial dust with smaller, more easily maneuverable cars that had more up-to-date styling. But what actually brought an end to the company before the Great Depression had a chance to weed out small producers was the demise of company leaders.

Most automobile manufacturers used slogans or catchy phrases to promote their products. Packard used the slogan "Ask the man who owns one" and Cadillac became known as "The standard of the world." McFarlan toyed with several different slogans beginning with "The Six at the Price of the Four." Several years later, "The Hercules of the Hills" appeared in ads. In the late teens, the slogan "By This Sign" appeared on some advertising. The origin of that phrase is credited to Constantine the Great, during his march on Rome in the year 312. He saw a luminous cross in the sky with the translated words "By this conquer." He did conquer, and the statement "By this sign shall ye conquer" became attributed to his efforts.[70] In the 1920s, the most often printed slogan and the one the company became best known for was "Custom Built by McFarlan." It was an appropriate description of how the company was doing business at the time.

Alfred Harry McFarlan, the organizer of the automobile effort, was a mere 43 years old when he left Connersville in 1925, placing the management of the business he had helped to build into the hands of trusted friends. Indeed, after he relocated to the southwest, Harry's health improved to the extent that he became active in several social activities.

The Ilco-Ryan-Lite headlamps were manufactured by the Indiana Lamp Company of Connersville, Indiana (*Automobile Trade Journal*, Jan. 1927).

CUSTOM-BUILT
MOTOR CARS
COACHWORK
MOTORS

McFarlan Motor Corporation
Connersville, Indiana, U. S. A.

CABLE ADDRESS
"CUSTOMBILT, CONNERSVILLE"
BENTLEY'S
COMPLETE PHRASE CODE

Jan. 23, 1928.

To Whom It May Concern:

    Lawrence Wilhite has been in our employ for a period of eight years and we can cheerfully recommend him as being industrious, honest, and capable.

    During his time of employment here he has been stock keeper, shipping clerk, and also had some office experience. We feel sure that he will prove satisfactory in any employment given him.

Very truly yours,
McFARLAN MOTOR CORPORATION,

E.W.Cotton,
Secretary.

MML

It became apparent in early 1928 that employees needed to be looking for more permanent employment. Efforts were made to help the long-time employees find suitable jobs (courtesy James Wilhite).

He never returned to Connersville until his ashes were brought back after his death. Harry died December 1, 1937, at his home near Phoenix.[71]

    Ned Cotton, one of the signers of the articles of incorporation, was the trusted salesman who made the deal with the Smith Funeral Home for their combination ambulance hearse. He also engineered several other high profile sales for McFarlan and became the company secretary, but after the factory closed, he drifted from one company to another trying to survive through the Great Depression hawking appliances or whatever product seemed to show promise. Other employees had equally difficult times as the company that had provided support for so many families for 72 years was no more.

Top: The big plant on Mount Street was closed in August of 1928 because of lack of leadership (*The McFarlan Six*). *Below:* New replacement bodies were available at bargain prices from McFarlan Motor Corporation, Kokomo, Indiana.

McFarlan prices had been high and resale values very low. The 1931 *Kelley Blue Book*, one common indicator of used car values, listed a three-year-old Twin-Valve Six 5-passenger sedan that sold new for $6,720 as being worth $335, less than 5 percent of its original cost. Even worse off was the customer who purchased a new Town Car for $9,000 in 1928 only to see it valued at $300 in 1931, just 3 percent of the original investment. True, 1931 was a depression year and McFarlan had become an orphan by then, but the value of those big machines skidded in a free-fall. The smaller Eight-in-Line sedan with the Lycoming engine didn't fare any better. Its original price was $3,380, but 36 months later it was valued at $120, a drop of 97 percent.[72] Many other cars

suffered a similar drop in value during this period. Paying a premium price to begin with didn't help much when the car had some wear on it and had lost its luster.

Whereas many Model T, Model A and other common cars spent their final days plowing farm fields or pulling hay wagons after being converted into tractors, the powerful engines of the McFarlan relegated those vehicles to become tow trucks, farm trucks, or often, the source of power for some stationary use.

6

McFarlans That Have Survived the Years

It is always a mystery why some makes of automobiles seem to have a higher survival rate than others. McFarlan is one of those with a better than average rate even though the number accounted for in the following list is small. For the average auto that had gone through the rigors of everyday use and abuse, 75 years later, there may be one remaining for every 1,000 that were produced. McFarlan's yearly production was never more than a few hundred and its total output in nearly 20 years of production only around 2,400. In their 1967 book *What Was the McFarlan?*, Keith Marvin, Alvin J. Arnheim and Henry H. Blommel identified 18 surviving vehicles. More than 40 years later, this author has accounted for a similar number of cars, for a ratio of one survivor for about each 135 produced. Most McFarlans just weathered away. The wood framing in bodies, though put together by master craftsmen to withstand the jostling of rough roads, was no match for the ravages of nature — sun, wind, rain and snow. When the bodies had long since lost their luster and were no longer keeping out the elements, their powerful engines were oftentimes removed to be used and abused running sawmills, pile driving rigs and other non-glamorous but necessary tasks. Other factors significantly reduced the number of old car survivors of all makes. One was the Great Depression, which reduced the values of used vehicles to nearly zero. Also, a social issue developed during these hard times when so many people were accepting public assistance just to survive. Being seen in ultra-luxurious automobiles such as the Twin Valve McFarlan, often chauffeur driven, was no longer advisable. Outright contempt was sometimes shown to those who openly flaunted their wealth. Then came World War II and the necessary scrap drives in which patriotic citizens often turned salvageable machines into scrap metal for armament. It is amazing that any McFarlans survived to be revered today.

1870s McFarlan Carriage

Built by J.B. McFarlan in the 1870s, this carriage represents the era of the horse-drawn vehicle. It is presently owned by the Fayette County Historical Museum, Connersville, Indiana. One interesting feature is the front seat backs that can be folded flat to permit the carriage to be driven from the back seat. The way home with a date could

This McFarlan built carriage from the 1870s is awaiting restoration. The carriage is owned by the Fayette County Historical Museum, Connersville, Indiana (photograph by author).

"J.B. McFarlan, Connersville, Ind." is identified as the maker of the carriage (photograph by author).

be a cozy affair with minimal attention to the route taken if the horse knew its way. This choice piece of local history was purchased on eBay in 2006 and is currently being restorated. The history of the carriage is unknown except that it came from northern Indiana. The name-tag "J.B. McFarlan — Connersville, Ind." indicates that this carriage was made before the McFarlan sons joined their father and formed the J.B. McFarlan Carriage Company in 1883.

1911 Toy Tonneau

This car had been out in a field for several years before it came into the possession of Bob Woodward of Bozeman, Montana. The man he got it from said his grandfather had bought two new McFarlans so he could get the dealership and thereby receive a discount. A hundred years ago, some enterprising customers could still give a lesson on how to save money while getting the car they desired. This McFarlan Little Six is the oldest known example of this marque. It is missing several key components including the Brownell engine, transmission, steering wheel and pedals.[1]

1917 Ninety Touring

The Harrah Automobile Collection in Nevada preserved hundreds of unusual automobiles including this 1917 model Ninety touring car that is powered by a Teetor-Hartley T head engine. After the Harrah collection was sold, this early McFarlan was purchased and has been restored by Harvey Harper, a car dealer in Eureka, California. It has been driven on numerous antique automobile tours and is thought to be the oldest McFarlan in running condition.

1917 McFarlan Ninety Touring owned by Harvey Harper. The car is a veteran of many antique automobile tours (courtesy Floyd Myers for Harper Motors Antique Auto Division, Eureka, California).

1919 Ninety owned by the Canton Classic Car Museum, Canton, Ohio (courtesy Char Lautzenheiser, Canton Classic Car Museum).

Originally a 7-passenger touring, this 1919 Ninety now carries a beautifully constructed boattail replacing the missing back part of the body (courtesy Char Lautzenheiser, Canton Classic Car Museum).

1919 McFarlan Ninety

This unusual automobile is owned by Canton Classic Car Museum, Canton, Ohio. The restoration is being done with a custom wood boattail body. It appears to have been a touring car with the back section removed, before the new rear deck was added. In the mid–1960s, the car was owned by Vernon Stone of Austerlitz, NY.[2]

1919 McFarlan Ninety Type 125

This 1919 McFarlan Type 125 4-passenger sport touring carries serial number 19133 and motor number 2692. The car was purchased new by Wallace "Wally" Reid, a star of the silent films. Once part of the Harrah Automobile Collection, it is now owned by the Fountainhead Antique Auto Museum in Fairbanks, Alaska. Special equipment includes a tonneau windshield, special side lamps and drum type headlamps from a later model McFarlan.

Wallace Reid's 1919 Ninety Type 125 Sport Touring is fitted with headlamps from a later McFarlan (courtesy Willy Vinton for the Fountainhead Antique Automobile Museum).

1921 Twin Valve Six Type 147 Seven Passenger Touring

Remarkably, this 90-year-old car, serial number 21368 and engine number D2236V, is almost entirely original. The leather upholstery is still the high-quality material installed by the factory and the paint, with the exception of that on the hood, is still what was carefully brushed on in 1921. (The hood was repainted after an engine fire.) Present owner Wellington Morton III of St. Johns, Florida, an avid car collector, was invited to drive

1921 Twin Valve Six Type 147 Seven Passenger Touring owned by Wellington Morton III (courtesy Wellington Morton III).

this car around the Indianapolis Motor Speedway and display it at the track as part of the Speedway's centennial celebration in 2011.

1923 Type 154 Knickerbocker Cabriolet

This Type 154 Knickerbocker Town Car was once owned by Fatty Arbuckle, a popular film comedian, screenwriter and director in the silent and early talkie period. The car had been ordered by Wallace "Wally" Reid, another film star, but Reid died before the car

1923 Knickerbocker Cabriolet, serial no. 23016 and engine no. D-2512V, was originally ordered by Wally Reid, but was completed for Roscoe "Fatty" Arbuckle upon Reid's death. It is now a choice attraction of the Nethercutt Collection (courtesy Skip Marketti).

The canopy fastened onto the McFarlan's roof, providing shade for actor/director Arbuckle (courtesy Randy Ema).

was finished, so Arbuckle assumed the contract and became the first owner. Some touches were added for Arbuckle: a red and white canopy that snapped onto the back of the roof provided a shaded rest area and the director's chair with his name embroidered on it made an acceptable place to observe the goings on. This red Knickerbocker Cabriolet is presently owned by the Nethercutt Collection, which purchased this rare vehicle July 31, 1968, from Tom Barrett and has since restored it. Previous owners were Milford H. Gould, Nelson Holmwood, Elliott Wiemer and Arbuckle. The serial number is 23016 and the engine number D-2512V.

1923 TV Sport Touring

Owned by John R. Gambs of Lafayette, Indiana, it is one of the few McFarlans whose complete history is known. This unusual Twin Valve 4-passenger Touring, serial

1923 Twin Valve 4-passenger Sport Touring owned by John Gambs of LaFayette, Indiana. David LeRoy Small was the original owner of the 1923 4-passenger Sport Touring. He earned enough while working for the Panama Canal Company to purchase his dream car when he returned home, but he died a few years later from malaria that he had contracted while in Panama (courtesy John Gambs).

number 23061 and motor number D2556V, was purchased new by LeRoy Small, who was born in 1871 in Berkeley County, West Virginia. After reaching adulthood, he took a job as an engineer for the Panama Canal Company soon after the new water passageway was opened. He earned and saved a considerable amount of money while working in the tropics during the teens and early '20s. When Small returned to the states, he made Pittsburgh his home and he sought out the fastest, most powerful, flashiest red motor-car he could find. This 1923 McFarlan 4-passenger sport touring fit the bill perfectly. He drove the car for a few years, but died of malaria on February 8, 1926, having contacted the disease while in Panama.[3] A nephew who lived in Martinsburg, West Virginia, inherited the sporty red chariot and in 1948, sold it to Ralph and Margaret Burkhart, who had a small automobile museum in Martinsburg. The red McFarlan became the prize of the collection. It was even pictured on the front cover of an issue of *Antique Automobile,* the bi-monthly organ of the Antique Automobile Club of America.[4] After Mr. Burkhart passed away, the current owner, John Gambs, an attorney from LaFayette, Indiana, heard about the car, flew down to see it and made the deal to purchase it. It has had just four owners and is now back in its home state of Indiana, where it was manufactured.

1924 Type 154 Town Car

From its introduction in 1917 through 1923, this body style was known as the Knickerbocker Cabriolet. For 1924, the more appropriate name Town Car became its

1924 Twin Valve Town Car owned by the Fayette County Historical Museum, Connersville, Indiana (photograph by author).

The driver's compartment of the 1924 Town Car was finished in quality materials but offered few creature comforts. The centralized control on the steering column includes ignition switches and starter button (photograph by author).

designation. This impressive vehicle, ID#2531, is owned by the Fayette County Historical Museum in Connersville, Indiana. The earliest history known about this car is that it is believed to have been part of the collection of D. Cameron Peck in the 1940s. He advertised it for sale in 1949. An article in a 1949 Tacoma, Washington, newspaper tells of the relic having been driven 2,250 miles from Chicago to Tacoma by two men who carried no tools. Ten days and six flat tires later, it was delivered to car collector Ed Griffin.[5] Later, the ownership of this prestige car passed to J.P. Wallerich, also of Tacoma. Eventually, Gary Anderson became the proud owner and the majestic Town Car took up residence in California. In 1987 it became the property of the Imperial Palace Collection and was restored by Joe Crusis who ran Crusis Classic Auto Restoration in Chico, California. In a telephone interview, Mr. Crusis said he remembered the big Town Car well. It was in good condition when it came to him. In restoring it, he did a repaint, replaced the upholstering and performed some mechanical work, but the original German silver plating on the radiator and headlights was not refinished and remains in excellent condition.[6] In the late 1990s, several cars from the Imperial Palace collection were sold to Dean Kruse of Auburn, Indiana. Kruse had no particular interest in the majestic TV Town Car and was willing to sell it at to the Fayette County Historical Museum in Connersville, Indiana, whose members were wanting to acquire a locally made automobile. The majestic Town Car is back home in Connersville and is the highlight of the museum display.

1924 Single Valve Coupe

This is the only Single Valve McFarlan with Wisconsin engine known to exist. The present owners are J.W. and Barbara Selveira of Oakland, California. Their research indicates that Jack Warner of Warner Bros. Studios had a fetish for McFarlans and bought several new ones to use in movie making. Supposedly, theirs was used to carry Rin-Tin-Tin around.[7] In the 1960s, it found a home in the Harrah Automobile Collection in Reno, Nevada. It carries serial no. 385 and engine no. 1397.

1924 McFarlan Single Valve Six Coupe. Its early history is not fully established, but by the mid–1960s, it was part of the Harrah Collection. Current owners are J.W. and Barbara Selveira of Oakland, California (courtesy Keith Marvin).

1924 Twin Valve Six Model 157 Suburban

This car, presently owned by Shawn Miller of Indianapolis, Indiana, features division glass and hydraulic brakes. Carrying serial number 23293 and engine number D2708V, it had an original selling price of $7,950. Previous known owners include Warner Bros. studios, the William Harrah Collection, Auto Gems Museum, and Mark Hyman.

Originally selling for $7,950, this 1924 Twin Valve Six Model 167 Suburban (serial no. 23293; engine no. D2708V) is owned by Shawn Miller of Indianapolis. Miller drove it on the Indianapolis Motor Speedway in May 2011, during the Speedway's 100th anniversary celebration (courtesy Gary L. Groves).

1924 Twin Valve Roadster

The history of this car, showing serial number 23131 and engine number D2649V, is also fairly complete. It was originally a graduation gift for a daughter of the Goodrich tire family. Most any young person would have yearned to start out adult life with transportation of this caliber, but few had such an opportunity. In 1950, this sporty roadster was purchased by E.J. Leap of Hyndman, Pennsylvania, and some of the family drove it on the 1951 Glidden Tour.[8] After Mr. Leap passed away, the roadster languished in storage for more than 50 years until it was finally auctioned off and purchased by Mark Smith. Mr. Smith has a museum in central Virginia where this car will be on display at times.

1925 Enclosed Limousine

It is always interesting when previous owners of an antique automobile have been documented, and it is especially intriguing when well known or interesting personalities have been involved. This limousine is one of the truly unique cars that McFarlan built and with an unusual and interesting history. Pure sentimentality may be the chief reason for the survival of this car. In 1923 a Russian nobleman fleeing from the uncertainties of post–Bolshevik Revolution Russia came to the safety and freedom of the United States, settling in Los Angeles. After purchasing a luxurious home in Hollywood Hills, he returned to Europe to collect his family and servants and bring them to their new home. On the way East, the nobleman stopped off at Connersville, Indiana, where he met with McFarlan factory representatives, ordered and paid for in gold, two monstrous McFarlan Twin Valve

Top: This impressive enclosed limousine was once owned by a Russian nobleman who paid in gold for the limousine and a McFarlan touring car. *Bottom:* An ornate Russian trunk was carried on the trunk rack. When the trunk was removed, the rack could be used to provide space for resting (both photographs courtesy Craig Karr).

Sixes: one 7-passenger touring car and this enclosed drive limousine with all of the amenities. Delivery was arranged to take place upon the return of the family from Europe in 1925. The entourage did make it back across the Atlantic and received their expertly crafted touring car and limousine. The nobleman drove one of the behemoths with his family and a chauffeur drove the other. They presumably enjoyed the prestige provided by the two McFarlans until the stock market crash in October 1929 wiped out their investments. With the onset of the Great Depression, the new immigrants were left in a strange country with few resources. The luxurious home was sold, as were the two McFarlans, and the Russians returned to Europe, believing that without their wealth, their hope of survival was more promising in Europe.

There was no real market for the McFarlans, but an Oldsmobile dealer in Glendale, H.F. Gearhart, obtained the cars to display in front of his dealership as an oddity. The touring car soon deteriorated due to sitting out in the weather and was junked. The limousine had a kinder fate. After Gearhart died in 1934, the dealership was taken over by Donald Bernette. He wasn't interested in keeping the old car, so, when approached to sell the big McFarlan, he grabbed the opportunity and Charles Bernhardt, a young enthusiast, became the new owner. Bernhardt tucked the giant limousine away hoping to restore it some day.[9] Years passed by with the most important thing being keeping bills paid and food on the table. Eventually finances improved and a new home with a large garage was built on a prime lot in Palos Verdes. Although the desire to restore the enclosed limousine remained, the opportunity never came and 40 years later, his health deteriorating, Bernhardt decided to sell. When approached by Craig Karr in 1974, Bernhardt at first refused, but upon reconsideration, decided it would be best for all concerned if he let the car go to someone with the resources and the ability to bring it back as a show piece. There have been just two owners in the past 75 years who have watched over this most unusual machine.

When Craig Karr got the limousine, he did what Bernhardt had dreamed of doing. He restored the limousine to its original glory. Some of the unusual features about this car include the large ornate Russian trunk that rests on the teakwood luggage deck at the rear. There is a long striped green and white tent that attaches to a row of metal fittings across the top of the leather at the rear roofline. The tent extends out nearly nine feet, held by two long brass and wood poles. At the top of the poles are brass eagles. The tent would give shelter from the sweltering sun on the family's trip West, or possibly provide overnight accommodations where none existed. By removing the trunk from the rear deck, a space was made to attach canvas cushions to the teakwood for comfortable sitting. The tent, poles, cushions and a lunch basket were stored inside the trunk.

A picture of the car as it appeared when new can be seen on page 202. The ornate Russian trunk, the side coach lamps and the correct fender mounted mirrors had been removed for restoration when the photos were taken. Karr believes that the wife of the nobleman was a sister of the Tsar of Russia. Karr is planning a trip to Russia hoping to build interest within the Russian government to purchase his car because of its connection to that country's past.

1925 McFarlan Roadster

This beautiful roadster is owned by the Indianapolis Motor Speedway Museum, Indianapolis, Indiana. It came from the St. Paul, Minnesota, area. The car had had an earlier restoration, but was showing signs of aging so it was restored again in 1997 by the museum.

1925 Twin Valve Six Roadster owned by the Indianapolis Motor Speedway Museum (courtesy Kenneth Lane).

1925 McFarlan Twin Valve Roadster

What a great ride could be had in this 1925 TV Roadster that was specially equipped with a factory installed instrument panel in the rumble seat. In the 1930s, the car was acquired by Don John Baumgart's father. The car had come from Brockton, Massachusetts, but spent many years in the Evansville, Indiana, area with the Baumgart family. In 1971, the "Big Mac" changed hands going to Joe Gruver of Phoenix, Arizona, in exchange for a Mercedes-Benz. Gruver completely restored the roadster even though it was in good condition when he got it.[10]

This once restored roadster was badly damaged by fire in the mid–1990s. The fire was started by a battery charger that was being used at the time. Since that unfortunate incident, this rare roadster has passed from one owner to another awaiting the needed repair. Dennis Gibbs is the current owner.

Cars don't always remain in mint condition as desired. This 1925 Twin Valve Roadster has been damaged by fire since it was photographed (courtesy Albert Mroz).

1926 TV Coupe

The only known Twin Valve Coupe to survive may have been the only one produced. Previous known owners include Craig Karr, Jack Passey and Johnny Crowell. It is currently owned by Dennis Gibbs.

This 1926 Twin Valve Six Coupe may have been the only one produced. It is presently owned by Dennis Gibbs (courtesy Jack Passey).

1926 TV Type 145 Touring

This 1926 Twin Valve Six Touring, serial no. 23407, engine no. D-2818V, is one of the McFarlans claimed to have been owned by Jack Dempsey. Since the accompanying photo was taken, the car has been restored by the Imperial Palace Collection and has found a new owner.

1926 Twin Valve Six Touring serial number 23407, engine number D-2818V, is claimed to have once been owned by Jack Dempsey. Since this photograph was taken, the car has been restored by the Imperial Palace Collection (author's collection).

1926 TV Roadster

Like several McFarlans, this roadster was purchased new by an important political figure, Connecticut governor John H. Trumbull. During the 1960s, it was restored by Anthony Pascucci. Known owners besides Trumball have included Otis Chandler, Jack Passey and currently, Stan Lucas.

Left: This beautifully restored 1926 Twin Valve Six Roadster was purchased new by Connecticut governor John H. Trumbull. *Right:* Twin spare tires were carried on the rear behind the rumble seat (both photographs courtesy Randy Ema).

1927 Eight-in-Line Roadster Type 842

This is the only Lycoming Straight-Eight McFarlan known to exist. During the 1990s, it was on display at the Petersen Museum in Los Angeles. The rear view shows a boattail body that may not be original to the car.

Left: 1927 Eight-in-Line Roadster is the only known surviving example using the Lycoming engine. *Right:* The boattail body probably was not original to this car (both photographs courtesy Randy Ema).

1927 Duesenberg Model X with Body by McFarlan

From the original purchaser, Arnold Kirkaby, to the present owner, Peter Heydon, several unidentified persons have helped this rare automobile survive. Kirkaby sold the car soon after the Great Depression set in, and for nearly 20 years, it was passed from one owner to another until being rescued and put in storage in 1950. Allen Sandburg, the Auburn Cord Duesenberg Club historian, purchased the car in 1960 and Bill Dreist acquired it in the 1970s. Heydon was encouraged to purchase it by Dreist, who had been impressed by the award-wining restoration Heydon had done with his 1923 Duesenberg Model A Roadster.

This Model X Duesenberg Boat Roadster is considered by many to be the rarest of the rare Duesenbergs. The Boat Roadster is the only early Duesenberg with this body style, and one of only two Model X chassis listed on the ACD Club's roster of cars. The car was equipped with its boattailed aluminum body at the McFarlan plant in Connersville. Heydon's restoration was carried out by three Michigan craftsmen, Brian Joseph in Troy, Larry Jordon who did the painting in Jackson, and Mark Larder of Homer who was responsible for the upholstering. Bright metal

A crowning achievement for the custom body department was this "Boat Roadster" body by McFarlan fitted to a 1927 Duesenberg "X" chassis. The car is owned by Peter Heydon of Ann Arbor, Michigan. The photograph of this beautifully restored car was taken at Meadow Brook Hall in Rochester, Michigan (courtesy Peter Heydon).

parts were replated, using nickel rather than chrome as nickel was the original finish. The original two-tone blue paint scheme was uncovered at the cowl vents and duplicated. A scrap of the original red leather was found far up underneath and behind the dashboard. Thus it was possible to match the materials and style used for the upholstering.[11] The magnificent condition of this Duesenberg is a testimony to Heydon's commitment to the early years of the marque and to the 2½ years of work by outstanding craftsmen. It has won numerous awards at Meadow Brook, Pebble Beach, Castle Hill, Newport and annual ACD reunions in Auburn, Indiana, since 2000, when it was awarded "Best of Show."

1928 Duesenberg Model J Prototype with Body by McFarlan

By June of 1928, the McFarlan Motor Corporation was in the process of being shut down. One of the last "custom" bodies to leave the factory was destined for a prestigious assignment: It was mounted on a Duesenberg Model Y chassis powered by a twin cam straight-eight engine. This car was used as a test goat while the famed Model J was in development. After the company no longer had a use for the car, the body was remounted on a Duesenberg Model A chassis and was sold to an Indianapolis businessman, Hugh R. Baylor. In the early 1950s, James T. Leeson, who lived in Mississippi, acquired the car.

This McFarlan body was originally mounted to a Duesenberg Model Y chassis in 1928 during development of the Model J. It was later transferred to the Model A chassis on which it remains (courtesy John Kruse, Worldwide Auctioneers).

He sold it in 1956 to a member of the Kershaw family, whose descendants still retain ownership. The building in the background is the Auburn Cord Duesenberg Museum in Auburn, Indiana (courtesy John Kruse, Worldwide Auctioneers).

1926 Maxim M-3 Fire Truck

During the 1920s and 1930s, some models of Maxim fire apparatus were powered by McFarlan engines. This example is a Maxim model M-3 that is powered by a 572.5 c.i.d.

Above: Maxim fire truck powered by a McFarlan engine, owned by Brian Anderson. *Left:* The 572.5 c.i.d. McFarlan engine powered this Maxim pumper (both photographs courtesy Brian Anderson).

McFarlan engine. It is owned by Brian Anderson, Jr. of Wilmington, Massachusetts. He bought it in 2007 from a person in Vermont. It had languished in a deteriorating barn for the previous 30 to 40 years. After buying it, Anderson added a little penetrating oil to each cylinder and replaced six of the eighteen spark plugs along with the battery. It started after a couple of cranks! Brian has driven his unusual piece of fire apparatus in a few parades. He reports that it tends to run a bit hot, but he is working on that issue.[12]

The same 572.5 cubic inch engine that powered McFarlan automobiles also received accolades from the Massachusetts Institute of Technology. They claimed it to be the most efficient power plant on the market, in the mid–1920s, for use with pumper trucks of 750 gallons per minute capacity. Although designed for an automobile, it had adequate power for the Maxim pumper.

McFarlan Memorabilia

Collecting memorabilia is one way for those not fortunate enough to own the "real thing" to express interest in the marque. Various McFarlan pieces have survived including the examples shown.

Above: McFarlan watch fob, rim-wind clock and ID plates on display at the Fayette County Historical Museum in Connersville, Indiana (photograph by author). *Right:* A real treasure is this Atlas desk piece believed to have been at one time in a St. Louis McFarlan dealership. It is now a treasure of John Lowell (courtesy John Lowell).

Appendix A:
McFarlan Automobile Models

Year	Model	Price	Whbse	Engine Make	Type	HP	CID	Bore × Stroke	Features/ Notes	Serial Nos.	Est. Prod.
1910	Touring & Toy Tonneau	$2000–$2100	120	Brownell	OHV	30–40	248	3⅝ × 4			100
1911	Little Six	$2000–$2100	120	Brownell	OHV	30–40	248	3⅝ × 4			100*
	Big Six	$2500–$2600	128	Wainwright	OHV	50–60	377	4 × 5			
1912	Little Six (early)	$2100	121	Brownell	OHV	35–40	248	3⅝ × 4	Firing order 1-4-2-6-3-5 Kellogg air starter	500–1000*	150*
	40–45 HP (late)	$2300	124	Herschell-Spillman	T-head	40–45	377	4 × 5	Firing order 1-4-2-6-3-5		
	Big Six / 55–60 HP	$2750	128	Wainwright	OHV	55–60	477	4½ × 5			
1913	S	$2300–$3100	124	Herschell-Spillman	T-head	40–45	377	4 × 5	Firing order 1-5-3-6-2-4	3000–4000*	175*
	T	$2500–$3700	124	Teetor	T-head	67	452	4 × 6			
	M	$2750–$4050	128	Wainwright	OHV	55–60	477	4½ × 5			
1914	T	$2590–$4000	128	Teetor	T-head	67	452	4 × 6	Lipman air starter	4000–5000*	200*
	X	$2900–$4310	128	Teetor	T-head	90	572.5	4½ × 6	Gray pneumatic gear shift		
1915	T	$2590–$4000	132	Teetor	T-head	67	452	4 × 6	Choice of air or electric starter	6000–7000*	200*
1916	X	$2900–$4310	132	Teetor	T-head	90	572.5	4½ × 6	Submarine body	9000–10000*	200*
	T	$2680–$2830	132	Teetor	T-head	67	452	4 × 6			
	X	$2990–$4400	132	Teetor	T-head	90	572.5	4½ × 6			
1917	Ninety	$3200–$5000	136	Teetor	T-head	90	572.5	4½ × 6	Government war work began	10001–11000*	176*
1918	Ninety	$3550–$5250	136	Teetor	T-head	90	572.5	4½ × 6	12 spark plugs; dual ignition	18000–19000*	168*
1919	Ninety	$4800–$6550	136	Teetor	T-head	90–100	572.5	4½ × 6		19001–20000*	193*
1920	Ninety	$4800–$6550	136	Teetor	T-head	90–100	572.5	4½ × 6		20001–21000*	207*
1921	Twin Valve 6	$6300–$9000	140	McFarlan	T-head	120	572.5	4½ × 6	Triple ignition (18 spark plugs) introduced		217*
1922	Twin Valve 6	$6300–$9000	140	McFarlan	T-head	120	572.5	4½ × 6		21000–21500*	235*

Year	Model	Price	W/bbse	Engine Make	Type	HP	CID	Bore × Stroke	Features/Notes	Serial Nos.	Est. Prod.
1923	Twin Valve 6	$5400–$9000	140	McFarlan	T-head	120	572.5	4½ × 6		21500–22000*	263*
1924	Single Valve 6	$2500–$3480	127	Wisconsin (Model Y)	OHV	70	268	3⅜ × 5		100–349	
1925	Twin Valve 6	$5400–$9000	140	McFarlan	T-head	120	572.5	4½ × 6	4-wheel hydraulic brakes standard	23000–23249	278*
	Single Valve 6	$2650–$3480	127	Wisconsin	OHV	70	268	3⅜ × 5	4-wheel hydraulic brakes standard	400–	262*
	Twin Valve 6	$5400–$9000	140	McFarlan	T-head	120	572.5	4½ × 6		23250–	
1926	Single Valve 6	$2650–$3480	127	Wisconsin	OHV	70	268	3⅜ × 5			197*
	Eight-in-Line	$2650–$4600	131	Lycoming (Series H)	Flathead	79	298.6	3³⁄₁₆ × 4½		1000–	
1927	Twin Valve 6	$5400–$9000	141¼	McFarlan	T-head	120	572.5	4½ × 6			
	Single Valve 6	$2650–$3480	127	Wisconsin	OHV	70	268	3⅜ × 5	143*		
	Eight-in-Line	$2650–$4600	131; 136	Lycoming	Flathead	79	298.6	3³⁄₁₆ × 4½			
	Twin Valve 6	$5400–$9000	141¼	McFarlan	T-head	120	572.5	4½ × 6			
1928	Eight-in-Line	$2650–$4600	136	Lycoming	Flathead	79	298.6	3³⁄₁₆ × 4½	175*		
	Twin Valve	$5400–$9000	141¼	McFarlan	T-head	120	572.5	4½ × 6			

*All models

Appendix B:
Body Styles Available, by Year

Year	Model	Body Style No.	Body Type	Price
1910	—	—	Toy Tonneau or Touring Car	$2000–$2100
1911	Little Six	26	5-Passenger Touring	$2100
		28	4-Passenger Torpedo	$2100
		30	Runabout	$2000
	Big Six	32	7-Passenger Touring	$2500
		34	Runabout	$2500
		36	4-Passenger Torpedo	$2600
1912	Little Six/	25	3-Passenger Colonial Coupe	$2900
	40–45 HP*	26	5-Passenger Touring	$2100
		28	4-Passenger Torpedo	$2100
		30	2-Passenger Runabout/Roadster	$2100
	Big Six	32	5-Passenger Touring	$2750
		33	7-Passenger Touring	$2750
		34	2-Passenger Runabout/Roadster	$2750
		36	4-Passenger Touring	$2750
		38	4-Passenger Special	$2750
1913	Series S	24S	Turtle Back Roadster	$2300
		25S	Standard Coupe	$3100
		26S	5-Passenger Touring	$2300
		28S	4-Passenger Touring	$2300
		29S	Turtle Back Coupe	$3100
		34S	Roadster	$2300
		35S	Roadster	$2300
	Series T	21T	Limousine	$3700
		24T	Turtle Back Roadster	$2500
		25T	3-Passenger Standard Coupe	$3300
		26T	5-Passenger Touring	$2500
		27T	6-Passenger Touring	$2500
		28T	4-Passenger Touring	$2500
		29T	2-Passenger Turtle Back Coupe	$3300
		34T	Roadster	$2500
		35T	Speedster	$2500
	Series M	21M	Limousine	$4050
		32M	5-Passenger Touring	$2750
		33M	7-Passenger Touring	$2750
		34M	Roadster	$2750

*Model change to 40–45 HP occurred at midyear, raising price by $200 on each body style.

Year	Model	Body Style No.	Body Type	Price
		35M	Speedster	$2750
		36M	4-Passenger Touring	$2750
		38M	Long-Distance Touring	$2750
1914	Series T	61	Roadster	$2590
		62	4-Passenger Touring	$2590
		63	5-Passenger Touring	$2590
		64	6-Passenger Touring	$2590
		65	7-Passenger Touring	$2590
		67	4-Passenger Coupe	$3300
		69	7-Passenger Limousine	$4000
	Series X	61	Roadster	$2900
		62	4-Passenger Touring	$2900
		63	5-Passenger Touring	$2900
		64	6-Passenger Touring	$2900
		65	7-Passenger Touring	$2900
		67	4-Passenger Coupe	$3610
		69	7-Passenger Limousine	$4310
1915	Series T	72	Roadster	$2590
		75	5-Passenger Touring	$2590
		76	6-Passenger Touring	$2590
		77	7-Passenger Touring	$2590
		78	4-Passenger Coupe	$3300
		79	7-Passenger Limousine	$4000
	Series X	72	Roadster	$2900
		75	5-Passenger Touring	$2900
		76	6-Passenger Touring	$2900
		77	7-Passenger Touring	$2900
		78	4-Passenger Coupe	$4000
		79	7-Passenger Limousine	$4310
		104	4-Passenger Submarine	$3140
1916	Series T	102	Roadster	$2680
		104	4-Passenger Submarine	$2830
		105	5-Passenger Touring	$2680
		106	6-Passenger Touring	$2680
		107	7-Passenger Touring	$2680
	Series X	102	Roadster	$2990
		104	4-Passenger Submarine	$3140
		105	5-Passenger Touring	$2990
		106	6-Passenger Touring	$2990
		107	7-Passenger Touring	$2990
		110	Semi-Touring	$4400
		111	Town Car	$4000
		113	Coupe	$3600
		116	6-Passenger Sedan	$4000
		117	Berline	$4300
		118	Limousine	$4200
		119	Landaulet	$4200
1917	Ninety	104	Submarine	$3230
		111	Town Car	$4740
		113	Coupe	$4000
		119	Landaulet	$4600
		122	Touring Roadster, 2-, 3- or 4-Passenger (wire wheels)	$3400
		125	Sport Touring	$3850

Year	Model	Body Style No.	Body Type	Price
		127	7-Passenger Touring	$3200
		127	7-Passenger Victoria	$3600
		134	Knickerbocker Cabriolet	$5000
		136	7-Passenger Sedan	$4300
		138	Limousine	$4450
1918	Ninety	122	Touring Roadster, 2-, 3- or 4-Passenger	$3500
		124	4-Passenger Destroyer	$4150
		125	Pasadena 5-Passenger Sport Touring (6 wire wheels)	$3900
		126	6-Passenger Touring	$3550
		127	7-Passenger Touring	$3550
		127	7-Passenger Victoria	$3550
		131	Town Car	$4000
		134	Knickerbocker Cabriolet	$5650
		136	Touring Sedan, Sloping V or Straight Front	$5000
		137	Philadelphia Berline	$5300
		138	Limousine	$5050
		141	Continental Landaulet	$5300
1919–1920	Ninety	122	Touring Roadster, 2-, 3- or 4-Passenger	$4800
		124	4-Passenger Destroyer	$5050
		125	4-Passenger Sport Touring	$5000
		126	6-Passenger Touring	$4800
		127	7-Passenger Touring	$4800
		131	Town Car	$5900
		134	Knickerbocker Cabriolet	$6550
		135	Sport Sedan	$6100
		136	Sedan, Sloping V or Straight Front	$5900
		137	Philadelphia Berline	$6200
		138	Limousine	$5950
		141	Continental Landaulet	$6200
1921–1922	Twin Valve 6	142	Roadster	$6300
		145	4-Passenger Sport Touring	$6300
		147	7-Passenger Touring	$6300
		151	Town Car	$7500
		153	Coupe	$7500
		154	Knickerbocker Cabriolet	$9000
		155	Sport Sedan	$7500
		157	7-Passenger Suburban Sedan	$7800
		158	Limousine	$7500
		161	Continental Landaulet	$8500
1923–1925	Twin Valve 6	142	Roadster	$5400
		145	4-Passenger Sport Touring	$5600
		147	7-Passenger Touring	$5700
		154	Knickerbocker Cabriolet	$9000
		157	Town Car, Enclosed Drive/ Special Berline	$9000
		158	Limousine	$6900
		159	Touring Sedan	$6720
		160	Sport Sedan	$6600
		163	4-Passenger Coupe	$6720
		165	6-Passenger Sedan	$6720

Year	Model	Body Style No.	Body Type	Price
		166	7-Passenger Sedan	$6810
		167	7-Passenger Suburban Sedan	$7000
		171	Landaulet	$8500
		—	Chassis only	$4550
1924	Single Valve 6	42	Roadster	$2500
		45	6-Passenger Touring	$2500
		47	7-Passenger Touring	$2650
		63	Coupe	$3000
		64	Brougham	$3000
		65	6-Passenger Sedan	$3000
		67	7-Passenger Sedan	$3100
		67	7-Passenger Suburban Sedan	$3480
1925	Single Valve 6	42	Roadster	$2650
		45	6-Passenger Touring	$2650
		47	7-Passenger Touring	$2750
		64	Brougham	$3180
		67	7-Passenger Sedan	$3280
		67	7-Passenger Suburban Sedan	$3480
		73	Coupe	$3180
		75	6-Passenger Sedan	$3180
		—	Chassis only	$2350
1926–1927	Single Valve 6	42	Roadster	$2650
		45	5-Passenger Touring	$2650
		47	7-Passenger Touring	$2750
		64	Brougham	$3380
		67	7-Passenger Sedan	$3480
		69	4-Door Brougham	$3480
		73	Coupe	$3380
		75	6-Passenger Sedan	$3380
1926–1928	Eight-in-Line	842	4-Passenger Roadster	$2650
		844	Sport Phaeton	$3180
		845	5-Passenger Touring	$2650
		854	Town Car	$4600
		872	Town Coupe	$3180
		873	Coupe	$3180
		874	Brougham	$3380
		875	5-Passenger Valencia Sedan	$3180
		876	7-Passenger Sedan	$3280
		879	Brougham w/ solid rear quarters	$3180
		880	5-Passenger Coupe	$3180
		886	7-Passenger Suburban Sedan	$3480
1926–1928	Twin Valve 6	142	4-Passenger Deluxe Roadster	$5400
		145	5-Passenger Touring	$5400
		147	7-Passenger Touring	$5600
		154	Town Car	$9000
		157	Town Car, Enclosed Drive	$9000
		159	Deluxe Touring Sedan	$6810
		165	6-Passenger Sedan	$6720
		166	7-Passenger Sedan	$6810
		176	7-Passenger Suburban Sedan	$7110
		177	7-Passenger Suburban Sedan with divider window	$7110

Chapter Notes

Chapter 1

1. "Local and Personal." *The Connersville Examiner*, Oct. 30, 1889, p. 3.
2. "Additional Local." *Cambridge City Tribune*, July 21, 1910, p. 2.
3. Barrows, Frederick I. "John B. McFarlan." *History of Fayette County Indiana*, 1917, p. 1009.
4. "John B. McFarlan." *The Carriage Monthly*, Sept. 1909, p. 17.
5. "The McFarlan Buggy Manufacturing Company." *The Daily News*, March 2, 1900, p. 4.
6. Barrows, Frederick I. *History of Fayette County, Indiana*, 1917, pp. 712–714.
7. "History of Old M'Farlan Corner." *The Evening News*, Jan. 22, 1914, p. 1.
8. *After Seventy Years of a Settled Plan*, McFarlan Motor Corp., 1926.
9. *History of Fayette County Indiana*, 1885, p. 150.
10. "F. B. McFarlan & Sons' Carriage Manufactury." *The Daily News*, Special Illustrated Edition, June 1896, p. 4.
11. *The Connersville Times*, Dec. 28, 1870, p. 2.
12. "To the Public." *The Connersville Times*, March 21, 1876, p. 4.
13. *The Connersville Examiner*, Nov. 4, 1868, p. 3.
14. "Local News." *The Connersville Times*, May 19, 1869, p. 3.
15. *The Connersville Times*, May 26, 1869, p. 3.
16. "Local and Personal." *The Connersville Examiner*, Dec. 24, 2867, p. 3.
17. "Local and Personal." *The Connersville Examiner*, March 4, 1868, p. 3.
18. "Local and Personal." *The Connersville Examiner*, Dec. 23, 1868, p. 3.
19. "Local and Personal." *The Connersville Examiner*, May 24, 1871, p. 3.
20. *The Connersville Times*, Dec. 23, 1868, p. 3.
21. *The Connersville Examiner*, Sept. 6, 1871, p. 2.
22. *The Connersville Times*, Sept. 15, 1869, p. 3.
23. "Premium List Concluded." *The Connersville Times*, Sept. 22, 1869, p. 3.
24. "The Wayne County Fair." *The Connersville Times*, Oct. 13, 1869, p. 2.
25. "Premiums Awarded at the Fayette County Fair." *The Connersville Examiner*, Sept. 21, 1870, p. 1.
26. "The Fair." *The Connersville Examiner*, Sept. 13, 1871, p. 1.
27. *The Connersville Examiner*, Sept. 15, 1881, p. 1.
28. *The Connersville Times*, Jan. 25, 1882, p. 1.
29. "Local and Personal." *The Connersville Examiner*, Sept. 13, 1882, p. 3.
30. "Additional Local." *The Connersville Examiner*, Sept. 20, 1871, p. 3.
31. "Local and Personal." *The Connersville Examiner*, May 9, 1876, p. 2.
32. "Local and Personal." *The Connersville Examiner*, July 12, 1876, p. 3.
33. "Additional Local." *The Connersville Examiner*, July 4, 1883, p. 2.
34. "Local Matters." *The Connersville Times*, June 27, 1888, p. 6.
35. "Local and Personal." *The Connersville Examiner*, April 24, 1872, p. 3.
36. "Local and Personal." *The Connersville Examiner*, June 5, 1872, p. 3.
37. "Local and Personal." *The Connersville Examiner*, Sept. 25, 1872, p. 3.
38. "Local and Personal." *The Connersville Examiner*, April 13, 1873, p. 3.
39. "Local and Personal." *The Connersville Examiner*, Oct. 8, 1873, p. 3.
40. "Local and Personal." *The Connersville Examiner*, May 21, 1873, p. 3.
41. *The Connersville Times*, Feb. 8, 1882, p. 1.
42. "Local News." *The Connersville Times*, Feb. 15, 1882, p. 1.
43. "Local and Personal." *The Connersville Examiner*, Feb. 15, 1882, p. 3.
44. "Local News." *The Connersville Times*, Feb. 15, 1882, p. 1.
45. "Local and Personal." *The Connersville Examiner*, Jan. 5, 1882, p. 3.
46. "Local and Personal." *The Connersville Examiner*, March 15, 1882, p. 3.
47. "Local and Personal." *The Connersville Examiner*, Aug. 13, 1884, p. 3.
48. "Local Matters." *The Connersville Times*, March 22, 1888, p. 6.
49. "Local News." *The Connersville Times*, Sept. 30, 1887, p. 7.
50. "Local and Personal." *The Connersville Examiner*, April 19, 1882, p. 3.
51. "Local and Personal." *The Connersville Examiner*, May 3, 1882, p. 3.
52. "Local and Personal." *The Connersville Examiner*, May 31, 1882, p. 3.
53. "Local and Personal." *The Connersville Examiner*, May 24, 1882, p. 3.
54. "Local and Personal." *The Connersville Examiner*, July 5, 1882, p. 3.
55. "Local and Personal." *The Connersville Examiner*, Oct. 24, 1883, p. 3.

56. "Local and Personal." *The Connersville Examiner*, Feb. 6, 1884, p. 3.
57. "Local and Personal." *The Connersville Examiner*, Aug. 27, 1884, p. 3.
58. "Local and Personal." *The Connersville Examiner*, Dec. 27, 1882, p. 3.
59. "Local and Personal." *The Connersville Examiner*, Dec. 12, 1888, p. 3.
60. "Local and Personal." *The Connersville Examiner*, July 25, 1883, p. 3.
61. "Local and Personal." *The Connersville Examiner*, Nov. 7, 1883, p. 3.
62. "Local and Personal." *The Connersville Examiner*, April 27, 1884, p. 3.
63. "Local and Personal." *The Connersville Examiner*, July 2, 1884, p. 3.
64. "Local and Personal." *The Connersville Examiner*, Dec. 24, 1884, p. 3.
65. Barrows, Frederick I. *History of Fayette County, Indiana*, 1917, pp. 714–715.
66. "Local and Personal." *The Connersville Examiner*, Nov. 7, 1883, p. 3.
67. "W. W. McFarlan Is to Retire." *The Connersville Times*, Sept. 2, 1908, p. 1.
68. Barrows, Frederick I. *History of Fayette County, Indiana*, 1917, pp. 706–707.
69. "Local and Personal." *The Connersville Examiner*, Sept. 19, 1883, p. 3.
70. "Local and Personal." *The Connersville Examiner*, Nov. 14, 1883, p. 3.
71. "Local and Personal." *The Connersville Examiner*, Aug. 13, 1884, p. 3.
72. "Local Matters." *The Connersville Times*, Feb. 23, 1887, p. 6.
73. "Local Matters." *The Connersville Times*, Feb. 16, 1887, p. 7.
74. "Local Matters." *The Connersville Times*, July 8, 1887, p. 6.
75. "Local Matters." *The Connersville Times* Aug. 19, 1887, p. 7.
76. "Local News." *The Connersville Times*, Sept. 30, 1887, p. 7.
77. "Local News." *The Connersville Times*, Dec. 16, 1887, p. 7.
78. "Local News." *The Connersville Times*, Feb. 17, 1888, p. 6.
79. "Local Matters." *The Connersville Times*, Nov. 21, 1888, p. 6.
80. "Local and Personal." *The Connersville Examiner*, Feb. 19, 1890, p. 3.
81. "J.B. McFarlan & Sons." *The Daily News*, June 1896, p. 4.
82. "Local and Personal." *The Connersville Examiner*, March 19, 1890, p. 3.
83. "Local and Personal." *The Connersville Examiner*, May 21, 1890, p. 3.
84. "Local and Personal." *The Connersville Examiner*, Jan. 15, 1890, p. 3.
85. "A Big Shipment." *The Daily News*, Jan. 3, 1891, p. 2.
86. "Local and Personal." *The Connersville Examiner*, Nov. 6, 1889, p. 3.
87. "City News." *The Daily Examiner*, June 4, 1891, p. 4.
88. "J.B. McFarlan, Sr." *Biographical and Genealogical History*, 1899, pp. 887–888.
89. "Local and Personal." *The Connersville Examiner*, Nov. 12, 1890, p. 3.
90. "Board of Trade." *The Daily Examiner*, Jan. 14, 1891, p. 4.
91. "City News." *Connersville Daily Examiner*, Feb. 18, 1891, p. 4.
92. Barrows, Frederick I. *History of Fayette County, Indiana*, 1917, p. 672.
93. "John Becraft McFarlan Has Been Called to Rest." *The Evening News*, Aug. 16, 1909, p. 5.
94. "No Hotel." *Connersville Daily Examiner*, Jan. 2, 1891, p. 4.
95. "Local and Personal." *The Daily News*, Nov. 4, 1892, p. 3.
96. "J.B. McFarlan & Sons." *The Daily News*, June 1896, p. 4.
97. *Connersville Daily Examiner*, Oct. 15, 1895, p. 4.
98. "A Double Somersault." *Connersville Daily Examiner*, April 18, 1895, p. 4.
99. "Local and Personal." *The Daily News*, April 13, 1900, p. 3.
100. "J. E. McFarlan Is Severely Injured." *The Evening News*, July 11, 1907, p. 1.
101. "Fortunes Made in Triple Signs." *The Daily News*, Feb. 22, 1900, p. 2.
102. *J.B. McFarlan Carriage Co. Vehicles*, 1900, p. 1.
103. "Largest Single Shipment." *The Connersville Courier*, Jan. 11, 1900, p. 1.
104. "Great Stroke of Enterprise." *The Daily News*, Jan. 9, 1900, p. 2.
105. "Dan M. Hankins's Work as Salesman." *The Evening News*, April 30, 1914, p. 1.
106. "A Big Display." *The Daily News*, April 14, 1900, p. 2.
107. *J.B. McFarlan Carriage Co.*, 1900.
108. "A New Deal." *The Daily News*, Sept. 7, 1901, p. 1.
109. "Potter Wins." *The Connersville Times*, April 26, 1899, p. 1.
110. "The McFarlan Buggy Manufacturing Company." *The Daily News*, March 2, 1900, p. 2.
111. "Failed to Gill Contract." *The Daily News*, Nov. 14, 1901, p. 2.
112. "Suit for Damages in Sum of $6,000." *The Evening News*, Feb. 10, 1904, p. 2.
113. "Local and Personal." *The Evening News*, Oct. 10, 1902, p. 3.
114. "Bright Outlook for Business in 1904." *The Evening News*, Feb. 18, 1904, p. 2.
115. "Big Combine of Carriage Makers." *The Evening News*, Sept. 11, 1907, p. 1.
116. *McFarlan Carriage Company*, 1908.
117. "News Industry Story Pleasing." *The Evening News*, June 12, 1909, p. 1.
118. "John Becraft McFarlan Has Been Called to Rest." *The Evening News*, August 16, 1909, pp. 1, 5.
119. "M'Farlan Auto Ranks as Finest." *Connersville News-Examiner* (IN), August 28, 1926, p. 1.
120. "Horse Vehicle Trade Fell Off." *The Evening News*, Jan. 7, 1910, p. 1.
121. "Manufacture of Auto Piano Parts." *The Evening News*, Sept. 21, 1912, p. 1.
122. *McFarlan Carriage Company*, Catalog 30, p. 50.
123. "To Sell McFarlan Property." *The Automobile*, Oct. 30, 1913, p. 837.
124. "Factory Sold." *The Evening News*, Dec. 31, 1913, p. 1.

Chapter 2

1. "Local News." *The Connersville Examiner*, August 7, 1872, p. 3.
2. "Local News." *The Connersville Examiner*, Dec. 30, 1868, p. 3.
3. "Local News." *The Connersville Examiner*, Nov. 16, 1870, p. 3.
4. "Automobile Was Dreamed of Here." *Connersville News-Examiner*, April 16, 1925, p. 1.
5. Barrows, Frederick I. "The First Horseless Vehicle." *History of Fayette County Indiana*, 1917, p. 625.
6. "Local and Personal." *The Connersville Examiner*, July 23, 1890, p. 3.
7. Smith, Harry M. "Connersville Once Known as Little Detroit." *Connersville, Indiana: A Pictorial History*, 1992, p. 86.
8. "Honk! Honk! The First Auto Arrives in C'ville." *Connersville News-Examiner*, Nov. 15, 1921, p. 1.
9. "Automobile Accident." *The Daily News*, Nov. 25, 1901, p. 2.
10. "Local and Personal." *The Connersville Examiner*, May 28, 1902, p. 8.
11. "Streets and Alleys to Be Paved with Brick." *The Connersville Times*, August 5, 1903, p. 2.
12. Barrows, Frederick, I. "Street Paving." *History of Fayette County Indiana*, 1917, p. 541.
13. "Some Auto Facts of Real Interest." *The Evening News*, June 21, 1910, p. 1.
14. "Central Manufacturing Company's Plant Almost Totally Destroyed." *The Evening News*, Oct. 27, 1905, p. 2.
15. "Automobile Plant May Locate Here." *The Evening News*, June 20, 1906, p. 2.
16. "Another Automobile Company Files Association Articles." *The Evening News*, Nov. 20, 1906, p. 1.
17. "The Ray Motor Co. Is Almost Ready." *The Evening News*, Feb. 6, 1907, p. 1.
18. "Hatfield Motor Company Assign." *The Evening News*, March 20, 1908, p. 1.
19. "Indiana Gains Two More Auto Makers." *The Automobile*, Nov. 29, 1906, p. 739.
20. "New Incorporations." *The Horseless Age*, Dec. 12, 1906, p. 840.
21. "New Connersville Industry Files Incorporation Articles." *The Evening News*, Nov. 20, 1906, p. 2.
22. "$50,000 Company Formed at Connersville, Ind." *Automobile Topics*, Dec. 1, 1906, p. 658.
23. "McFarlan Carriage Co. to Manufacture Cars." *The Evening News*, June 11, 1909, p. 1.
24. *The Connersville Times*, Nov. 24, 1881, p. 1.
25. "A Pleasant Event." *Connersville Daily Examiner*, Nov. 20, 1895, p. 4.
26. "Minor Mention." *The Horseless Age*, June 23, 1909, p. 567.
27. "Minor Mention." *The Horseless Age*, Sept. 29, 1909, p. 359.
28. "Two Fine Samples to First Be Built." *The Evening News*, August 6, 1909, p. 1.
29. "The McFarlan 40 on Streets Today." *The Evening News*, August 18, 1909, p. 1.
30. "Making Autos at M'Farlan's." *The Evening News*, Sept. 4, 1909, p. 1.
31. Marvin, Keith and others. *What Was the McFarlan?*, Alvin Arnheim, 1967, p. 2.
32. "Oh Yez! Oh Yez!" *Connersville News-Examiner*, Oct. 25, 1967, p. 3.
33. "The McFarlan Car Had Fine Showing." *The Evening News*, Nov. 4, 1909, p. 1.
34. "Test Car Struck." *The Evening News*, Feb. 21, 1910, p. 1.
35. *Introducing the Makers of McFarlan*, McFarlan Motor Company, 1913.
36. "McFarlan Auto Plant Running." *The Evening News*, Nov. 20, 1909, p. 1.
37. McFarlan, A. H., unpublished correspondence to William S. Crowe, Dec. 1, 1909.
38. "Announcement for the Motorist." *Motor Print*, April 1910, p. 20.
39. "The NAAM Show." *The Automobile*, Feb. 3, 1910, pp. 7–10.
40. Moore, Erma. Personal interview, March 27, 2008.
41. "Brownell Motor in McFarlan 6." *San Francisco Bulletin*, April 18, 1910.
42. "An Important Vehicle Change in San Francisco." *San Francisco Record*, March 1910.
43. "McFarlan Available Here." *San Francisco Bulletin*, March 26, 1910.
44. "To Handle McFarlan Cars." *San Francisco Post*, June 11, 1910.
45. "Gets Coast Agency for Two Popular Indiana Cars." *The San Francisco Evening Post*, Oct. 2, 1910.
46. "Demonstrator Returns." *San Francisco Globe*, Oct. 26, 1910.
47. "All Signs Point to an Active Auto Market." *San Francisco Post*, Nov. 29, 1910.
48. "Big Car Carries Off Prize at Santa Rosa Carnival." *The San Francisco Call*, June 25, 1910.
49. "Honk Honks from Gasoline Row." *San Francisco Globe*, Sept. 12, 1910.
50. "Vern Dumas with His Family in Their McFarlan Six Car." *San Francisco Chronicle*, June 12, 1910.
51. "Convince Rancher of McFarlan's Worth." *San Francisco Chronicle*, July, 17, 1910.
52. "New Auto Agency." *Noblesville Ledger*, April 1910.
53. "M'Farlan Six at Hoosier Capital." *The Evening News*, Feb. 11, 1910, p. 1.
54. "McFarlan Six—1911." *McClure's*, Dec. 1910, p. 64.
55. "Better Cars and Not Too Cheap." *The Evening News*, July 13, 1910, p. 1.
56. "Australia Man Contracts for 25 McFarlans." *The Daily Examiner*, Nov. 21, 1910, p. 1.
57. "One Standard Chassis for McFarlan Six Next Season." *The Horseless Age*, Sept. 27, 1910.
58. "New Six Cylinder Motor." *The Horseless Age*, August 17, 1910, p. 251.
59. "Wainwright Engineering." bugladyconsulting.com/genealogy, May 21, 2007, p. 1.
60. "McFarlan Motor Given Final Test." *The Evening News*, August 18, 1910, p. 1.
61. "New 1911 Motors for McFarlan Six." *The Evening News*, Nov. 23, 1910, p. 8.
62. *Catalogue of the McFarlan Six Cylinder Automobiles*, McFarlan Carriage Co., pp. 17–23.
63. "Details of Passenger Automobiles." *The Automobile*, Jan. 5, 1911, pp. 86–87.
64. *Catalogue of the McFarlan Six Cylinder Automobiles*, McFarlan Carriage Co., pp. 12–13.
65. "Garden Display to Show Year's Progress." *Motor Age*, Dec. 22, 1910, p. 12.
66. "McFarlan Six in Great Show." *The Daily Examiner*, Dec. 22, 1910, p. 1.
67. McNaughton, Charles. Personal interview, Oct. 25, 2001.
68. "Bert Adams with a M'Farlan Six." *The Evening News*, Oct. 11, 1911, p. 1.

69. "Big Rush Sale of M'Farlan Cars." *The Evening News*, Sept. 4, 1911, p. 1.
70. "McFarlan Six—1912." *Indianapolis Star*, May 28, 1911, Auto Section p. 8.
71. "Little Sixes Have All Latest Features." *The Evening Post* (CA), Dec. 2, 1911.
72. "McFarlan Cars." *The Motor World*, Jan. 18, 1912, p. 418.
73. "McFarlan Sixes." *Automobile Trade Journal*, Jan. 1, 1912, p. 279.
74. *McFarlan Six*. McFarlan Motor Car Company, Catalog No. 31.
75. "McFarlan Cars." *The Motor World*, Jan. 18, 1912, p. 418.
76. "The Start of the Starter." *Automobile Trade Journal*, Dec. 1, 1924, p. 82.
77. "McFarlan Six." *The Motor World*, Jan. 18, 1912, p. 418.
78. "We Are Selling Cars." *The Evening News*, July 1, 1912, p. 1.
79. *Motor Age*, April 10, 1913, p. 19.
80. "M'Farlan Cars in Show at Buffalo." *The Evening News*, Feb. 1, 1913, p. 1.
81. "New Agencies Established During the Week." *The Automobile*, March 6, 1913, p. 619.
82. Woodburn, Bob. Telephone interview, Feb. 2008.
83. "McFarlan." *Motor*, Nov. 1912, p. 153.
84. "The McFarlan New Series." *Automobile Trade Journal*, Jan. 1913, pp. 179–181.
85. "McFarlan." *Automobile Engineering*, Vol. III, American Technical Society, Chicago, Ill., 1918, p. 155.
86. "McFarlan Adopts Floating Axle." *The Automobile*, Jan. 9, 1913, p. 124.
87. *Self Starting McFarlan Six*, McFarlan Motor Car Co., Connersville, Indiana, Catalog 32, p. 9.
88. *Introducing the Makers of McFarlan*, McFarlan Motor Car Company, 1913.
89. "Automobiles Costing from $2000 to $2999." *The Automobile*, Jan. 9, 1913, p. 107.
90. "The Self Starter." *Self Starting McFarlan Six*, McFarlan Motor Car Co., Catalog 32, p. 20.
91. "Officers Visited Town of Everton." *The Daily Examiner*, Sept. 2, 1916, p. 1.
92. "To Make One License Do." *Motor Age*, June 19, 1913, p. 15.
93. "Restricted Credit Hampers Pope Finances." *The Automobile*, Oct. 30, 1913, p. 837.
94. "M'Farlan Company Awards Contract." *The Evening News*, Sept. 27, 1913, p. 1.
95. "M'Farlan Motor Company Formed." *The Evening News*, Sept. 25, 1913, p. 1.
96. "Form McFarlan Motor Co." *Motor Age*, Oct. 9, 1913, p. 23.
97. "To Sell McFarlan Property." *The Automobile*, Oct. 30, 1913, p. 837.
98. "Factory Sold." *The Evening News*, Dec. 31, 1913, p. 1.
99. "Cambridge City and Environs 50 Years Ago." *The National Road Traveler*, Feb. 23, 1961, p. 1.
100. "Ten Big Sixes in Three Short Days." *The Evening News*, Nov. 22, 1913, p. 1.
101. *McFarlan Six*, McFarlan Motor Company, Catalog 33.
102. "New McFarlan Six." *The Horseless Age*, Oct. 22, 1913, pp. 693–694.
103. "Gray Pneumatic Gearshift Eliminates Both Hand Levers." *Motor Age*, June 19, 1913, p. 30.
104. "McFarlan Has Pneumatic Gear Shift." *Automobile Trade Journal*, Feb. 1914, p. 100A.
105. "McFarlan Concentrates on Six for 1914." *The Automobile*, Nov. 13, 1913, pp. 916–917.
106. "McFarlan Putting Out a Six." *The Automobile*, Jan. 1, 1914, p. 70.
107. "Engineering Aspects." *The Automobile*, Jan. 29, 1914, pp. 295–296.
108. "Right or Left Control—Which?" *The Automobile*, August 1, 1912, pp. 209–213.
109. "New McFarlan Six." *The Horseless Age*, Oct. 22, 1913, p. 694.
110. "Test Cars Raise the Public Wrath." *The Evening News*, Oct. 5, 1914, p. 1.
111. McNaughten, Charles. Personal interview, Oct. 25, 2001.
112. "Cambridge City and Environs 47 Years Ago." *The National Road Traveler*, Sept. 20, 1962, p. 1.
113. "Agency Opportunities." *Automobile Trade Journal*, Sept. 1914, p. 176.
114. "New McFarlan Models Have Longer Wheelbase." *Motor World*, August 19, 1914, p. 10.
115. "Improvements in the McFarlan Six." *The Horseless Age*, August 26, 1914, pp. 319–320.
116. "McFarlan Is Longer and Lower." *Automobile Topics*, August 15, 1914, p. 5.
117. "Specifications of Gasoline Pleasure Cars." *The Horseless Age*, Oct. 14, 1914, p. 562.
118. "Passenger Cars for 1915." *The Automobile*, Dec. 31, 1914, pp. 1224–1225.
119. "Light Dimmers for Cars in City." *The Evening News*, Sept. 23, 1915, p. 1.
120. "McFarlan Six." *The Automobile*, August 20, 1914, p. 88.
121. "The McFarlan Submarine." *The Horseless Age*, June 2, 1915, p. 734.
122. *The Horseless Age*, Dec. 15, 1915, p. 54.
123. "McFarlan Six Series T and X." *The Automobile Journal*, August 25, 1915, p. 41.
124. "Refinement in New McFarlan Six." *The American Chauffeur*, Nov. 1915, pp. 490–491.
125. "1916 Passenger Automobiles." *The Automobile*, Dec. 30, 1915, pp. 1250–1251.
126. "McFarlan Six Series T and X." *The Automobile Journal*, August 25, 1915, p. 42.
127. "A New Achievement." *The Theatre*, Feb. 1917, p. 123.
128. "McFarlan Ninety Shows Refinement." *The Horseless Age*, June 15, 1916, pp. 478–479.
129. Brown, Arch, "McFarlan TV Series." *Special Interest Autos*, Feb. 1990, p. 38.
130. "McFarlan Magnetic Transmission." *Motor World*, Dec. 27, 1916.
131. *McFarlan Six, By This Sign—*, McFarlan Motor Company, 1917, pp. 3–6.
132. "Seventeenth Annual Car Review." *Automobile Trade Journal*, Dec. 1916, pp. 182–183.
133. "Newest McFarlan Lower and Roomier." *Motor World*, June 14, 1916, pp. 18–19.
134. "1917 McFarlan Built on Single Chassis." *The Automobile*, June 15, 1916, pp. 1088–1089.
135. "Wilson to Review Motor Car Parade." *The Daily Examiner*, Sept. 28, 1916, p. 1.
136. "Reply Given to Local Critic." *The Daily Examiner*, July 3, 1919, p. 1.
137. "McFarlan Plant to Do Government Work." *The Daily Examiner*, Dec. 21, 1917, p. 1.
138. "McFarlan Plant Is Mentioned in Word." *The Evening News*, Nov. 25, 1918, p. 1.

139. "Joy Car Factories Advised to Change." *The Evening News*, August 10, 1918, p. 2.
140. "M'Farlan Working on Federal Order." *The Evening News*, March 10, 1919, p. 1.
141. "McFarlan Company in Front Column." *The Daily Examiner*, March 17, 1919, p. 1.
142. "McFarlan Cars Are Driven to Seaside." *The Evening News*, April 8, 1919, p. 1.
143. "McFarlan Price Increase." *Automobile Industries*, April 11, 1918, p. 749.
144. "McFarlan Ninety for 1918 Carries Wide Range of Bodies." *Automobile Topics*, August 11, 1917, p. 39.
145. Meyer, Marjorie Teetor. *One Man's Vision*, 1995, p. 51.
146. "Ansted Brothers Turn a Big Deal." *The Evening News*, April 4, 1918, p. 1.
147. "Auto Companies to Return to Making." *The Evening News*, Nov. 13, 1918, p. 1.
148. "Local Auto Makers Given Attention." *The Evening News*, March 12, 1919, p. 1.
149. "McFarlan Company Acquires the Title." *The Evening News*, Nov. 18, 1919, p. 1.
150. "M'Farlan Company Is Making a Change." *Connersville News-Examiner*, March 18, 1920, p. 1.
151. *Automobile Trade Journal*, March 1920, p. 315.
152. Barrows, Barton. Letter to Commercial Union Assurance Co., April 21, 1920 (unpublished).
153. "Home Cars Attract Attention." *The Connersville News and Examiner*, Jan. 5, 1920, p. 1.
154. "M'Farlans Catch Handful of Prizes." *Connersville News-Examiner* (IN), April 15, 1920, p. 1.
155. "Connersville Was Up Front." *Connersville News-Examiner*, March 13, 1920, p. 8.
156. "Auto Expansion Programs Seen." *The Evening News*, Nov. 25, 1916, p. 1.
157. Olsson, Igamar, and Mats Heder. "Lexington in Sweden." December 3, 2002 (unpublished).
158. "The Hatch Affair." *Air Cooled News*, Issue 16, June 1958, p. 2.
159. Hubbard, Thomas H. "The Case for Franklin." *Automobile Quarterly*, vol. 5, no. 3, 1967, p. 240.

Chapter 3

1. "McFarlan Six." *Cycle and Automobile Trade Journal*, Jan. 1, 1910, pp. 36–37.
2. Kimes. "The Rise and Fall of the Empire." *Automobile Quarterly*, v. 12 no. 1, 1974, p. 72.
3. "McFarlans at Speedway." *The Daily Examiner*, Aug. 26, 1910, p. 1.
4. "Speed Kings Ready for Coming Strife." *The Indianapolis Star*, Sept. 2, 1910, p. 1.
5. "Nationals First in Speedway Feature." *The Indianapolis Star*, Sept. 6, 1910, p. 1.
6. "Labor Day Events." *The Automobile*, Sept. 8, 1910, pp. 17–20.
7. "Equaled the Speedway Record." *Connersville Daily Examiner*, Sept. 7, 1910, p. 1.
8. "McFarlan Six—1911." *The Saturday Evening Post*, Nov. 12, 1910, p. 52.
9. "Wonderful Feat of M'Farlan Six." *The Evening News*, Sept. 7, 1910, p. 1.
10. "Indianapolis Races." *The Automobile*, Sept. 8, 1910, p. 423.
11. "Business Change at Upper Garage." *The Evening News*, August 24, 1909, p. 1.
12. "McFarlans Go to Atlanta, Ga." *Connersville Daily Examiner*, Oct. 18, 1910, p. 1.
13. "Glenaw in Falcar Captures Coca-Cola Cup." *Motor Age*, Nov. 10, 1910, pp. 1–5.
14. "McFarlans Are Making Fine Showing." *Connersville Daily Examiner*, Nov. 5, 1910, p. 1.
15. "Great Day for McFarlan Six." *Connersville Daily Examiner*, Nov. 8, 1910, p. 1.
16. *Cincinnati Enquirer*, Nov. 7, 1910.
17. "City of Atlanta Races." *The Automobile*, Nov. 10, 1910, p. 780.
18. "Great Showing of McFarlan Six Cars." *San Francisco Post-Globe*, Nov. 16, 1910.
19. "500 Mile Sweepstakes Run Off." *The Automobile*, June 1, 1911, pp. 23–27.
20. "Cars and Drivers Named in Big Race." *The Indianapolis Star*, May 3, 1911, p. 9.
21. "The Drivers and Their Histories." *The Indianapolis Star*, May 28, 1911, p. 6.
22. Marquette, Phillip. Personal interview, June 8, 2009.
23. Davidson, Donald. Personal interview, Jan. 26, 2009.
24. Bentley, John. "The First '500.'" *Great American Automobiles*, 1957, pp. 195–196.
25. Catlin, Russ. "Who Really Won the First Indy 500?" *Automobile Quarterly*, v. 7, no. 4, 1969, p. 383.
26. "500 Mile Sweepstakes." *The Automobile*, June 1, 1911, p. 23.
27. Catlin, Russ. "Who Really Won the First Indy 500?" *Automobile Quarterly*, v. 7, no. 4, 1969, p. 384.
28. "500 Mile Sweepstakes." *The Automobile*, June 1, 1911, p. 23.
29. "Twenty-one Cars Have Qualified." *The Evening News*, May 28, 1912, p. 1.
30. "New Pilots Arrive Here." *The Indianapolis Star*, May 3, 1912, p. 11.
31. "Entrants in the 500 Mile Race." *Motor Age*, May 9, 1912, p. 15.
32. "McFarlan Six Qualified Today in the 500 Mile Speedway Race." *The Evening News*, May 27, 1912, p. 1.
33. "All Roads Lead to Speedway." *The Evening News*, May 29, 1912, p. 1.
34. "Dawson in a National Wins Thrilling 500-Mile Indianapolis Race." *Horseless Age*, June 5, 1912, p. 986.
35. "Accidents Befell Local Racing Cars." *The Evening News*, May 31, 1912, p. 1.
36. Robinson, Mary Fowler. Personal interview, August 2007.
37. "In M'Farlan Cars." *The Evening News*, May 27, 1914, p. 1.
38. "Four-States Tour Begins Tomorrow." *The Evening News* (IN), July 8, 1912, p. 1.
39. "Four-States Tour Success." *The Automobile*, July 20, 1912, pp. 114–115.
40. "McFarlan Cars Are Winners." *The Evening News*, July 22, 1912, p. 1.
41. "Local Autos in 1912 Big Run." *The Illustrated Buffalo Express*, Sept. 8, 1912, p. 44.
42. "First Day for Auto Run." *The Illustrated Buffalo Express*, Sept. 12, 1912, p. 13.
43. "Auto on Tour Turns Turtle." *The Illustrated Buffalo Express*, Sept. 13, 1912, p. 11.
44. "Car Is Penalized for Its Accident." *The Evening News*, Sept. 16, 1912, p. 1.
45. "Coast List Fills." *Motor Age*, June 19, 1913, p. 10.
46. Blakely, A. S. "Cavalcade Plans Parade Before Official Start." *Indianapolis Star*, July 1, 1913, p. 1.

47. "Local Cars in a Tour to Pacific." *The Evening News*, July 1, 1913, p. 1.
48. Quigley, Barbara. "Going West." *Traces of Indiana and Midwestern History*, Winter 2003, p. 22.
49. "Eighteen Cars Start in Indiana-Pacific Tour." *The Automobile*, July 3, 1913, p. 8.
50. "Indiana-Pacific Reaches Kansas." *The Automobile*, July 10, 1913, pp. 43–45.
51. "The Climb Begins Over Great Divide." *The Evening News*, July 14, 1913, p. 4.
52. "Snow and Sleet." *The Evening News*, July 15, 1913, p. 4.
53. "Hoosier Run Finished." *The Automobile*, August 7, 1913, p. 261.
54. "Long Trip Ended." *The Evening News*, August 4, 1913, p. 1.

Chapter 4

1. "Motorized Fire Fighting Apparatus." *The Automobile Journal*, April 25, 1915, p. 51.
2. "Motor Car Is Hero at Fire." *The Daily Examiner*, March 8, 1918, p. 4.
3. "Bright Lights on All Fire Wagons." *The Evening News*, Dec. 20, 1913, p. 1.
4. "Motor Power for Fire Department." *The Evening News*, July 28, 1914, p. 1.
5. "Contract Let for Motor Fire Wagon." *The Evening News*, August 18, 1914, p. 1.
6. "Automatic Truck in Lower Station." *The Evening News*, Nov. 27, 1914, p. 1.
7. "Fire Truck Accepted by Council on Modified Payments." *The Evening News*, Dec. 1, 1914, p. 1.
8. "Exit the Horse from City Plans." *The Evening News*, Jan. 16, 1915, p. 1.
9. Barrows, Frederic I. "Fire Department." *History of Fayette County, Indiana*, B. F. Bowen, 1917, p. 535.
10. Moore, J. Willard F. "Fire Horses Have Found Good Homes." *The Daily Examiner*, Jan. 3, 1917, p. 1.
11. "Fire Truck Crashed into Tree at Sixth." *The Daily Examiner*, Sept. 28, 1919, p. 1.
12. "Fire Truck Skids Throwing One Man." *The Evening News*, April 17, 1918, p. 1.
13. "Fire Truck Struck Cottom Auto." *The Daily Examiner*, July 5, 1919, p. 3.
14. "Two Fire Trucks Go Out of Commission." *The Evening News*, Nov. 7, 1919, p. 1.
15. "Council Studying Truck Situation." *The Evening News*, Nov. 11, 1919, p. 1.
16. "New Apparatus to Fight Fires So Badly Needed." *The Connersville News and Examiner*, Jan. 5, 1920, p. 1.
17. "Council in Next Grind." *Connersville News-Examiner*, Jan. 31, 1920, p. 1.
18. "Weak Kneed Truck Gives Down Again." *Connersville News-Examiner*, March 18, 1920, p. 1.
19. "Fire Truck Gives Down on a Journey." *Connersville News-Examiner*, Dec. 14, 1920, p. 1.
20. "Pumper Bought." *Connersville News-Examiner*, March 22, 1921, p. 1.
21. "Fire Equipment Contracts Let." *Connersville News-Examiner*, April 4, 1922, p. 1.
22. "New Truck to Be Ready Next Week." *Connersville News-Examiner*, July 1, 1922, p. 1.
23. "Fireman Hurt in Crash of a Truck." *The Daily Free Press*, Jan. 11, 1925, p. 1.
24. "Hybrid Truck." *The Daily Free Press*, Jan. 14, 1925, p. 1.
25. "Commissioners Court." *Commissioners Record*, Book 6, Connersville, Indiana, April 1918, pp. 327–328.
26. "Fayette County First Road Truck." *Connersville Evening News*, Oct. 19, 1918, p. 6.
27. Whitcomb, Joseph C. "Maxim's First Fifty Years." *The Middleborough Antiquarian*, June 1964, p. 1.
28. Smith, Howard T. *Maxim Fire Apparatus Photo History*. Hudson, WI: Iconografix, 2004, p. 15.
29. "M'Farlan Auto Ranks as Finest." *Connersville News-Examiner*, August 28, 1926, p. 1.
30. "A Funeral Car of Splendid Appearance." *The Evening News*, July 22, 1915, p. 4.
31. Walters, H. Max. "1916 McFarlan Hearse at the Smith Funeral Home." *The Making of Connersville and Fayette County* Vol. II, Gateway Press, 1989.
32. "Local and Personal." *The Connersville Examiner*, May 7, 1890, p. 3.
33. "Two Local Plants Make Auto Bodies." *The Evening News*, Feb. 1, 1910, p. 1.
34. "Candy Car." *The Evening News*, Nov. 23, 1914, p. 1.
35. Meyer, Marjorie Teetor. *One Man's Vision: The Life of Automotive Pioneer Ralph R. Tector*. Indianapolis: Guild Press of Indiana, 1995, p. 48.
36. *By This Sign*, McFarlan Motor Company, 1917, p. 8.
37. "McFarlan Body Types." *Motor Age*, Oct. 4, 1917, p. 49.
38. Brown, Arch. "McFarlan TV Series — Most Powerful American Car of 1926," *Special Interest Autos*, Feb. 1990, p. 42.
39. Stanley, Richard A. *The Lexington Automobile: A Complete History*. Jefferson, NC: McFarland, 2007, p. 182.
40. "M'Farlan Company Trucking Bodies." *The Daily Free Press*, Feb. 16, 1925, p. 1.
41. "The Locomobile Company of America." *Automobile Trade Journal*, Dec. 1, 1924, p. 81.
42. Lamm, Michael, and Holls, Dave. *A Century of Automotive Style*. Stockton, CA: Lamm-Morada Publishing, 1997, p. 40.
43. "M'Farlan Auto Ranks as Finest." *Connersville News-Examiner*, August 28, 1926, p. 1.
44. "McFarlan Company Has Large Order." *The Daily Free Press* (IN), March 25, 1925, p. 1.
45. Peterson, West. "Duesenberg Straight 8." *Cars & Parts*, Oct. 2003, pp. 42–45.
46. Heydon, Peter. Correspondence to Richard Stanley, April 2009.
47. Roe, Fred. "It All Began with 'A.'" *Automobile Quarterly*, v. 30 no. 4, 1992, pp. 42–43.

Chapter 5

1. "McFarlan Six Is a Wonderful Car." *Connersville News-Examiner*, March 16, 1923, p. 10.
2. *Motor Age*, May 6, 1922, p. 61.
3. "Adjustment and Maintenance." *Motor World*, May 3, 1922, pp. 28–29.
4. *McFarlan Six — By This Sign*, McFarlan Motor Company, Connersville, Indiana, p. 3.
5. "Test Car Driver Gravely Hurt in Wreck Above City." *Connersville News-Examiner*, August 9, 1920, p. 1.
6. "M'Farlan Motor Turns a Big Trick." *Connersville News-Examiner*, Feb. 9, 1921, p. 1.
7. "M'Farlan Car Is Found in Southland." *Connersville News-Examiner*, Feb. 16, 1921, p. 1.

8. "McFarlan Automobiles Win Place Among Men of Fame." *Connersville News-Examiner*, June 7, 1921, p. 6.
9. "Film Star's Visit Here Is Recalled." *Connersville News-Examiner*, Jan. 19, 1923, p. 1.
10. "M'Farlan Liked by the Movie Folk." *Connersville News-Examiner*, March 13, 1920, p. 1.
11. "Arbuckle Now Behind Bars." *Connersville News-Examiner*, Sept. 12, 1921, p. 1.
12. "Arbuckle Free, Quick Verdict." *Connersville News-Examiner*, April 13, 1922, p. 1.
13. Adler, Dennis. "McFarlan & Fatty." *Car Collector*, May 2009, pp. 30–39.
14. "Arbuckle Films in the Discard." *Connersville News-Examiner*, Jan. 22, 1923, p. 1.
15. Meredith, Alex. "Conspicuous Consumption." *Special Interest Autos*, Feb. 1990, pp. 44–45.
16. "Monte Blue." *The Internet Movie Database*, 2009.
17. "Connersville Made Product Ranks High in Motor World." *Connersville News-Examiner*, Sept. 15, 1922, p. 1.
18. "Home-Made Car." *Connersville News-Examiner*, March 19, 1920, p. 1.
19. "McFarlan Autos Billed to Spain." *The Daily Free Press*, Feb. 1, 1925, p. 1.
20. Bergreen, Laurence. *Capone: The Man and the Era*. New York: Simon & Schuster, 1996, pp. 233–235.
21. McNaughton, Charles. Personal interview, Oct. 25, 2001.
22. Smith, Glen. Personal interview, May 2, 2007.
23. Mezzrow, Milton, and Wolfe, Bernard. *Really the Blues*. New York: Random House, 1946, pp. 62–68.
24. "Paul Whiteman." *Wikipedia*, 2008.
25. Cangany, Harry J., Jr. Unpublished material, July 21, 2008.
26. "Connersville Made Product." *Connersville News-Examiner*, Sept. 15, 1922, p. 1.
27. "Gold Plated McFarlan Motor Car." *Motor Vehicle Monthly*, Dec. 1922, p. 24.
28. "The Highest Priced Car." *Motor Age*, Feb, 1, 1923, p. 16.
29. "Automobile to Be Gold Plated." *Connersville News-Examiner*, Oct. 26, 1922, p. 1.
30. "Gold Plated Car to Be Displayed." *Connersville News-Examiner*, Jan. 9, 1923, p. 1.
31. "Gold Plated Car Draws Interest." *Connersville News-Examiner*, Jan. 31, 1923, p. 1.
32. "Chicago Man Owns Gold Plated Car." *Connersville News-Examiner*, Feb. 3, 1923, p. 1.
33. McNaughton, Charles. Personal interview, Oct. 25, 2001.
34. McCombs, Nancy. Personal interview, March 2008.
35. McCombs and Sons ledger, ca. 1923–24 (unpublished).
36. "Car Prices and Weights." *Automobile Trade Journal*, June 1, 1923, p. 126.
37. "Passenger Car Specifications." *Automobile Trade Journal*, June 1, 1923, pp. 136–137.
38. *The National Used Car Service*. P. C. Zeigler Publishing, 1926, p. 215.
39. "McFarlan." *Motor Age*, Jan. 31, 1924, p. 28.
40. *The New and Lighter McFarlan Six*. Connersville, Indiana: McFarlan Motor Corporation, 1925.
41. *McFarlan Motor Company*. Connersville, Indiana: McFarlan Motor Company, Dec. 1923.
42. "McFarlan and Anderson Carry 4-Wheel Brakes." *Automotive Industries*, Nov. 22, 1923, p. 1077.

43. "Prices and Weights." *Motor Age*, Dec. 25, 1924, p. 45.
44. "Here and There at the Automobile Show." *Motor Age*, Jan. 29, 1925, p. 24.
45. "Ascendency of Enclosed Type Car." *Motor Age*, Dec. 25, 1924, p. 281.
46. "Connersville Products to Play Big Part at National Automobile Show." *Connersville News-Examiner*, Dec. 4, 1924, p. 1.
47. "Personal." *Connersville News-Examiner*, Jan. 20, 1925, p. 8.
48. "Good Speed." *The Daily Free Press*, May 3, 1925, p. 1.
49. "Local Factories Are Busy Indeed." *The Daily Free Press*, July 24, 1925, p. 1.
50. Belknap, R. B. Unpublished correspondence to George W. Sutton, Jr., Dec. 23, 1925.
51. "Gasoline Passenger Car Specifications." *Automobile Trade Journal*, Oct. 1, 1926, p. 108.
52. "McFarlan Produces Eight Series in Eleven Models." *Motor Age*, Oct. 22, 1925.
53. "Buyers Guide for 1926 Cars." *Motor Age*, Jan. 7, 1926, p. 87.
54. "M'Farlan Auto Ranks as Finest." *Connersville News-Examiner*, August 28, 1926, p. 1.
55. *After Seventy Years of a Settled Plan*. Connersville, Indiana: McFarlan Motor Company, 1926.
56. "Passenger Car Manufacturers." *Automobile Trade Journal*, Jan. 1, 1927, p. 96.
57. "Booth to Booth Trip at the Show." *Automobile Trade Journal*, Feb. 1, 1927, p. 26.
58. "Lexington Cars to Enter Great Shows." *The Daily Free Press*, Jan. 6, 1926, p. 1.
59. Kimes, Beverly Rae. "It Was a Very Good Year." *Automobile Quarterly*, v. 14, number 3, 1976, p. 277.
60. "Adds Phaeton 5-Passenger." *Motor Age*, July 14, 1927.
61. "Ilco-Ryan-Lite." *Automobile Trade Journal*, Feb. 1927, pp. 44–45.
62. "Gasoline Passenger Cars." *Automobile Trade Journal*, Jan. 1, 1927, pp. 100–103.
63. "Civic Business Leader Killed." *Connersville News-Examiner*, March 31, 1928, p. 1.
64. "McFarlan Motor Corporation." *Automobile Industries*, July 30, 1928.
65. "McFarlan in Receivership." *Automobile Trade Journal*, August 1, 1928, p. 69.
66. Stanley, Richard A. *The Lexington Automobile: A Complete History*. Jefferson, NC: McFarland, 2007, p. 192.
67. "M'Farlan Plant Is Sold to Auburn Co." *Connersville News-Examiner*, April 1, 1929, p. 1.
68. Squires, Donald. Personal interview, Feb. 2008.
69. *McFarlan Six—By This Sign*. Connersville, Indiana: McFarlan Motor Company, p. 2.
70. Stevensen, Burton. *The Home Book of Proverbs*. New York: Macmillan, 1956.
71. "Harry McFarlan, 55, Expires in Arizona." *Connersville News-Examiner*, Dec. 1, 1937, p. 1.
72. "1928 Twin Valve Six." *Kelley Blue Book*, July–August 1931, p. 128.

Chapter 6

1. Woodward, Bob. Telephone interview with the author, March 17, 2009.
2. Marvin, Keith, and Arnheim, Alvin J., and Blom-

mel, Henry H. *What Was the McFarlan?* Privately published, 1967, p. 65.
   3. Gambs, John R. Correspondence with the author, December 2008.
   4. Bomgardner, William, E. "The Burkhart Museum." *Antique Automobile*, Vol. 48, No. 5, Sept.–Oct. 1984, front cover, p. 18.
   5. Leubker, Earl, "What Is a McFarlan?" *The Tacoma Sunday Ledger-News Tribune*, Dec. 11, 1949.
   6. Crusis, Joe. Telephone interview with the author, March 2000.
   7. Selveira, F.W. and Barbara. Telephone interview with the author, May 2009.
   8. Marvin and Arnheim and Blommel, p. 67.
   9. Williams, Mike Worthington. "The Russian's McFarlan." *Old Cars*, Oct. 10, 1978, pp. 6 and 18.
   10. Thomas, Diane. "McFarlan 'Brought It All Together.'" *Old Cars*, June 15, 1976, p. 10.
   11. Kurtz, Dave. "Best-of-Show Car Is One of a Kind." *The Evening Star*, Sept. 7, 2000, p. A1.
   12. Anderson, Brian. Telephone interview with the author, June 25, 2008.

Bibliography

Newspaper Articles

"Accidents Befell Local Racing Cars." *Connersville Evening News*, May 31,1912, p. 1.

"Additional Local." *Cambridge City Tribune* (IN), July 21, 1910, p. 2.

"Additional Local." *The Connersville Examiner*, July 4, 1883, p. 2.

"All Roads Lead to the Big Speedway." *The Evening News* (IN), May 29, 1912, p. 1.

"All Signs Point to an Active Auto Market." *San Francisco Post*, Nov. 29, 1910.

"Another Automobile Company Files Association Articles." *The Evening News* (Connersville, IN), Nov. 21, 1906, p. 1.

"Ansted Brothers Turn a Big Deal." *Connersville Evening News*, April 5, 1918, p. 1.

"Arbuckle Films in the Discard." *Connersville News-Examiner*, Jan. 22, 1923, p. 1.

"Arbuckle Free; Quick Verdict." *Connersville News-Examiner*, April 3, 1922, p. 1.

"Arbuckle Now Behind Bars." *Connersville News-Examiner*, Sept. 12, 1921, p. 1.

"Australia Man Contracts for 25 McFarlans." *The Daily Examiner* (IN), Nov. 21, 1910, p. 1.

"Auto Companies to Return to Making of Pleasure Cars Somewhat as They Did Before War." *The Evening News* (Connersville, IN), Nov. 13, 1918, p. 1.

"Auto Expansion Programs Seen." *The Evening News* (Connersville, IN), Nov. 25, 1916, p. 1.

"Auto on Tour Turns Turtle." *The Illustrated Buffalo Express* (NY), Sept. 13, 1912, p. 11.

"Automatic Truck in Lower Station." *The Evening News* (Connersville, IN), Nov. 22, 1914, p. 1.

"Automobile Accident." *The Daily News* (Connersville, IN), Nov. 25, 1901, p. 2.

"Automobile Plant May Locate Here." *The Evening News* (Connersville, IN), June 20, 1906, p. 2.

"Automobile to Be Gold Plated." *Connersville News-Examiner*, Oct. 26, 1922, p. 1.

"Automobile Was Dreamed of Here." *Connersville News-Examiner*, April 16, 1925, p. 1.

"Bert Adams with a M'Farlan Six." *The Evening News* (Connersville, IN), Oct. 11, 1911, p. 1.

"Better Cars and Not Too Cheap." *The Evening News* (Connersville, IN), July 13, 1910, p. 1.

"Big Combine of Carriage Makers." *The Evening News* (Connersville, IN), Sept. 11, 1907, p. 1.

"Big Contract for M'Farlan Plant." *Connersville News-Examiner*, April 12, 1923, p. 1.

"A Big Display." *The Daily News* (Connersville, IN), April 14, 1900, p. 2.

"Big Rush Sale of M'Farlan Cars." *The Evening News* (Connersville, IN), Sept. 4, 1911, p. 1.

"A Big Shipment." *The Daily News* (Connersville, IN), Jan. 3, 1891, p. 2.

Blakley, A. S. "Cavalcade Plans Parade Before Official Start." *Indianapolis Star*, July 1, 1913, p. 1

"Board of Trade." *The Daily Examiner* (Connersville, IN), Jan. 14, 1891, p. 4.

"Bright Lights on Fire Wagons." *The Evening News* (Connersville, IN), Dec. 19, 1913, p. 1.

"Bright Outlook for Business in 1904." *The Evening News* (Connersville, IN), Feb. 18, 1904, p. 2.

"Brownell Motor in McFarlan 6." *The San Francisco Bulletin*, April 18, 1910.

"Business Change at Upper Garage." *The Evening News* (Connersville, IN), August 24, 1909, p. 1.

"Cambridge City and Environs 50 Years Ago — As Told by the Local Newspapers." *The National Road Traveler* (Cambridge City, IN), Feb. 23, 1961, p. 1.

"Cambridge City and Environs 47 Years Ago — As Told by the Local Newspapers." *The National Road Traveler* (Cambridge City, IN), Sept. 20, 1962, p. 1.

"Candy Car." *The Evening News* (Connersville, IN), Nov. 23, 1914, p. 1.

"Car Is Penalized for Its Accident." *The Evening News* (Connersville, IN), Sept. 16, 1912, p. 1.

"Cars and Drivers Named in Big Race." *The Indianapolis Star*, May 3, 1911, p. 9.

"Car Turns Turtle." *The Evening News* (Connersville, IN), Sept. 13, 1912, p. 1.

"Cavalcade Plans Parade Before Official Start." *The Indianapolis Star*, August 1, 1913, p. 1.

"Central Manufacturing Company's Plant Almost Totally Destroyed." *The Evening News* (IN), Oct. 27, 1905, p. 2.

"Chicago Man Owns Gold Plated Car." *Connersville News-Examiner*, Feb. 3, 1923, p. 1.

Cincinnati Enquirer, Nov. 7, 1910.

"City News." *The Daily Examiner* (Connersville, IN), Feb. 18, 1891, p. 4.

"City News." *The Daily Examiner* (Connersville, IN), June 4, 1891, p. 4.

"Civic, Business Leader Killed." *Connersville News-Examiner*, March 31, 1928, p. 1.

"The Climb Begins Over Great Divide." *Connersville Evening News*, July 14, 1913, p. 4.

Connersville Daily Examiner, Oct. 15, 1895, p. 4.

Connersville Examiner, Nov. 4, 1868, p. 3; Sept. 6, 1871, p. 2; Sept. 18, 1881, p. 1.

"Connersville Made Product Ranks High in Motor World." *Connersville News-Examiner*, Sept. 15, 1922, pp. 1, 10.

"Connersville Products to Play Big Part at National Automobile Show." *Connersville News-Examiner*, Dec, 4, 1924, p. 1.
Connersville Times, Dec, 23, 1868, p. 3; May 19, 1869, p. 3; May 26, 1869, p. 3; Sept. 15, 1869, p. 3; Dec. 28, 1870, p. 2; Nov. 24, 1881, p. 1; Jan. 25, 1882, p. 1; Feb. 8, 1882, p. 1.
"Connersville Was Up at the Front." *Connersville News-Examiner*, March 13, 1920, p. 8.
"Contract Let for Motor Fire Wagon." *The Evening News* (Connersville, IN), August 18, 1914, p. 1.
"Convince Rancher of McFarlan's Worth." *San Francisco Chronicle*, July 17, 1910.
"Council in Next Grind." *Connersville News-Examiner*, Jan. 31, 1920, p. 1.
"Council Studying Truck Situation." *The Evening News*, Nov. 11, 1919, p. 1.
"Dan M. Hankins Work as Salesman." *The Evening News* (IN), April 30, 1914, p. 1.
"Demonstrator Returns." *San Francisco Globe*, Oct. 26, 1910.
"A Double Somersault." *Connersville Daily Examiner*, April 18, 1895, p. 4.
"The Drivers and Their Histories." *The Indianapolis Star*, May 28, 1911, p. 6.
"Equaled the Speedway Record." *Connersville Daily Examiner*, Sept. 7, 1910, p. 1.
"Exit the Horse from City Plans." *The Evening News* (Connersville, IN), Jan. 26, 1915, p. 1.
"Factory Sold." *The Evening News* (Connersville, IN), Dec. 31, 1913, p. 1.
"Failed to Fill Contract." *The Daily News* (Connersville, IN), Nov. 14, 1901, p. 2.
"The Fair." *The Connersville Examiner*, Sept. 13, 1871, p. 1.
"Fayette County First Road Truck." *Connersville Evening News*, Oct. 19, 1918, p. 6.
"Film Star's Visit Here Is Recalled." *Connersville News-Examiner*, Jan. 19, 1923, p. 1.
"Fire Equipment Contracts Let." *Connersville News-Examiner*, April 4, 1922, p. 1.
"Fire Truck Accepted by Council on Modified Payments." *The Evening News* (Connersville, IN), Dec. 1, 1914.
"Fire Truck Crashed into Tree at Sixth." *The Daily Examiner* (Connersville, IN), Sept. 28, 1916, p. 1.
"Fire Truck Gives Down on a Journey." *Connersville News-Examiner*, Dec. 14, 1920, p. 1.
"Fire Truck Skids Throwing One Man." *Connersville Evening News*, April 17, 1918, p. 1.
"Fire Truck Struck Cotton Auto." *The Daily Examiner* (Connersville, IN), July 3, 1919, p. 3.
"Firemen Hurt in Crash of a Truck." *The Daily Free Press* (Connersville, IN), Jan. 11, 1925, p. 1.
"First Day of Auto Run." *The Illustrated Buffalo Express* (NY), Sept. 12, 1912, p. 13.
"Fortunes Made in Triple Signs." *The Daily News* (Connersville, IN), Feb. 22, 1900, p. 2.
"Four-States Tour Begins Tomorrow." *The Evening News* (Connersville, IN), July 8, 1912, p. 1.
"A Funeral Car of Splendid Appearance." *The Evening News* (IN), July 22, 1915, p. 4.
"Gets Coast Agency for Two Popular Indiana Cars." *The San Francisco Evening Post*, Oct. 2, 1910.
"Gold-Plated Car Draws Interest." *Connersville News-Examiner*, Jan. 31, 1923, p. 1.
"Gold Plated Car to Be Displayed." *Connersville News-Examiner*, Jan. 9, 1923, p. 1.
"Good Speed." *The Daily Free Press* (Connersville, IN), May 3, 1925, p. 1.

"Great Day for McFarlan Six." *The Connersville Daily Examiner*, Nov. 8, 1910, p. 1.
"Great Showing of McFarlan Six Cars." *San Francisco Post-Globe*, Nov. 16, 1910.
"Great Stroke of Enterprise." *The Daily News* (Connersville, IN), Jan. 9, 1900, p. 2.
"Harry McFarlan, 55, Expires in Arizona." *Connersville News-Examiner* (IN), Dec. 1, 1937, p. 1.
"Hatfield Motor Company Assign." *The Evening News* (Connersville, IN), March 20, 1908, p. 1.
"History of Old M'Farlan Corner." *The Evening News* (Connersville, IN), Jan. 22, 1914, p. 1.
"Home Cars Attract Attention in New York Show." *The Connersville News and Examiner*, Jan, 5, 1920, p. 1.
"Home-Made Car." *Connersville News-Examiner*, March 19, 1920, p. 1.
"Honk! Honk! The First Auto Arrived in C'ville Twenty Yrs. Ago Today." *Connersville News-Examiner*, Nov. 25, 1921, p. 1.
"Honk Honks from Gasoline Row." *San Francisco Globe*, Sept. 12, 1910.
"Horse Vehicle Trade Fell Off." *The Evening News* (Connersville, IN), Jan. 7, 1910, p. 1.
"Hybrid Truck." *The Daily Free Press* (Connersville, IN), Jan. 14, 1925, p. 1.
"An Important Vehicle Change in San Francisco." *San Francisco Record*, March 1910.
"In M'Farlan Cars." *The Evening News* (Connersville, IN), May 27, 1914, p. 1.
"J.B. McFarlan & Sons Carriage Manufactory." *The Daily News Special Illustrated Edition* (Connersville, IN), June 1896, reprint 1996, p. 4.
"J. E. McFarlan Is Severely Injured." *The Evening News* (Connersville, IN), July 11, 1907, p. 1.
"John Becraft McFarlan Has Been Called to Rest." *The Evening News* (Connersville, IN), August 16, 1909, pp. 1, 5.
"Joy Car Factories Advised to Change." *The Evening News* (Connersville, IN), August 10, 1918, p. 2.
Kurtz, Dave. "Best-of-Show Car Is One of a Kind." *The Evening Star* (Auburn, IN), Sept. 7, 2000, p. A1.
"Largest Single Shipment of Vehicles Ever Sent Out of the State." *The Connersville Courier*, Jan. 11, 1900, p. 1.
"Lexington Cars to Enter Great Shows." *The Daily Free Express* (Connersville, IN), Jan. 6, 1926, p. 1.
"Light Dimmers for Cars in City." *The Evening News* (Connersville, IN), Sept. 23, 1915, p. 1.
"Little Sixes Have All Latest Features." *The Evening Post* (San Francisco, CA), Dec. 2, 1911.
"Local and Personal." *The Connersville Examiner*, Dec. 24, 1867, p. 3; March 4, 1868, p. 3; Dec. 23, 1868, p. 3; May 24, 1871, p. 3; Sept. 20, 1871, p. 3; April 24, 1872, p. 3; June 5, 1872, p. 3; Sept. 25, 1872, p. 3; April 16, 1873, p. 3; May 21, 1873, p. 3; Oct. 8, 1873, p. 3; May 9, 1876, p. 2; July 12, 1876, p. 3; Jan. 5, 1882, p. 3; Feb. 15, 1882, p. 3; March 15, 1882, p. 3; April 19, 1882, p. 3; May 2, 1882, p. 3; May 24, 1882, p. 3; May 31, 1882, p. 3; July 5, 1882, p. 3; Sept. 13, 1882, p. 3; Dec. 27, 1882, p. 3; July 25, 1883, p. 3; Sept. 19, 1883, p. 3; Oct. 24, 1883, p. 3; Nov. 7, 1883, p. 3; Nov. 14, 1883, p. 3; Feb. 6, 1884, p. 3; April 27, 1884, p. 3; July 2, 1884, p. 3; August 13, 1884, p. 3; August 27, 1884, p. 3; Dec. 24, 1884, p. 3; Dec. 12, 1888, p. 3; Oct. 30, 1889, p. 3; Nov. 6, 1889, p. 3; Jan. 15, 1890, p. 3; Feb. 19, 1890, p. 3; March 19, 1890, p. 3; May 7, 1890, p. 3; May 21, 1890, p. 3; July 23, 1890, p. 3; Nov. 12, 1890, p. 3; Nov. 4, 1892, p. 3; April 13, 1900, p. 3; May 28, 1902, p. 8.

_____. *The Evening News* (Connersville, IN), Oct. 10, 1902, p. 3.
"Local Automakers Given Attention." *The Evening News* (Connersville, IN), March 12, 1919, p. 1.
"Local Autos in 1912 Big Run." *The Illustrated Buffalo Express* (NY), Sept. 8, 1912, p. 44.
"Local Cars in a Tour to Pacific." *The Evening News* (Connersville, IN), July 1, 1913, p. 1.
"Local Factories Are Busy Indeed." *The Daily Free Press* (Connersville, IN), July 24, 1925, p. 1.
"Local Matters." *The Connersville Times*, Feb. 16, 1887, p. 7; Feb. 23, 1887, p. 6; August 19, 1887, p. 7; March 22, 1888, p. 6; June 27, 1888, p. 6; Nov. 21, 1888, p. 6.
"Local News." *The Connersville Times*, Dec. 30, 1868, p. 3; May 19, 1869, p. 3; Nov. 16, 1870, p. 3; August 7, 1872, p. 3; Feb. 15, 1882, p. 1; Sept. 30, 1887, p. 7; Dec. 16, 1887, p. 7; Feb. 17, 1888, p. 6.
"Long Trip Ended." *The Evening News* (Connersville, IN), August 4, 1913, p. 1.
Luebker, Earl. "What Is a McFarlan?" *The Tacoma Sunday Ledger-News Tribune* (WA), Dec. 11, 1949.
"Making Autos at M'Farlan's." *The Evening News* (Connersville, IN), Sept. 4, 1909, p. 1.
"Manufacture of Auto Piano Parts." *The Evening News* (Connersville, IN), Sept. 21, 1912, p. 1.
"Man Who Induced Late Mr. M'Farlan." *The Evening News* (Connersville, IN), July 9, 1910, p. 1.
"McFarlan Automobiles Win Place Among Men of Fame in Ring and Before Camera." *Connersville News-Examiner*, June 7, 1921, p. 6.
"McFarlan Auto Plant Running." *The Evening News* (Connersville, IN), Nov. 20, 1909, p. 1.
"McFarlan Autos Billed to Spain." *The Daily Free Press* (Connersville, IN), Feb. 1, 1925, p. 1.
"McFarlan Available Here." *San Francisco Bulletin*, March 26, 1910.
"The McFarlan Buggy Manufacturing Company." *The Daily News* (Connersville, IN), March 2, 1900, p. 4.
"The McFarlan Car Had Fine Showing." *The Evening News* (Connersville, IN), Nov. 4, 1909, p. 1.
"McFarlan Carriage Company to Manufacture Cars." *The Evening News* (Connersville, IN), June 11, 1909, p. 1.
"McFarlan Cars Are Driven to Seaside." *The Evening News* (Connersville, IN), April 8, 1918, p. 1.
"McFarlan Cars Are Winners." *The Evening News* (Connersville, IN), July 22, 1912, p. 1.
"McFarlan Cars in Show at Buffalo." *The Evening News* (Connersville, IN), Feb. 1, 1913, p. 1.
"McFarlan Company in Front Column." *The Daily Examiner* (Connersville, IN), March 17, 1919, p. 1.
"McFarlan Company Is Making a Change." *Connersville News-Examiner*, March 18, 1920, p. 1.
"McFarlan Plant to Do Government Work." *The Daily Examiner* (Connersville, IN), Dec. 21, 1917, p. 1.
"McFarlan Six at Hoosier Capital." *The Evening News* (Connersville, IN), Feb. 11, 1910, p. 1.
"McFarlan Six in Great Show." *The Connersville Daily Examiner*, Dec. 22, 1910, p. 1.
"McFarlan Six — 1912." *The Indianapolis Star*, May 28, 1911, Auto Section p. 8.
"The McFarlan Six Is a Wonderful Car." *Connersville News-Examiner*, March 16, 1923, p. 10.
"McFarlans Are Making Fine Showing." *The Connersville Daily Examiner*, Nov. 5, 1910, p. 1.
"McFarlans at Speedway." *The Connersville Daily Examiner*, August 26, 1910, p. 1.
"McFarlans Go to Atlanta GA." *The Connersville Daily Examiner*, Oct. 18, 1910, p. 1.
"McFarlan Six Did Very Well." *The Connersville Daily Examiner*, Nov. 4, 1910, p. 1.
"McFarlan Sixes at the Speedway." *The Evening News* (Connersville, IN), Sept. 6, 1910, p. 1.
"McFarlan Six Handicapped." *The Connersville Daily Examiner*, Nov. 2, p. 1.
"McFarlan Six in Today's Race." *The Connersville Daily Examiner*, Nov. 7, 1910, p. 1.
"M'Farlan Auto Ranks as Finest." *Connersville News-Examiner*, August 28, 1926, p. 1.
"M'Farlan Cars in Great Race." *The Daily News* (Connersville, IN), Sept. 5, 1910, p. 1.
"M'Farlan Car Which Mysteriously Left Between Days, Six Months Ago, Is Found in Possession of Thieves in Southland." *Connersville News-Examiner*, Feb. 16, 1921, p. 1.
"M'Farlan Company Acquires the Title." *The Evening News* (Connersville, IN), Nov. 4, 1919, p. 1.
"M'Farlan Company Awards Contract." *The Evening News* (Connersville, IN), Sept. 27, 1913, p. 1.
"M'Farlan Company Has Big Order." *The Daily Free Press* (Connersville, IN), March 25, 1925, p. 1.
"M'Farlan Company Trucking Bodies." *The Daily Free Press* (Connersville, IN), Feb. 16, 1925, p. 1.
"M'Farlan Motor Company Formed." *The Evening News* (Connersville, IN), Sept. 25, 1913, p. 1.
"M'Farlan Motor Given Final Test." *The Evening News* (Connersville, IN), August 18, 1910, p. 1.
"A M'Farlan Motor of Brand New Kind Turns a Big Trick." *Connersville News-Examiner*, Feb. 9, 1921, p. 1.
"M'Farlan Motor Turns a Big Trick." *Connersville News-Examiner* (IN), Feb. 9, 1921, p. 1.
"M'Farlan Plant Is Mentioned in Word." *The Evening News* (Connersville, IN), Nov. 25, 1918, p. 1.
"M'Farlan Plant Is Sold to Auburn Co." *Connersville News-Examiner*, April 1, 1929, p. 1.
"M'Farlans Catch Handful of Prizes." *Connersville News-Examiner*, April 15, 1920, p. 1.
"M'Farlan Six in Great Coast Tour." *The Evening News* (Connersville, IN), August 9, 1913, p. 1.
"M'Farlan Six in Notable Victory." *The Evening News* (Connersville, IN), Sept. 5, 1910, p. 1.
"M'Farlan Six in Today's Races." *The Evening News* (Connersville, IN), Sept. 3, 1910, p. 1.
"M'Farlan Six Is a Wonder Car." *Connersville News-Examiner*, March 19, 1923, p. 1.
"M'Farlans Liked by the Movie Folk." *Connersville News-Examiner*, March 13, 1920, p. 1.
M'Farlan Six Qualified Today in the 500 Mile Speedway Race." *The Evening News* (IN), May 27, 1912, p. 1.
"M'Farlan Working on Federal Order." *The Evening News* (Connersville, IN), March 10, 1919, p. 1.
Moore, J. Willard F. "Fire Horses Have Found Good Homes." *The Daily Examiner* (Connersville, IN), Jan. 3, 1917, p. 1.
"Motor Car Is Hero at Fire." *The Daily Examiner* (Connersville, IN), March 8, 1918, p. 4.
"Motor Power for Fire Department." *The Evening News* (Connersville, IN), July 28, 1914, p. 1.
"Nationals First in Speedway Feature." *The Indianapolis Star*, Sept. 6, 1910, p. 1.
"New 1911 Motors for M'Farlan Six," *The Evening News* (Connersville, IN), Nov. 23, 1910, p. 8.
"New Apparatus to Fight Local Fires So Badly Needed." *The Connersville News and Examiner*, Jan. 5, 1920, p. 1.
"New Auto Agency." *Noblesville Ledger* (IN), April 1910.
"New Connersville Industry Files Incorporation Articles." *The Evening News* (Connersville, IN), Nov. 20, 1906, p. 2.

"A New Deal." *The Daily News* (Connersville, IN), Sept. 7, 1901, p. 1.

"New Pilots Arrive Here." *The Indianapolis Star*, May 3, 1912, p. 11.

"New Truck to Be Ready Next Week." *Connersville News-Examiner*, July 1, 1922, p. 1.

"News Industry Story Pleasing." *The Evening News* (Connersville, IN), June 12, 1909, p. 1.

"No Hotel." *The Connersville Daily Examiner*, Jan. 2, 1891, p. 4.

"Officers Visited Town of Everton." *The Daily Examiner* (Connersville, IN), Sept. 2, 1916, p. 1.

"Oh Yez! Oh Yez!" *Connersville News-Examiner*, Oct. 25, 1967, p. 3.

"Only Car That Had No Trouble." *The Evening News* (Connersville, IN), Nov. 8, 1910, p. 2.

"Personal." *Connersville News-Examiner*, Jan. 20, 1925, p. 8.

"A Pleasant Event." *Connersville Daily Examiner*, Nov. 20, 1895, p. 4.

"Potter Wins." *The Connersville Times*, April 26, 1899, p. 1.

"Premiums Awarded at the Fayette County Fair." *The Connersville Examiner*, Sept. 21, 1870, p. 1.

"Premium List Concluded." *Connersville Times*, Sept. 22, 1869, p. 3.

"The Ray Motor Co. Is Almost Ready." *The Evening News* (Connersville, IN), Feb. 6, 1907, p. 1.

"Real Estate Transfers." *Connersville Times*, Dec. 23, 1868, p. 3.

"Reply Given to Local Critic." *The Daily Examiner* (Connersville, IN), July 3, 1919, p. 1.

"Snow and Sleet." *The Evening News* (Connersville, IN), July 15, 1913, p. 4.

"Some Auto Facts of Real Interest." *The Evening News* (Connersville, IN), June 21, 1910, p. 1.

"Speed Kings Ready for Coming Strife." *The Indianapolis Star*, Sept. 2, 1910, p. 1.

"Splendid Showing for M'Farlan Six." *Connersville Evening News*, Sept. 5, 1910, p. 5.

"Streets and Alleys in Business Section to Be Paved with Brick." *The Connersville Times*, August 5, 1903, p. 2.

"Suit for Damages in Sum of $6,000." *Connersville Evening News*, Feb. 10, 1904, p. 2.

"Ten Big Sixes in Three Short Days." *Connersville Evening News*, Nov. 22, 1913, p. 1.

"Test Car Driver Gravely Hurt in Wreck Above City." *Connersville News-Examiner*, August 9, 1920, p. 1.

"Test Car Struck." *The Evening News* (Connersville, IN), Jan. 21, 1910, p. 1.

"Test Cars Raise the Public Wrath." *The Evening News* (Connersville, IN), Oct. 5, 1914, p. 1.

"The M'Farlan 40 on Streets Today." *The Evening News* (Connersville, IN), August 18, 1909, p. 1.

"To Handle McFarlan Cars." *San Francisco Post*, June 11, 1910.

"To the Public." *Connersville Times*, March 21, 1876, p. 4.

"Twenty-One Cars Have Qualified." *The Evening News* (Connersville, IN), May 28, 1912, p. 1.

"Two Fine Samples to First Be Built." *The Evening News* (Connersville, IN), August 6, 1909, p. 1.

"Two Fire Trucks Go Out of Commission." *The Evening News* (Connersville, IN), Nov. 7, 1919, p. 1.

"Two Local Plants Make Auto Bodies." *The Evening News* (Connersville, IN), Feb. 1, 1910, p. 1.

"Vern Dumas with His Family in Their McFarlan Six Car." *San Francisco Chronicle* (CA), June 12, 1910.

"A Very Important Industrial Move." *The Evening News* (Connersville, IN), Jan. 5, 1914, p. 1.

"The Wayne County Fair." *Connersville Times*, Oct. 13, 1869, p. 2.

"We Are Selling Cars." *The Evening News* (Connersville, IN), July 1, 1912, p. 1.

"Weak Kneed Truck Gives Down Again." *Connersville News-Examiner*, March 18, 1920, p. 1.

"Wilson to Review Motor Car Parade." *The Daily Examiner* (Connersville, IN), Sept. 28, 1916, p. 1.

"Wonderful Feat of M'Farlan Six." *The Evening News* (Connersville, IN), Sept. 7, 1910, p. 1.

"W. W. McFarlan Is to Retire." *The Connersville Times*, Sept. 2, 1908, p. 1

Other Articles

"Adds Phaeton 5-Passenger." *Motor Age*, July 14, 1927.

"Adjustment and Maintenance of the Borg & Beck Clutch." *Motor World*, May 3. 1922, pp. 28–29.

Adler, Dennis. "McFarlan & Fatty." *Car Collector*, May 2009, pp. 30–39.

"Agency Opportunities." *Automobile Trade Journal*, Sept. 1, 1914, p. 176.

"Announcement for the Motorist." *Motor Print*, April 1910, p. 20.

"Ascendancy of Enclosed Type Car Shown in Fisher Booklet." *Motor Age*, Dec. 25, 1924, p. 35.

Automobile Trade Journal, March 1, 1920, p. 315.

"Automobiles Costing from $2000 to $2999." *The Automobile*, Jan. 9, 1913, p. 107.

Bomgardner, William E. "The Burkhart Museum." *Antique Automobile*, vol. 48, no. 5, Sept–Oct. 1984, front cover, p. 18.

"Booth to Booth Trip at the Show." *Automobile Trade Journal*, Feb. 1, 1927, p. 26.

Brown, Arch. "McFarlan TV Series—Most Powerful American Car of 1926." *Special Interest Autos*, Feb. 1990, pp. 28, 42.

"Buyers Guide for 1926 Cars." *Motor Age*, Jan. 7, 1926, p. 87.

"Car Prices and Weights—Maker's List." *Automobile Trade Journal*, June 1, 1923, p. 126.

Catlin, Russ. "Who Really Won the First Indy 500?" *Automobile Quarterly*, vol. 7, no. 4, 1969, pp. 383–384.

"Coast List Fills." *Motor Age*, June 19, 1913, p. 10.

"Current Passenger Car Specifications." *Motor Age*, Dec. 25, 1924, p. 46.

"Dawson in a National Wins Thrilling 500-Mile Indianapolis Race." *The Horseless Age*, June 5, 1912, p. 30.

"Details of Passenger Automobiles on the American Market for 1911." *The Automobile*, Jan. 5, 1911, pp. 56–87.

"Eighteen Cars Start in Indiana-Pacific Tour." *The Automobile*, July 3, 1913, p. 8.

"Engineering Aspects of Chicago Show." *The Automobile*, Jan. 29, 1914, pp. 295–296.

"Entrants in 500-Mile Race on Indianapolis Speedway." *Motor Age*, May 9, 1912, p. 15.

"$50,000 Company Formed at Connersville, Ind." *Automobile Topics*, Dec. 1, 1906, p. 658.

"500 Mile Sweepstakes Run Off at the Indianapolis Speedway." *The Automobile*, June 1, 1911, pp. 22–27.

"Form McFarlan Motor Co." *Motor Age*, Oct. 9, 1913, p. 23.

"Four-States Tour Success." *The Automobile*, July 18, 1912, pp. 114–115.

"Garden Display to Show Year's Progress." *Motor Age*, Dec, 22, 1910, p. 12.

"Gasoline Passenger Car Specifications." *Automobile Trade Journal*, Jan. 1, 1927, pp. 100–103.

"Glenaw in Falcar Captures Coca-Cola Cup." *Motor Age*, Nov. 10, 1910, pp. 1–5.

"A Gold Plated McFarlan Motor Car." *Motor Vehicle Monthly*, Dec. 1922, p. 24.

"Gray Pneumatic Gearshift Eliminates Both Hand Levers." *Motor Age*, June 19, 1913, p. 30.

"The Hatch Affair." *Air Cooled News*, Issue 16, June 1958, p. 2.

"Here and There at the Automobile Show." *Motor Age*, Jan. 29, 1925, p. 24.

"The Highest Priced Car." *Motor Age*, Feb. 1, 1923, p. 16.

"Hoosier Party Reaches Pacific Ocean." *The Automobile*, July 31, 1913, pp. 211–212.

"Hoosier Run Finished." *The Automobile*, August 7, 1913, p. 261.

The Horseless Age, Dec. 15, 1915, p. 54.

Hubbard, Thomas H. "The Case for Franklin." *Automobile Quarterly*, vol. 5, no. 5, 1967, p. 240.

"Ilco-Ryan-Lite." *Automobile Trade Journal*, Feb. 1927. pp. 44–45.

"Improvements in the McFarlan Six." *The Horseless Age*, August 26, 1914, pp. 319–320.

"Indiana Gains Two More Auto Makers." *The Automobile*, Nov. 29, 1906, p. 739.

"Indiana-Pacific Reaches Kansas." *The Automobile*, July 10, 1913, pp. 43–45.

"Indiana-to-Coast Tourists at Goldfield." *The Automobile*, July 24, 1913, pp. 144–145.

"Indiana Tourists Reach Grand Junction." *The Automobile*, July 17, 1913, pp. 102–103.

"John B. McFarlan." *The Carriage Monthly*, Sept. 1909, p. 17.

Kimes, Beverly Rae. "It Was a Very Good Year." *Automobile Quarterly*, vol. 14, no. 3, 1976, p. 277.

_____. "The Rise and Fall of the Empire." *Automobile Quarterly*, vol. 12, no. 1, 1974, p. 72.

"Labor Day Events at Indianapolis." *The Automobile*, Sept. 8, 1910, pp. 17–20.

"List Prices and Weights — Passenger Cars." *Automobile Trade Journal*, March 1, 1920, p. 315.

"The Locomobile Company of America." *Automobile Trade Journal*, Dec. 1, 1924, p. 81.

"McFarlan." *Motor*, Nov. 1912, p. 153.

"McFarlan." *Motor Age*, Jan. 31. 1924, p. 28.

"McFarlan Adopts Floating Axle." *The Automobile*, Jan. 9, 1913, p. 124.

"McFarlan and Anderson Carry 4-Wheel Brakes." *Automotive Industries*, Nov. 22, 1923, p. 1077.

"McFarlan Body Types." *Motor Age*, Oct. 4, 1917, p. 49.

"McFarlan Cars." *The Motor World*, Jan. 18, 1912, p. 418.

"McFarlan Concentrates on Six for 1914," *The Automobile*, Nov. 13, 1913, pp. 916–917.

"McFarlan Has Pneumatic Gear Shift." *Automobile Trade Journal*, Feb. 1914, p. 100A.

"McFarlan in Receivership." *Automobile Trade Journal*, August 1, 1928, p. 69.

"McFarlan Is Longer and Lower." *Automobile Topics*, August 15, 1914, p. 5.

"McFarlan Magnetic Transmission." *Motor World*, Dec. 27, 1916.

"McFarlan Motor Car Co." *Motor Age*, April 10, 1913, p. 19.

"McFarlan Motor Corporation." *Automotive Industries*, June 30, 1928.

"The McFarlan New Series." *Automobile Trade Journal*, Jan. 1913, p. 179–181.

"McFarlan Ninety for 1918 Carries Wide Range of Bodies." *Automobile Topics*, August 11, 1917, p. 39.

"McFarlan Ninety Shows Refinement." *The Horseless Age*, June 15, 1916, pp. 478–479.

"McFarlan Price Increase." *Automobile Industries*, April 11, 1918, p. 749.

"McFarlan Produces Eight Series in Eleven Models." *Motor Age*, Oct. 22, 1925.

"McFarlan Putting Out a Six." *The Automobile*, Jan. 1, 1914, p. 70.

"McFarlan Six." *The Automobile*, August 20, 1914, p. 88.

"McFarlan Six." *Cycle and Automobile Trade Journal*, Jan. 1, 1910, pp. 36–37.

"McFarlan Six." *Motor World*, Jan. 18, 1912, p. 418.

"McFarlan Six —1911." *McClure's*, Dec. 1910, p. 64.

"McFarlan Six —1911." *The Saturday Evening Post*, Nov. 12, 1910, p. 52.

"McFarlan Six Series T and X." *The Automobile Journal*, August 25, 1915, pp. 41–43.

"A New Achievement." *The Theatre*, Feb. 1917, p. 123.

"McFarlan Sixes." *Automobile Trade Journal*, Jan. 1, 1912, p. 279.

"The McFarlan Submarine." *Horseless Age*, June 2, 1915, p. 734.

Meredith, Alex. "Conspicuous Consumption — Fatty Arbuckle's Fabulous Pierce Arrow," *Special Interest Autos*, Feb. 1990, p. 45.

"Minor Mention." *The Horseless Age*, June 23, 1909, p. 867.

"Minor Mention." *The Horseless Age*, Sept. 29, 1909, p. 359.

Motor Age, April 10, 1913, p. 19; May 6, 1920, p. 61.

"Motor Age Monthly Passenger Car Specification Tables," *Motor Age*, May 6, 1920, p. 61.

"Motorized Fire Fighting Apparatus." *The Automobile Journal*, April 25, 1915, p. 51.

"The N A A M Show." *The Automobile*, Feb. 3, 1910, p. 7–10.

"National Show Issue Specification Number." *Motor Age*, Jan. 7, 1926, p. 84.

The National Used Car Service, P. C. Zeigler Publishing, 1926, p. 215.

"New Agencies Established During the Week." *The Automobile*, March 6, 1913, p. 619.

"New Incorporations." *The Horseless Age*, Dec. 12, 1906, p. 840.

"New McFarlan Models Have Longer Wheelbase." *Motor World*, August 19, 1914, p. 10.

"New McFarlan Six." *The Horseless Age*, Oct. 22, 1913, pp. 693–694.

"New Six Cylinder Motor." *The Horseless Age*, August 17, 1910, p. 251.

"New Vehicles and Parts." *Horseless Age*, August 26, 1914, pp. 319–320.

"Newest McFarlan Lower and Roomier." *Motor World*, June 14, 1916, pp. 18–19.

"1916 Passenger Automobiles Listed with Technical Specifications." *The Automobile*, Dec. 30, 1915, pp. 1250–1251.

"1917 McFarlan Built on Single Chassis — A Bigger Car." *The Automobile*, June 15, 1916, pp. 1088–1089.

"1928 Twin Valve Six." *Kelly Kar Blue Book*, July–August 1931, p. 128.

"One Standard Chassis for McFarlan Six Next Season." *The Horseless Age*, Sept. 27, 1910, p. 12.

"Open Cars for Five Passengers at $2400 to $3000." *The Automobile*, Jan. 9, 1913, p. 83.

"Passenger Car Manufacturers, Car Prices and Weights." *Automobile Trade Journal*, Jan. 1, 1927, p. 93.

"Passenger Car Specifications." *Automobile Trade Journal*, March 1, 1920, pp. 322–323.
"Passenger Car Specifications." *Automobile Trade Journal*, June 1, 1923, pp. 136–137.
"Passenger Cars for 1915 Listed with Their Principal Specifications." *The Automobile*, Dec. 31, 1914, pp. 1224–1225.
Peterson, West. "Duesenberg Straight 8 — The Next Generation." *Cars & Parts*, Oct. 2003, pp. 42–45.
"Prices and Weights of Current Passenger Car Models." *Motor Age*, Dec. 25, 1924, p. 45.
Quigley, Barbara. "Going West." *Traces of Indiana and Midwestern History*, Winter 2003, p. 22.
"Refinement in New McFarlan Six." *The American Chauffeur*, Nov. 1915, pp. 490–491.
"Restricted Credit Hampers Pope Finances." *The Automobile*, Oct. 30, 1913, p. 837.
"Right or Left Control — Which?" *The Automobile*, August 1, 1912, pp. 209–213.
Roe, Fred. "It All Began with "A." *Automobile Quarterly*, vol. 30, no. 4, 1992, pp. 42–43.
"Seventeenth Annual Complete Car Review." *Automobile Trade Journal*, Dec. 1, 1916, pp. 182–183.
"Specifications of Current Passenger Car Models." *Motor World*, May 3, 1922, p. 48b.
"Specifications of Gasoline Pleasure Cars." *The Horseless Age*, Oct. 14, 1914, p. 562.
"The Start of the Starter." *Automobile Trade Journal*, Dec. 1, 1924, p. 82.
Thomas, Diane. "McFarlan 'Brought It All Together.'" *Old Cars*, June 15, 1976, p. 10.
"To Make One License Do." *Motor Age*, June 19, 1913, p. 15.
"To Sell McFarlan Property." *The Automobile*, Oct. 30, 1913, p. 837.
The Vehicle Dealer, March 1906, p. 522.
Whitcomb, Joseph C. "Maxim's First Fifty Years." *The Middleborough Antiquarian*, June 1962, p. 1.
Williams, Mike Worthington. "The Russian's McFarlan: A 20th Century Survival Story." *Old Cars*, Oct. 10, 1978, pp. 6, 18.

Books and Public Records

"Articles of Incorporation." *Fayette County Miscellaneous Records*, Book 6, Connersville, Indiana, p. 497.
Barrows, Frederic Irving. "Edward W. Ansted." *History of Fayette County Indiana*. Indianapolis, IN: B. F. Bowen, 1917, p. 672.
_____. "Charles E. J. McFarlan." *History of Fayette County Indiana*. Indianapolis, IN: B. F. Bowen, 1917, pp. 714–715.
_____. "Fire Department." *History of Fayette County Indiana*. Indianapolis, IN: B. F. Bowen, 1917, p. 535.
_____. "John B. McFarlan." *History of Fayette County Indiana*. Indianapolis, IN: B. F. Bowen, 1917, pp. 1008–1010.
_____. "John B. McFarlan, Jr." *History of Fayette County Indiana*. Indianapolis, IN: B. F. Bowen, 1917, pp. 706–707.
_____. "The First Horseless Vehicle." *History of Fayette County Indiana*. Indianapolis, IN: B. F. Bowen, 1917, p. 625.
_____. "Street Paving." *History of Fayette County Indiana*. Indianapolis, IN: B. F. Bowen, 1917, p. 541.
Bentley, John. "The First "500." *Great American Automobiles*. New York: Prentice-Hall, 1957, pp. 195–196.
Bergreen, Laurence. *Capone: The Man and the Era*. New York: Simon & Schuster, 1996, pp. 233–235.
Blommel, Henry. *Indiana's Little Detroit 1846–1964*. Connersville, IN, 1964, p. 3.
"Commissioners Court." *Commissioners Record*, Book 8, Connersville, IN, April 1918, pp. 327–328.
History of Fayette County, Indiana. Chicago: Warner Beers, 1885, p. 150.
"J.B. McFarlan, Sr." *Biographical and Geneological History of Wayne, Fayette, Union and Franklin Counties, Indiana*. Chicago: Lewis Publishing, 1899, pp. 887–888.
Kimes, Beverly Rae. "McFarlan." *Standard Catalog of American Cars 1805–1942*, Volume 3. Iola, WI: Krause Publications.
Lamm, Michael, and Holls, Dave. "Le Baron Carrossiers." *A Century of Automotive Style: 100 Years of American Car Design*. Stockton, CA: Lamm-Morada Publishing, 1997, p. 40.
Marvin, Keith, and Arnheim Alvin J., and Blommel, Henry H. *What Was the McFarlan?* New York: Alvin Arnheim, 1967, pp. 2, 65.
"McFarlan." *Automobile Engineering*, Volume III. Chicago: American Technical Society, 1918, p. 155.
Meyer, Marjorie Teetor. *One Man's Vision: The Life of Automotive Pioneer Ralph R. Teetor*. Indianapolis: Guild Press of Indiana, 1995, p. 51.
Mezzrow, Milton, and Wolfe, Bernard. *Really the Blues*. New York: Random House, 1946, pp. 62–68.
1920 Automobile Reference Book, Glens Falls Insurance Company, Glens Falls, NY, 1920, p. 95.
Scharz, Rev. Julius F. *Pen and Camera of Connersville, Indiana*. Connersville, IN, 1906, pp. 21, 88, 89.
Smith, Harry M. "Connersville Once Known as Little Detroit." *Connersville, Indiana: A Pictorial History*. St. Louis: G. Bradley Publishing, 1992, p. 86.
Smith, Howard T. *Maxim Fire Apparatus Photo History*. Hudson, WI: Iconografix, 2004, p. 15.
Stanley, Richard A. *The Lexington Automobile: A Complete History*. Jefferson, NC: McFarland, 2007, pp. 182, 192.
Stevensen, Burton. *The Home Book of Proverbs, Maxims and Familiar Phrases*. New York: Macmillan, 1956.
Walters, H. Max. "A 1916 McFarlan Hearse at the Smith Funeral Home." *The Making of Connersville and Fayette County* Volume II. Baltimore: Gateway Press, 1989, pp. 481–485.
Williams, Harriet E. *Historical Pageant of Connersville, Fayette County, Indiana, July 5th, 1916*. Connersville, IN: Examiner Pub., 1916, p. 58.

Factory Literature

After Seventy Years of a Settled Plan. Connersville, IN: McFarlan, 1926.
Catalogue of the McFarlan Six Cylinder Automobiles. Connersville, IN: McFarlan, 1911, pp. 12–13, 17–23.
Instruction Book for All Models Series X Cars. Connersville, IN: McFarlan, [1916].
Introducing the Makers of the McFarlan. Connersville, IN: McFarlan, 1913.
J.B. McFarlan Carriage Company Business and Pleasure Vehicles. Connersville, IN: McFarlan, January 1, 1896.
J.B. McFarlan Carriage Company Business and Pleasure Vehicles. Connersville, IN: McFarlan, 1900, p. 1.
Marmon. Indianapolis, IN: Nordyke & Marmon, 1923.
McFarlan Carriage Company. Connersville, IN: McFarlan, 1908.

McFarlan Carriage Company, Catalog 30. Connersville, IN: McFarlan, 1911, p. 50.
McFarlan Custom Built 1856–1927. Connersville, IN: McFarlan, 1927.
The McFarlan Eight-In-Line. Connersville, IN: McFarlan, 1926.
McFarlan Eight-In-Line. Connersville, IN: McFarlan, 1928.
McFarlan Motor Company. Connersville, IN: McFarlan, Dec. 1923.
The McFarlan Ninety. Connersville, IN: McFarlan, 1919.
McFarlan Six. Connersville, IN: McFarlan, 1911, pp. 17–23.
McFarlan Six, Catalog 33. Connersville, IN: McFarlan, 1914.
McFarlan Six, By This Sign—. Connersville, IN: McFarlan, 1917, pp. 3–9.
McFarlan Six, "By This Sign." Connersville, IN: McFarlan, 1918.
McFarlan Six—By This Sign. Connersville, IN: McFarlan, 1921, pp. 2–3.
The McFarlan Six (Custom Built). Connersville, IN: McFarlan, 1925.
Self Starting McFarlan Six, Catalog 31. Connersville, IN: McFarlan, 1912.
Self Starting McFarlan Six, Catalog 32. Connersville, IN: McFarlan, 1913, pp. 9, 20.
The New and Lighter McFarlan Six. Connersville, IN: McFarlan, 1925.
"A New McFarlan Body at Less Than Half Price." Kokomo, IN: McFarlan, [1929].

Correspondence and Unpublished Material

Barrows, Burton. Letter to Commercial Union Assurance Co., April 21, 1920.
Belknap, R. B. Correspondence to George W. Sutton, Jr., Dec. 23, 1925.
Cangany, Harry J., Jr. Correspondence to Richard Stanley, July 21, 2008.
Heydon, Peter. Correspondence to Richard Stanley, April 2009.
McCombs and Sons. Ledger, ca. 1923–24 (unpublished).
McFarlan, A. H. Correspondence to William S. Crowe, Dec. 1, 1909.
Olsson, Igamar, and Heder Mats. "Lexington in Sweden," Dec. 6, 2002 (unpublished).

Interviews

Crusis, Joe. Telephone interview with Richard Stanley, March 2000.
Davidson, Donald. Personal interview, Indianapolis, IN, Jan. 26, 2009.
Heydon, Peter. Telephone interview with Richard Stanley, March 2009.
Marquette, Phillip G. Personal interview, Connersville, IN, June 8, 2009.
McCombs, Nancy. Personal interview, Connersville, IN, March 2008.
McNaughton, Charles. Personal interview, Muncie, IN, Oct. 25, 2001.
Moore, Erma. Telephone interview, March 17, 2008.
Robinson, Mary Fowler. Personal interview, Connersville, IN, August 2007.
Smith, Glen. Personal interview, Connersville, IN, May 2, 2007.
Squires, Donald. Personal interview, Connersville, IN, Feb. 2008.
Woodburn, Bob. Telephone interview with Richard Stanley, March 17, 2009.

Internet Sources

"Monte Blue." *The Internet Movie Database*, imdb.com, 2009.
"Paul Whiteman." *Wikipedia*, 2008.
"Wainwright Engineering." bugladyconsulting.com/genealogy, May 21, 2007, p. 1.

Index

Acme truck 154
Adams, Bert 70, 72, 128, 130, 131, 132, 134, 142, 143, 144, 146
Ahrens-Fox fire apparatus 153, 154
Alco automobile 59, 68, 134, 180
Allison, James 126
American automobile 141, 144
American Automobile Association 126
American Motors, Indianapolis, Indiana 87
Amplex automobile 134, 143
Anderson, Brian, Jr. 236, 237
Anderson, C.L. 135
Anderson, Gary 227
Ansted, Edward W. 24, 50, 88, 90, 116
Ansted, Frank B. 114
Ansted, George 114
Ansted Engineering Company
Ansted Spring and Axle Co. 24, 29, 88
Applegate, Deacon 51
Apperson automobile 59, 68, 134, 135, 144, 211
Arbuckle, Rosco (Fatty) 176, 179, 180, 223, 224, 225
Arnheim, Alvin J. 2, 219
Association of Licensed Automobile Manufacturers 70
Atlanta, Georgia 28, 29, 65, 130
Auburn automobile 1, 160, 161, 165, 166, 169, 208
Auburn Automobile Company 166, 168, 211
Auburn Sales Co. 154
Australia 21, 67

Baily, J.L. 18
Banks, Johnny 122
Barbin, Knowles 95
Barndollar, W.J. 127–130
Barnes, F.M. 197
Barrett, Tom 223
Barrows, Burton M. 88, 89, 163, 165, 198, 203, 209
Barrows, Frederick I. 163, 164
Barrows, Paul 207, 209
Barry, Dave 183
Baumgart, Don John 231
Baylor, Hugh R. 235
Beaver, Dora 152

Beeson, Lycurgus 10
Beeson, Wellington 10
Belknap, Robert B. 200, 203, 209
Benson, E.A. 189
Benson, Leslie L. 172
Benton, L.E. 146
Bernette, Donald 230
Bernhardt, Charles 230
Bertch, William 10
Bertsh, Malinda 153
Bessemer Motor Truck Co. 154
Black-Crow automobile 130
Blanchard Brothers & Lane 188
Blommel, Henry viii, 2, 219
Blommel, John viii
Blommel, William viii, 57
Blue, Monte 180, 181
Board of Trade 26
Bosler, F.A. 79
Bowen System 202, 206
Brady, Matthew F. 180
Braun, Mayor Phillip 150
Broeding, Herman 154
Brooks & Tittle 160
Brown, (A.J.) 62, 64
Brown, Ezra 72
Brown, James A. 62, 64, 133
Brown, William 29
Brown truck 144, 146
Brownell engine 55, 58, 62, 67, 69, 70, 85, 127, 221
Bryant, Allen 62
Bryant, Arthur 62
Buck Board Company 17
Buffalo, New York 79, 142–144; reliability tour 142–144
Buffalo New York Automobile Club 142, 143
Buggyabout automobile 53, 54
Buick (Marquette) automobile 102, 131, 132–134, 138
Burkhart, Margaret 226
Burkhart, Ralph 226
Burns, Frank 53
Buxton, George 188

Cadillac Auto Truck Co. 154
Cadillac automobile 53, 76, 79, 172, 194, 200
Cambridge City, Indiana 4, 5
Canton Classic Car Museum 222
Capone, Al 1, 184

Carson, Enoch 9
Carter, George R. Leather Company 24
Carthage Motor Car Company, Rochester, New York 82
Case automobile 134, 135, 138
Catley top lift 46
C.B. Swan, Old Town, Main 82
Cedar Rapids, Iowa 22
Central Manufacturing Company 24, 53, 160, 165, 211
Chadwick automobile 68
Chambers, C.A. 64
Chandler, Otis 233
Cheviot, Ohio 4
Chicago Manufacturing Company 53
Chicago steam car 53
Cincinnati, Ohio 4, 5, 29, 57
Cincinnati Hamilton & Dayton Railroad (C.H. & D.) 19–21, 29, 71
Cino automobile 130
City of Atlanta races 130–132
Clark, Ralph 154
Clark, Rylie 62
Clemens, Fred 127–131, 134
Clifford, Horry 10
Coey, C.A. 65
Cole automobile 127, 130, 134, 141
Coller-Reitz Motor Company, St. Louis, Missouri 82
Collins curtains 91
Conner, John 3
Conner and Conner 37
Connersville, Indiana 1, 3, 5, 53, 71, 138, 139; city council 149–151, 153, 154; fire department 96, 149–153
Connersville Axle Company 24, 29
Connersville Blower Company 24, 44
Connersville Buck Board Company 17
Connersville Buggy Company 15
Connersville Carriage Shop 6
Connersville Furniture Company 19
Connersville Land and Improvement Company 22–24, 44
Connersville Lounge Company 24

Connersville Motor Vehicle Company 54
Connersville Natural Gas Company 17, 24
Connersville Wagon Company 29, 37
Connersville Woodworking Company 24
Consolidated Vehicle Company 62, 64, 133
Constantine the Great 215
Corbin, Alf 10
Cord, Errett Lobben 166, 168
Cord automobile 211
Core, Guy C. 145
Cottom, Harry 152
Cotton, Edward W. 89, 156, 157, 159, 203, 216
Cotton States Exhibition 28
Cox, Christopher 145, 146
Crane & Breed ambulance 156, 158
Crowell, Johnny 232
Crusis, Joe 227
Cunningham automobile 201
Cutler Hammer 93
Cutting automobile 134, 138
Cutting Motor Car Company 88

Dallas, Texas 29
Dalton, Dorothy 176
Daniels Eight automobile 116
Dart truck 154
Davis, Maud 11
Dawson, Joe 139
Dayton wire wheels 202
Dempsey, Jack 1, 182–184, 233
Denver, Colorado 15
DePalma, Ralph 138, 139
Derbyshire, Kathryn 52
Des Moines, Iowa 29
DeTamble automobile 141
Diamond T truck 154
Disbrow 129
Dixon, Arthur 89, 145, 146
Dodge Brothers automobile 149
Donner, Mr. 175
Dorsey, H.O. 51
Dreist, Bill 234
Duesenberg, Augie 170
Duesenberg automobile 1, 168–170, 234, 235
Dumas, Vern 64
Dupont automobile 201
Durant, William C. 166
Durant automobile 167

Edenburn, W.D. 141
Edgewood 22, 24
Edwards, Alex 10
Edwards, John 46
Elliott, R.N. 46, 88
Ellis, L.M. 54
Empire automobile 53, 126, 144
Enid, Oklahoma 42
Erb, Maynard 212

F.A.L. (Falcar) 127, 128, 130–132, 134

Farley, Dorothy 176, 177
Faversham, William 107
Fayette Banking Company 44
Fayette County, Indiana 3, 7, 53, 110
Fayette County Commissioners 154
Fayette County Fair (Free Fair) 8–10, 79
Fayette County Historical Museum 219, 220, 226, 227, 237
Fayetteville (Orange) Indiana 10
Federal truck 154
Fiat automobile 132, 134–136, 138
Firestone-Columbus automobile 128, 130, 132, 134, 138
Fishbach, Fred 179
Fisher, Carl G. 126, 133, 135, 144, 146
Flint, Michigan 29
Flint automobile 166
Ford, Henry 94
Ford automobile 94, 201, 218
Four-States Tour 141, 142
Fowler, Edna 139, 140
Fowler, Ray 138–140
Franklin automobile 59, 68, 121–123, 125, 171, 201
French, C.C. 121
Fries Brick Works 24
Frost, Hyatt 211

G & J truck 144, 146
Gambs, John R. 225, 226
Ganley, Mike 46
Gearhart, H.F. 230
Geiger Candy Company 161
General Parts Corporation 211
Gerlinger Motor Car Company, Portland, Oregon 82
Gibbs, Dennis 231, 232
Gipe's Fruit Store 18
Glover, John 135
Gould, Milford H. 225
Grand Central Palace 70
Gray, Edward E. 91
Gray Pneumatic Gearshift 91, 93, 95
Great Western automobile 141
Green Bay Motor Car Company, Madison, Wisconsin 82
Greer, Joshua 14
Griffin, Ed 227
Gruver, Joe 231

Halladay automobile 132
Handley, O.V. 46
Hankins, Dan M. 29
Hanson, Karl L. 154
Harper, Harvey 221
Harrah Automobile Collection 221, 223, 228
Harris, Harry L. 188, 189
Harroun, Ray 136, 138
Hartford shock absorbers 90, 120
Hartley, Charles 84
Hassett, Fire Chief Edward 149

Hatch, Frank 121
Hatfield Motor Company 53, 54
Haynes, Elwood 144
Haynes automobile 141, 144, 146, 211
Heeb, Phillip and Sons 10
Heil & Company 155
Henderson automobile 144
Henry, John 13, 51
Herida, Antonio 182
Heroun, Ray 136, 138, 144
Herreshoff automobile 130
Herschell-Spillman engine 72, 78, 82
Heydon, Peter 234, 235
Hibbs, Clem 152
Hitchcock, Frank 185
Holmwood, Nelson 225
Holter, Wright 35
Hoosier Castings Company 24
Houk wire wheels 114
Howard automobile 53
Hudson automobile 102
Hughes, Ella S. 17
Hupmobile automobile 143
Huston, J.E. 79
Huston, R.T. 46
Huzell, August 121
Huzell, Eskil 121

Ilco-Ryan-Lite 208, 215
Imperial Palace Collection 227, 233
Indiana Automobile Manufacturers' Association 141, 144
Indiana French Mirror Company 24
Indiana Furniture Company 44
Indiana Lamp Company 24, 88
Indiana to Pacific Tour 88, 144
Indiana Wheelman 52
Indianapolis, Indiana 141, 145, 176
Indianapolis Bicycle Club 52
Indianapolis Motor Speedway (Brickyard) 65, 126, 134, 141, 228, 231; 1910 Labor Day races 127–130; 1911 132–136; 1912 Indianapolis 500 137–140
Indianapolis Motor Speedway Museum 231
Indianapolis Truck Sales 154
Industrial park 23, 25
Inland Motor Sales Corp. 154
Inter-State automobile 134

Jackson, Andrew 35
Jackson, Charles 10
Jackson, Edward 64
Jackson, Lydia 4
Jackson automobile 134
Jacobs, Charlie 29
Jagersberger, Joe 135
Jameson, William 13
Jemison, Elijah 10
John's Corn Patch 24
Johnson, Captain 51
Jordan, Larry 234

Index

Jos. B. Deibler Motor Car Company, Chicago, Illinois 81
Joseph, Brian 234

Kansas City, Missouri 21, 29, 31, 42
Karl L. Hanson Co. 154
Karr, Craig 230, 232
Kellogg air compressor 79, 80, 86
Kennedy, Clyde C 62.
Kensinger, John 13
Kepler, Jesse 172
Kepler, Stanley 57, 130, 131, 172
Kershaw family 236
Kettering, Charles F. 76
Kimball coachwork 161
Kirkeby, Arnold 169, 234
Kirkpatrick, John 13
Kissel Kar (Kissel) automobile 59, 180
Kline Kar automobile 59
Knight, Harry 135, 137, 139
Knox automobile 134, 138
Kokomo, Indiana 19, 211
Krell Auto Grand Piano Company 46
K-R-I-T automobile 143
Kruse, Dean 227

Lamb, Rev. G.C. 46
Larder, Mark 234
Leap, E.J. 229
Leedy, Ulysses S. 185, 186
Leeman, Ray 141
Lehman, E.J. 161
Leland, Henry M. 76
Lexington automobile 53, 68, 135, 137-139, 141, 162, 163, 211
Lexington Motor Company 114
Light Inspection Car Company 84, 87, 114
Lincoln, Nebraska 29
Lincoln automobile 175, 200, 201
Lincoln Highway Association 86
Lipman air compressor 91, 98
Little Giant truck 154
Locomobile automobile 1, 68, 167, 201, 208
Locomobile Motor Company of America, Inc. 167
Long, Moses 8
Loper, George and Sons Company 9, 15
Louis F. Benton Company, Los Angeles, California 82
Lowell, John 237
Lozier automobile 59, 131-133, 135, 136, 138
Lycoming engine 200, 208, 210
Lycoming Motor Company 168, 207
Lyons, Quincy T. 154

Madison Square Garden 70
Madrid, Spain 182
Manlove, Jessica 55, 56
Manlove, John 9, 10
Manufacturers' Club 53

Marion automobile 144
Marmon automobile 102, 127-129, 131, 132, 136, 141, 144, 160, 164, 165, 208
Marquette, Melvin (Mel) 132, 134-139, 141
Marquette, Phillip 135
Marshall, Gov. Thomas R. 126
Marvin, Keith 2, 219
Massachusetts Institute of Technology 156, 237
Master truck 154
Matheson automobile 68, 127, 130
Maxim, Carlton W. 155, 156
Maxim, Ernest 155, 156
Maxim fire apparatus 155, 156, 236
Maxwell automobile 141, 143, 175
Maxwell-Brisco band 127, 128
McCombs and Sons 191-193
McConegle, Edward 172
McCready, B.F. 149
McDaniel, Tom 14
McFarlan, Alfred Harry 17. 54-57, 67, 88-90, 134, 142, 143, 197, 198, 203, 209, 211, 212, 215, 216
McFarlan, Ann 4
McFarlan, Charles E.J. 4, 5, 7, 11, 15-17, 54, 203
McFarlan, Edward 4
McFarlan, Elizabeth 4
McFarlan, Herbert M. 18, 52, 56, 70, 142, 143, 145
McFarlan, James 4
McFarlan, James Edward 4, 7, 15-17, 29
McFarlan, James Edward, Jr. 17
McFarlan, John B. (J.B.) 1, 4, 7, 8, 11, 12, 15-19, 21, 22, 24, 26, 42, 44, 46, 54-56, 90, 160, 211, 219, 220
McFarlan, John B., Jr. 4, 5, 11, 16, 18
McFarlan, John B., III 18
McFarlan, Lucy 4
McFarlan, Maria J. 4
McFarlan, Martha 4
McFarlan, Mary 4
McFarlan, Robert 4
McFarlan, Roe Mount 18
McFarlan, Thomas 4
McFarlan, William W. 4, 11, 15-18, 52
McFarlan automobile 1, 53, 55-61, 65, 71, 73, 74, 77, 79, 101, 141-147, 171, 176, 215; ambulance-hearse 96, 156-159; automobile bodies 160-170, 174, 203, 204, 207, 208, 217, 234, 235; Big Six 66-68, 75, 240, 242; county highway truck 96, 154, 155; Eight-in-Line 168, 199-201, 204, 207-210, 212, 213, 217, 233, 234, 240, 245; fire trucks 96, 150-154; gold plated McFarlan 186-189; Knickerbocker Cabriolet (Town Car) 109, 117, 171, 172, 174, 180, 181, 187-189,

191, 192, 196, 202, 224, 225, 227, 229, 244, 245; Little Six 63, 64, 67, 68, 72, 74, 76, 78, 221, 240, 242; Ninety (90) 107, 109-113, 118-123, 221, 222, 223, 240, 243, 244; racecars 127-140; Series "M" 82-84, 86, 240, 242, 243; Series "S" 82, 83, 240, 242; Series "T" 82-85, 87, 90-94, 96, 97, 99, 102-104, 240, 242, 243; Series "X" 90-94, 96, 97, 99, 102-107, 240, 243; Single-Valve (SV) 193, 194, 196-201, 207, 228, 241, 245; Submarine (Destroyer) 100, 102, 103, 113, 117, 160, 243, 244; Twin-Valve (TV) 156, 171-175, 187-201, 206-208, 212, 214, 217, 219, 223-233, 240, 241, 244, 245; wartime products 111, 115
McFarlan Building Company 27, 44
McFarlan Car Company 55
McFarlan Carriage Company 12, 14, 15, 17-23, 27-31, 35, 38, 42, 46, 50, 52, 54, 55, 57, 88, 116, 203
McFarlan horse-drawn vehicles 8, 10, 13-16, 26, 32-41, 43-45, 47-49, 88, 203
McFArlan Hotel 26-28, 32, 55, 176
McFarlan Motor Car Company 81, 88
McFarlan Motor Company 88, 89, 116, 141, 156
McFarlan Motor Corporation 116, 117, 187, 211, 217
McFarlan Reality Company 17
McFarlan Sales Company 62, 64
McFarlan Six Club 140
McFarlan's ware room 6, 18, 28
McFarlantown (McFarlan Plat) 7, 8. 42
McGraw, Charles 79
McNaughton, Charles 71, 72, 184, 190
Meek, Berry 10
Menocal, Pres. Mario García 181, 182
Mercedes automobile 134 138
Mercer automobile 138
Merida, Antonio 182
Meridian, Missouri 176
Merrell, Hurry Up Geezer 79
Merrell, William 6
Meyers, Mart 32
Mezzrow, Milton 185
Michener, Scott 54
Middleboro, Massachusetts 156
Midland automobile 127, 130
Miller, George C. and Sons 4
Miller, Glen 62
Miller, Shawn 228
Moberly, Missouri 29
Moerschbaecher, Edward 189
Moffett, Joe 52
Moore, David 154

Index

Moore, Edward 35, 46, 97
Moore, J.F.L. 52
Morrison, Dr. Joshua H. 54
Morton, Wellington III 223
Mount, Helen Louise 18
Mount, Howard 79
Mulford, Ralph 135
Murphy, John 10
Myers, Harry 150

National automobile 68, 127, 129, 130, 134, 138
National Paving Brick Manufacturers' Association 126
National Road (U.S. Highway 40) 4, 5, 145
Nethercutt Collection 225
New Departure 75
New York City to Montreal race 121–123, 125
Newby, Arthur 126
Nittie, Frank 185
Noble, John 79
Noblesville, Indiana 30
Norris, Tom G. 4, 203, 209
Nyberg truck 141

O. Armleader Co. 154
O'Brian, Judge Daniel 179
Oldsmobile automobile 52, 68, 102
Omaha, Nebraska 42
Opel automobile 138
O.R. Crutcher, Lexington, Kentucky 82
Osborne, Marie 176
Overland band 128
Overlesse, William 79

Packard automobile 171, 194, 200, 201
Paige-Detroit automobile 143
Palmer-Singer automobile 35, 72
Parry automobile 141
Parry Manufacturing Company 14, 24, 38
Parsehel, Fred 11
Pascucci, Anthony 233
Passey, Jack 232, 233
Pathfinder automobile 141, 144
Pawtucket, Rhode Island 148
Peck, D. Cameron 227
Peerless automobile 68, 194, 200
Pelan, Rev. William 4
Petersen Museum 233
Peterson, Charles T. 62
Pickford, Mary 178
Pierce-Arrow automobile 57, 68, 94, 143, 171, 175, 180
Pike, Levi 9
Pilot automobile 144
Polo, Eddie 176
Pope-Hartford automobile 131, 132, 134
Pope Manufacturing Company 87
Porter, Clark 10
Potter, William 36, 37

Premier automobile 1, 68, 141, 143, 144, 146, 160, 163, 208
Purcell, Frank 153

Ralston, Governor 145
Rappe, Virginia 179
Ray Motor Company 53
R.C.H. automobile 143
Reeder, Charles 35, 203
Reid, Wallace (Wally) 1, 176–178, 180, 223, 224
Renault automobile 171
Reo Speed Wagon truck 153, 154
Republic truck 154
Rex Manufacturing Company 15, 29
Richmond, Indiana 17
Richwine, G.C. 30
Rieder, Charles 46
Riggs, Fire Chief O.S. 149
Rin-Tin-Tin 228
Roberts, Lee 10
Robinson, Frank 64
Robinson, Mary Fowler 139, 140
Rolls Royce automobile 106, 108, 171, 180, 190, 212
Roots, F.M. 3, 4
Roots, P.H. 3, 4
Roots Blower Company 24
Roots Positive Rotary Principal 3
Russell Bros., Kenoshe, Wisconsin 82
Ryan, Ellis W. 211
Ryan, Walter D'Arcy 208

St. Louis, Missouri 145, 146
Sandburg, Allen 234
San Diego, California 146
Santa Barbara, California 146
Sarvan Wheel Company 32, 38, 42
Schacht automobile 138
Schebler carburetor 205
Scheidel-Thompson Manufacturing Company 88
Schenck, Joseph 180
Schlobohm, Art 122
Schrank, Fanny 13
Seagrave Manufacturing Company 156
Sellers, D.H. 7
Selveira, Barbara 228
Selveira, J.W. 228
Service Truck Sales Co. 154
Sheridan, H.C. 50
Sherman, Lowell 179
Sherry, Dora W. 154
Shields, Tom 7
Silvers, Will 35
Simler, Lewis 10
Simplex automobile 131–134, 138
Simpson, Alma 179
Skaneatelas, New York 149
S.M. Foote, Middletown, Connecticut 82
Small, LeRoy 225, 226
Smith, Carl C. 156–159
Smith, Fred 15, 28, 35

Smith, John 154
Smith, Leslie 184
Smith, Mark 229
Smith, Millie 185
Smith, Thomas L. 156, 157
Smith Funeral Home 156–159
Sparks, Doc 10
Speedwell automobile 127, 130
Splitdorf 59
Springer, Raymond S. 211
Springfield, Illinois 12
Squires, Don 212
Star automobile 167
Staver automobile 130
Stearns-Knight automobile 201
Stevens-Duryea 69, 180, 201
Stoddard-Dayton 135
Stone, Vernon 223
Stromberg 59, 75, 90, 173
Studebaker, Mr. 11
Studebaker automobile 102, 143
Stutz automobile 72, 134, 144, 146
Swartz & Company, New Orleans, Louisiana 82
Sweden 121

Taylor, William D. 84, 176
Teetor, Charles 84
Teetor, John 84
Teetor, Ralph 161
Teetor-Hartley engine 84, 97, 105, 110
Teetor-Hartley Motor Corporation 84, 114
Teetor-McFarlan engine 113, 172
Terre Haute, Indiana 145
Thistlewaite, Mark 126
Thomas, Scott 52
Thomas automobile 69
Trinkle, Gov. Elbert Lee 181, 182
Trinz, Joseph J. 197
Trumbull, Gov. John H. 181, 233
Tryon, Fannie 51, 52
Tryon, Harvin 51, 52
Tunney, Gene 183

Updyke Automobile Company, Indianapolis, Indiana 116

Van Auken Electric automobile 53
Velie automobile 134
velocipede 51, 52
Vesta lighting 82, 108, 190, 208
Vincent, J. Werle 89

Wagner, Fred 128, 137
Wagner, L.R. 146
Wainwright, E. Pierre 213
Wainwright, Harry 67
Wainwright, William Warren 53
Wainwright engine 66, 134, 137
Wainwright Engineering 57, 66, 67, 68
Walker, Earl 52
Wallerich, J.P. 227
Ward, J.M. 144
Ware and Veatch 5
Warner, Jack 228

Warner Brothers Studio 228
Webb, Scott 35
Wellman, Fred 146
Wertlake Brothers 19
Wescott automobile 131, 132, 134, 135
West Chester, Pennsylvania 148
Westinghouse 98, 99, 105, 117, 194
Weston-Mott 55
What Was the McFarlan? viii, 2, 219

Wheeler, Frank H. 126
White automobile 138
White Water Canal (Whitewater Canal) 3, 4
White Water River (Whitewater River) 3
Whiteman, Paul 185, 186
Whitesides truck 141
Wiedley, Walter 146
Wiemer, Elliott 224
Williams, Harry 152

Williams, T.L. 197
Wills, Dr. N.G. 153
Willys Overland 175
Wilson, Pres. Woodrow 110
Winton automobile 57, 59, 69
Wisconsin engine 156, 194, 200, 207
Woodward, Bob 221
Woverton, Leon 174, 175
Woverton, Leora 175
Wright & Updike undertakers 156